Chase

and other stories

Edited by Ginger Mayerson

The Wapshott Press

Chase and Other Stories

Published by
The Wapshott Press
An Imprint of J LHLS
PO Box 31513
Los Angeles, CA 90031

The Wapshott Press
www.WapshottPress.com

Compilation copyright © 2007 by Ginger Mayerson

Copyrights for the individual works are held by their respective author(s). Also see page 187.

First printing October 2007

All rights reserved. Being works of fiction, any resemblance herein to persons living or dead is astonishing and purely coincidental. No part of this is publication may be reproduced or transmitted in any form or by any means, electronic or mechanical, including photocopy, recording, or any information storage and retrieval system now known or to be invented, without permission in writing from the publisher, except by a reviewer who wishes to quote brief passages in connection with a review written for inclusion in a magazine, newspaper, or broadcast.

ISBN: 978-0-6151-6846-3

06 05 04 03   4 3 2 1

Wapshott Press logo by Molly Kiely

This collection is dedicated to Jane Seaton, Lynn Loper, Laurel Sutton, Molly Kiely, Perla Kiely, Robin Austin, Kelly Taylor, Annie Proulx, Satoru Kanagi, Dani F., Leigh D., Kate K., and to our readers. Thanks for reading us all these years.

Steve, by Molly Kiely

Contents

Introduction	*i*
Tally Keller	
The Lawn Fags	1
Turk Albany	
Humu Humu	15
Lene Taylor	
Nul Gravity	27
Valessa Smith	
The Accompanist	35
Amy Throck*-Smythe	
Jewel of My House	51
Colleen Wylie	
Mage Vows	75
Kathryn L. Ramage	
Chiaroscuro	85
Ginger Mayerson	
The Fall	95
Laura Dearlove	
The Omega Men	115
Kitty Johnson	
The Dipsy Doodle Inn	123
Karmen Ghia	
Chase	165
Anastasia Witchhazel	
Permissions	187

Introduction

You hold in your hand a slim volume that is a delightfully varied sampler from a genre of fiction that continues to puzzle, fascinate, and outrage readers all over the globe. This, my friend, is homoerotica written by women (usually), for women (usually) that features men having sex with other men (and sometimes women, aliens, elves, and furries).

Why, the critics of this type of erotica ask, would heterosexual (usually) women want to write and read about gay sex? And there's the problem. Women writing homoerotica for other women are treading an unbeaten path, but do have the author of "Brokeback Mountain," Annie Proulx as their idol. If Ms. Proulx can get her story published in the New Yorker and made into a major motion picture, what's to stop other women from writing homoerotica? As hardly needs to be pointed out, male-male pairings featuring two objects of female desire going at it like crazed weasels with no competing females in sight are an optimal fantasy scenario for fans of this genre. Perhaps if we called it "hot two boy action" instead of homoerotica even people at truck stops could better understand the appeal.

Other writers have looked at homoerotica as an expression of women's dissatisfaction with the inequalities of conventional heterosexual relationships. In male-male pairs no one has to automatically be the one-down partner because of their gender. Personality, intelligence, and ability all take greater precedence in the on-going competitions to determine who is the more dominant partner. In the stories in this volume, you'll find that there is a lot of ink devoted to such playful (and sometimes not so playful) negotiations. I was particularly interested to find so many of these stories were set in academia or peopled with academics. The constant shift and play between which partner is student and which is teacher is a vital part of the dynamics of each of these stories.

Finally, homoerotica written by women also appeals to readers simply because it is taboo. Nice girls don't write about men having anal sex and fellating each other - nice girls write about home décor and having babies. But, as you will see in this collection, nice girls do and do so very well. These writers bring their own romantic and romance writer sensibilities to each situation and character without getting (too) mushy. In several of these stories, writers push themselves to put unlikely partners together in even more unlikely situations. Part of the fun in these stories is having the "Oh, no! They couldn't possibly...!" reaction, only to read on and find, "but, oh yes, they did!" This erotica playfully thumbs its nose at conventional morality, tastefulness, and all other things that proper young ladies are supposed to happily accept as their lot.

So, dear reader, gird your loins to enjoy this collection of audaciously erotic fictions. Enter into the fun and games with each of these pairs of lovers as they battle with brains and other assorted body parts to outwit, outlast, and out delight each other. Why do we love homoerotica written by women? After you finish this book, let me know.

Tally Keller
October 2007

The Lawn Fags

Turk Albany

Professor Southern looked up from his desk at his lover. "I'll only be gone a month," he said. "I can't impose on Dr. Vromsky's goodwill for longer than that, but the fact he's letting me look at his work and his study groups is a minor miracle."

"But, Lee, why can't I go with you?" Ed asked for the nth time.

"Because you're not a linguist, Edward, and someone has to look after the lawn while I'm gone."

Lawns and the palatalization of the phoneme /t/ were Lee Southern's twin obsessions. Somewhere in between he made room in his life for Edward Aurillac, who was getting a PhD in history.

Their lawn—because Ed could either hate Lee's lawn or love *their* lawn in the happy yard of *their* happy home—was magnificent. Verdant, lush, manicured: it was the envy of the block, with the exception of another gay couple three doors down across the street who were even more obsessed than Lee. It was a pleasant competition for best lawn between them, but this was West Los Angeles: gay couples with domestic partnerships and high-maintenance lawns were *de rigueur*.

Of course Ed took an interest in the lawn, but the lack of domestic partnership commitment held him back from giving himself entirely to Lee and the lawn. He didn't doubt Lee loved him, and were gay marriage legal in California, they'd be married. Ed blamed the Byzantine legalities of acquiring a domestic partnership and Lee's lawyer-phobia for his unnotarized ménage.

So it was more difficult for Ed to care deeply about the yard, which was lovely. Spice bush and plumbago banked the walls and fences on all sides; there were islands of jasmine, sages, lilies and roses, and anything else colorful and fragrant that Lee could find scattered in the lush lawn, but it was just another distraction from Ed's dissertation whenever he happened to notice how lovely it was. He'd even moved his desk so his back was to the window, thus limiting his view to his computer monitor and whatever the solitude-seeking Irish monks were doing in his head.

There were no gardens in his dissertation. There was speculation on Irish monks going from mainland Ireland to the Irish islands, in search of solitude, and instead bumping into the first waves of Viking exploration in the 6th and 7th centuries, which sent some of the monks—again in search of solitude—to Iceland. There were Vikings finding Irish monks seeking solitude there in 9th century. There were Irish monks moving on to Greenland when the Viking colonization of Iceland got on their nerves. There was speculation, near the end of his dissertation, that Irish monks crossed the North Atlantic, from Greenland to Labrador to Newfoundland to possibly what is now the US. The Places of Stones in Massachusetts, the Ogham carvings in West Virginia, the legends of St. Brendan the Navigator seemed to indicate that solitude seeking Irish monks were in America 300 years before the Pilgrims. There was all that in his dissertation, but not one garden anywhere.

Occasionally the irony of Ed, who loathed being alone, and his obsession with Irish monks who so loved being alone they lived in the harshest conditions imaginable, was thrown into stark relief. The prospect of being on his own for a month, with only the garden and his dissertation to keep him occupied worried him. And he didn't especially worship the garden; he drew no strength from it. Rather, when the fecundity of the garden surrounding his home wore on his spirit, he took comfort in the icy wastes that were the background of his research and his refuge from the frustrations of the modern world. Not that Ed wanted to be anywhere near those wastes where there were no dentists, indoor plumbing, libraries, high-speed internet, any kind of internet, or café lattes, not to mention lawns or lawn services.

"Don't be sulky, Edward," Lee sighed, drawing him close that night in bed.

"I'm not, I'm just going to miss you while you're gone," Ed sighed, giving up even the pretense of reluctance.

"Mmmm, I'll miss you, too," Lee murmured into Ed's neck, working his hand into his lover's pajama bottoms. "Take these off."

Ed complied, giving his hardening cock some much-needed freedom. As Lee stroked him to full hardness, he fumbled at the waistband of his lover's pants, but was gently restrained.

"Shhh, Edward, shhhh." Lee pressed a soft kiss to his lips and another to his jaw. Working his way slowly to Ed's chest, nuzzling each nipple and ending with a light nip. He pushed Ed's knees farther apart and slid between them as he licked and tasted from Edward's chest to abdomen and into the younger man's downy blond thatch. Lee playfully prodded the base of Ed's shaft with his chin before sliding his lips up and over the head, licking a drop of pre-cum off the dusky pink tip before easing it into his mouth and down his throat.

As always, Ed marveled at how good a cocksucker his stodgy professor lover was. Lee claimed it was something he'd learned in grad school. It wasn't especially funny, so Ed never mentioned it again, but he never failed to respond to the man who could make lights dance behind his eyes and waves of pleasure ripple from his head down to his toes. He just wished it happened more often. But he knew the drill, and at a minor slowing in Lee's ministrations, he knew he wasn't coming that way that night. He also knew it was time to get the lube out of the nightstand drawer and grab a towel from underneath it. The fact that Lee was good at fellatio made up for his clockwork lovemaking in other areas. That is, when he could be bothered to make love; if they got each other off more than three times a week, that was a good week for them both.

But tonight was their farewell for a month, and Edward was all obedience and acquiescence as he licked his scent off Lee's lips. He obligingly tilted his hips so Lee could slide in one slippery finger.

"Ready?" Lee asked, rolling on his back. He grabbed a condom and rolled it down his erection. He handed Ed the lube and drew him astride his lap.

This was not Ed's favorite position, but it was their last night for a while. He put lots of lube on Lee's latex-clad shaft and positioned his ass over the head. Lee's hands rested on his thighs, gently massaging them as Ed eased down. The darkness hid Ed's wince at the initial discomfort, but not his gasp of pleasure as his body accepted Lee's fullness, the sparks as the shaft brushed his prostate and a sigh as his balls nestled into Lee's pubic hair.

Lee let Edward rest there a moment, sliding his hands up to pinch his nipples and then down to stroke his cock. Encouragement enough; Lee rolled his hips slightly, urging his lover to move before the mood was lost.

Adjusting his seat, Ed began to move at his own pace, which was in slow, short pulses. This was a game they played; Lee would put the impetus for pleasure on Ed, Ed would respond in a way that was not quite what Lee was after. Not inherently lazy, Ed knew Lee's patience with such a laid-back performance wouldn't last long.

Sure enough, Lee thrust firmly into Edward and held his hips in place as he rolled him onto his back. Arranging Edward's legs around him, Lee leaned down for a long, sweet kiss, before he started pumping gently into his lover. Ever the gentleman, he reached between them and jerked Edward off. With that out of the way, Lee lengthened his thrusts and came with a muffled roar into Edward's neck. He rested on Edward's heaving chest until his breathing got close to normal. "I must be heavy," he said, as he always said before rolling off and heading into the bathroom.

Ed used the towel on his chest and abdomen. His ass felt fine; he didn't especially like condoms but they did make clean-up easier. He shifted to his side of the bed when Lee came back. "I'll miss you..." Ed ran his hand though the salt and pepper hair on Lee's rapidly cooling chest.

"You'll miss this..." Lee said, bringing the hand to his lips.

"I'll miss you doing this." Ed turned Lee's lips to his, but didn't linger. It was late, and Lee had a plane to catch first thing in the morning.

"Thanks for the clarification, Edward," Lee murmured, wrapping his arms around Edward and falling asleep.

The next morning, Lee kissed him hard when the airport shuttle pulled into their driveway. "This will give you a solid month to work on your dissertation," he said, letting him go and picking up his bags. "Don't forget to look after the lawn."

"I won't forget." Ed dutifully followed him to the shuttle and stood there until it was out of sight. Then he turned and looked at the lawn. "I guess it's just you and me for a month, lawn," he murmured, and immediately felt foolish for it. It was only seven a.m., but two of his neighbors were watering their lawns so, for the sake of form, Ed got out the hose and watered a few shrubs. This was unnecessary because the yard was on a state-of-the-art sprinkler timer system and was watered more accurately than mere humans were capable of doing. Either science hadn't devised or Lee simply hadn't found a robotic lawn mowing system, and Ed recalled that today was the lawn service day. This didn't affect him, but he was aware of it. He put the hose away, went inside and took a shower. The urge to take a nap was huge, but he was strong. He made the bed and then settled into his office for some serious frowning at his dissertation.

After several hours of frowning over anti-social monks, likely with chilblains, vs. god-like Viking warriors, there was a knock on the front door. Annoyed by the interruption of his meditations on freezing Irish monks, Ed headed for the door. On the way he caught a glimpse of the lawn service truck, its side emblazoned with "Happy Lawns," at the curb. He hadn't noticed them in the yard, or had they just gotten there? So much for those soft scientist powers of observation. He wondered what they wanted; Lee usually handled this stuff. Damn Lee for not being around. Oh well.

Ed opened the front door and the only thought in his head was, "Oh my God, why didn't I study the Aztecs?" Standing before him was a tall, bronze god in a tight wife-beater, denim shorts, and sturdy work boots. It was an effort not to stare at the man's powerful chest and muscular arms, but after a quick glace at his legs, Ed was afraid to look any lower than his visitor's solar plexus. He looked bravely up into large brown eyes above tanned cheekbones. The man's nose was wide, but not out of proportion to his face and his lips were full, distractingly full.

"I am sorry, Mr. Southern?" he asked hesitantly, looking at the paper in his hand. His voice was rough, but polite. "I am Ramon Juarez, I'm here to..." He trailed off and gestured to the mower in the yard. He was young, too, definitely out of his teens and somewhere in his early twenties.

"Um..." Ed pulled himself together and switched to Spanish. "Can we speak Spanish, Ramon?" he asked. "My Spanish isn't very good, but if that's not a problem–"

"Oh, no, señor, you speak very well!" Ramon looked visibly relived.

"Thank you, I don't speak enough, so it will be good for me to speak Spanish with you." Ed was starting to feel like a Berlitz lesson. "Mr., I mean, Dr. Southern isn't here, but I can help you."

"Señor Garrel asked me to give Dr. Southern this envelope when I finished today," Ramon said. He was more assured in his own language and this made him even sexier in Ed's eyes.

"Thank you." Ed took the envelope from him and thanked Mrs. Vasquez in seventh grade for making Spanish class so much fun that he'd kept at it all through high school and college. It came in handy in LA; although Lee had managed without it for decades, Ed would have been lost without it. "So are you finished with the yard?" he asked, looking around.

"I haven't begun yet," Ramon said, smiled and turned to go.

"I, ack–" Ed's statement was choked off this first view of Ramon's magnificent ass.

Ramon turned back with a quizzical look.

"I'm Ed."

"Excuse me?" Ramon asked.

"My name is Ed," Ed said more firmly.

"It is a pleasure to meet you, Mr. Ed," Ramon said, politely.

"It's just Ed, Ramon," Ed said. "I call you Ramon, you can call me Ed. I don't even know your last name."

"It's Juarez."

"Oh, that's right! You told me, I'm sorry, I–"

"But call me Ramon, please," Ramon said.

"I will, thanks." Ed stood there trying to think of something to say.

Ramon nodded and excused himself to go to work.

Ed closed the door and leaned against it. "Jesus, he must think I'm a total idiot," he thought. He banged his head against the solid stained oak and it felt good. He was half hard; he hoped Ramon hadn't noticed. "Nah," Ed thought. "A macho stud like that would have kicked my ass if he'd noticed."

But then the racist definition of macho flitted through his head: Macho means you don't just fuck women, you fuck everyone.

Even Ed realized that this train of thought was unproductive. After making a cup of coffee, he ambled back to his study and stared out the window at Ramon getting sweatier and sweatier...

"Okay! That's it!" The first thing Ed did was scrabble for the phone and leave a message on Dr. LaGonda's machine. "Can you fit me in ASAP?" he pleaded. She was probably the worst shrink in LA, but she worked late, was cheap, and let her clients get whatever it was out of their systems. She had few steady customers; no one could take her bored and sardonic gaze and chainsmoking for very long.

The second thing he did was act on a bad impulse in a good way. This was also part of the LaGonda method: you may think whatever you like, but your actions must be positive for the object of your thoughts. There were rumors that she worked with pedophiles, whom she made give money, and lots of it, to children's hospitals and medical charities. But Ed was hardly a pervert, he was just young and horny...and in a relationship he didn't want to mess up with a fling with the gardener. He stopped in the bathroom for a quick cold shower and then into the kitchen where he grabbed a big bottle of Evian. He had to hurry because Ramon was packing up.

"Ramon!" Ed trotted up to the truck where Ramon was rippling his muscles lifting the mower into the truckbed with one hand.

"Señor?" Ramon asked, wiping his forehead with a grass-stained palm.

Ed kept his eyes firmly on Ramon's, not daring to stray to the wifebeater sweat-plastered to his pecs and his nipples showing dark brown through the flimsy fabric. Oh no! He would be strong for...for...for Lee! That's right! Lee! "I thought you'd like some water," he stammered in Spanish.

"Thank you very much," Ramon said, smiling beautifully with his yellow teeth. "I was wondering, um, if I could..." He hesitated. "Thank you for the water."

"Were you asking me something?" Ed asked.

"Your bathroom..." This was almost inaudible, so he had to say it twice.

"Of course!" Ed nearly shouted. "Of course," he said more calmly. "Right this way," and led the blushing gardener into the house. "Okay, this is my chance," he thought, pacing before the open front door. "No, no, it's not. C'mon, LaGonda, call me." He transferred his pacing to the front yard and waved at one of the Lawn Fags down the street who was way too interested in Ed's pacing. "Oh God, if he sees Ramon come out of the house..."

Fortunately at that moment, Ramon came around from the back of the house. "He must have gone out the back door," Ed thought with relief.

"Thank you, señor," Ramon said politely.

"Oh, it's nothing," Ed replied cheerfully. "So, in two weeks then?"

"I will see you in two weeks," Ramon said in halting English.

"Okay," Ed said, also in English. "Two weeks." It took a supreme act of will not to watch Ramon and the truck drive away. He went back into the house and waited for LaGonda to call.

"So, you have a beautiful new gardener and your husband is away?" LaGonda sighed out a lungful of smoke.

"Lee isn't my husband," Ed muttered guiltily.

"In a PERFECT WORLD, he would be," LaGonda yelled. She raised her voice when Ed started muttering or whining or both. "And I am only interested in a PERFECT WORLD."

Ed looked up, puzzled. "What?"

"Well, at least I have your attention, Edward." She smiled bitterly, crushed out her cigarette and lit a new one. "So why are you panicked? You were just looking at Estaban, weren't you?"

"His name is Ramon."

"Of course it is," she said leaning back. "But you were just looking; what were you thinking?"

"Nothing," Ed said too quickly and too softly.

"Nothing? You come running in here looking like a scared rabbit and YOU WERE THINKING NOTHING?" she asked at full volume. It was not for nothing that her home office was soundproof.

"Well...I was admiring him," Ed said at a normal volume.

"And?"

This was LaGonda's usual prompt for a full description of a lurid sexual fantasy. But Ed wasn't buying it.

"And nothing," he said coolly. "I didn't get any farther than admiring."

"Why not?"

"Um, because my faculty advisor called, I had errands to run, and you had a spot open this afternoon," Ed rattled off.

"How is the dissertation going?" she asked. Her dissertation had been on the patterns of guilt and relief of women who'd lost custody of their children to the State. She'd spent three years counseling for Child Protective Services as research. Publicly she concluded that more attention should be paid to early education of girls, with an emphasis on self-esteem and money management. Less publicly, but still publicly enough to cause an uproar, she concluded that the nuclear family was doomed and the sooner an alternative—group child raising, 24-hour schools, state-funded unlimited pre-school starting at birth—was found, the better. She also felt that sex education, easy access to birth control, and free sterilization for both sexes should be seriously considered, but the only time she mentioned these out loud in a public forum she was nearly lynched. Her dissertation was accepted and shelved in the University of California Berkeley Library where only a few brave souls have opened its dusty covers. Dr. LaGonda and her work were so controversial in the Bay Area, she had to move to Los Angeles to have any kind of practice at all.

"It's going well, thanks," Ed said.

"Still fantasizing about Vikings raping Irish monks?" she asked blandly.

Ed rolled his eyes. "I told you that I'm trying to get over that."

"Why? So you can fantasize about someone like Ramon who could actually fuck you?" she asked with a sneer.

"Why do I come here?" Ed asked.

"To talk about the worst so you DON'T DO IT! Why the hell do you think they call it the talking cure?" She ground her cigarette out and lit another one. "If you don't have any dark thoughts to tell me, then come back when you do." She sat back, waiting, gazing out the window as if she were alone in the room.

"...He's very handsome..." Ed swallowed hard and leaned back in his chair. "Mowing lawns is hard work. He gets all hot and sweaty, so I take him water. One day he's in the shed in the back yard. It's cool and dark in there. My eyes haven't adjusted to the gloom, so I call out to him.

"'Ramon?'

"A large warm hand encircles my wrist and pulls me inside. I drop the bottle of Evian as I'm pulled tight against his powerful chest. He whispers, 'Aqui,' against my lips. He takes my lower lip gently between his teeth. I moan and turn my head. He crushes my limp form in his arms and his kisses devour me."

"I'm hard and I can feel his erection against mine. He cups my ass in his hands and grinds us together as I cling helplessly to his neck like a drowning man. He half-carries half-drags me to the workbench in the far shadows of the shed. Leaning against it, we fumble savagely at our pants. I struggle furiously at the button and zipper of his jeans. He laughs as he easily snaps the drawstring of my cut-off sweat pants. They fall to my ankles. My penis is engulfed by his hand. He gives it a few powerful strokes and smears the pre-cum around the head. With his other hand, he fondles my balls and strokes teasingly behind them.

"Growling with frustration, I finally free his cock and it is magnificent. I drop to my knees in awe and take the head in my mouth. Ramon reaches down and strokes my hair, gently calling my name, and sighing with pleasure.

"At some signal only known to himself, Ramon pulls me to my feet and bends me over the workbench. He strokes some pre-cum off my cock and rubs it around my asshole. Gentle at first, then rougher as he presses his fingertip in, working his whole middle finger inside me. Alternately panting against my neck and nipping at it, he finger fucks me until I beg, 'Please...please fuck me...' He laughs softly and withdraws his finger. He caresses and then spreads my butt cheeks. I feel a large slippery head push against my ring and then the head pops inside. I gasp and he asks, 'Okay?' I say, 'Yes,' and push against him. He holds my hips firmly in place and thrusts slowly all the way in.

"We are both panting like mad dogs when he is inside and begins to fuck me in long powerful strokes. I cling to the workbench with all my might because if I let go, I'll be swept away by this force of nature invading my body, my mind, my soul. Just as I think I might lose my mind, he reaches around and takes a firm grip on my dick. He strokes me in the same rhythm as he's fucking me. I can only moan helplessly into the bench and surrender to this dual ravishment.

"'I can't...I can't...' I cry out as I come. Ramon thrusts his full length into me and comes with a strangled shout against my shoulder that shakes my body to its core. I am limp, the only thing holding me up are Ramon's arms around me."

Edward stopped his narrative to take a deep breath and swallow. A box of Kleenex landed in his lap.

"Don't make a mess," LaGonda said, rising from behind her desk. "I'll make some tea." She walked from the room as she usually did in these sessions.

Once she was gone, Ed gratefully unzipped his chinos and pretended his hand was Ramon's.

He found LaGonda at her kitchen table with two cups of tea. She shoved one of them at him. "Feel better?" she asked.

"I don't want to be unfaithful to Lee," Edward mumbled.

"Then don't be." LaGonda had amazing hearing when she wanted. "What you do in the privacy of your head is between you and your imagination. There's no need to drag anyone else into it. If more people just fantasized most of their sex lives, it would be a better world all around."

"But I feel guilty."

"Over a fantasy? And a fantasy you're not going to indulge in? Or are you?" she asked calmly.

Ed met her eyes. "I'm not going to cheat on Lee," he said firmly. "With anyone," he added.

"Good lad," she said, patting him on the bicep. "You're paying cash for today, yes?"

In order to give his overworked penis a break, Edward alternated jackoff sessions with cold showers and hours of writing about his Irish monks meditating in their icy wastes. Ramon's next visit was not as devastating as his debut. Ed had pretty much had all the mental sex he could stand with Ramon and the prospect of the real thing, although tantalizing, wasn't such a thrill anymore. Even so, Ed was still fucking and getting fucked by Ramon in his fantasies three times a day. He called LaGonda to ask her why his sex drive was so high with a fantasy and so low with Lee. She said because Lee was a real flesh-and-blood person with his own thoughts and desires, and not some mental cum-splashed, sticky, obedient, mute blow-up doll for Edward to work his dominance and control issues out with in his head. She added that Lee loved Edward as a person, and not as a sex toy.

"Well, I should think not, Dr. LaGonda," Ed nearly snapped at her.

"Well, I should hope not, Edward," she snapped back. "But stranger things have happened."

"Not with us!"

"That's good," she said, sounding bored. "You know where to mail my check, of course."

Edward put the phone down and made a quick mental calculation of what he owed her for that conversation. Then he doubled it because if she could piss him off in such a short time, she'd done him some good.

Lee called from New York and said don't wait up, he'd get a cab home. Since Ed was in the shower when he called, he left the message on Ed's cell phone. Ed figured he'd just pick him up at the airport anyway, but realized Lee was coming back a week late, so he had no idea what flight or even airline he was on. He tried to call him back to tell him he'd pick him up at the airport if Lee could tell him his flight, but the call went straight to voicemail.

The Lawn Fags

"Typical," Ed thought. "He tells me what to do and then makes it impossible to argue with him. But, damn, I've missed him."

Ed called Dr. LaGonda to tell her the good news.

"What about your idol, Ramon?" she asked, sounding like she was lighting a cigarette at the same time.

Ed laughed. "He can still be my idol after my lover comes home."

LaGonda said, "Hmph," and hung up without asking for payment. Ed stared at the phone for a few minutes, wondering if this meant he was cured or he'd just rendered her speechless for once.

Later that night, Ed woke to loud banging on the front door. He chuckled evilly as he padded down the hallway to let Lee in.

"If you knew I was coming home, why did you put the deadbolt on?" Lee, jetlagged, asked.

"I didn't want to be scared to Jesus when you came into the bedroom. Like last time you told me not to wait up," Ed said, following Lee into the bedroom. "What? No kiss hello?"

Lee swung around, scowling, but couldn't stop his arms from closing around Ed when Ed stepped into them. If it was possible to keep scowling while kissing the man you love, Lee Southern was not capable of it. "Hello," he said with a little laugh when he came up for air. "Edward, I'm on Moscow time, I've been trapped in airports, I'm–"

"Stinky and cranky," Ed helpfully supplied. "Why don't you take a shower and relax? Want some food?"

"No."

"Then go bathe," Ed said, gathering up Lee's coat and briefcase. "And brush your teeth," he added as Lee, with unnecessary modesty, closed the bathroom door.

Ed opened the window and let the mild, grass-scented air refresh the room. He crawled back into bed and if it hadn't been so late, would have called LaGonda to get her odds on whether he was going to get laid that night or not. Based on the erection in Lee's pants, and if the shower didn't relax him too much, chances were very very much in Ed's favor. "I really have to stop depending on LaGonda," he told himself as he smoothed Lee's pillow. "She's not expensive, but it adds up eventually."

Lee came out, toweling his hair and smiling. "I do feel better. Sorry I bit your head off."

"Jetlag does that," Ed said pleasantly. "Come to bed."

Lee pulled Ed into his arms and kissed him deeply. "I'm jetlagged, Ed, don't expect very much."

"I understand," Ed breathed, and began to move down Lee's body.

"Well, I can manage that," Lee said vaguely, and maneuvered them into a sixty-nine. He liked this position, sliding his lips over Ed's rapidly hardening cock was always such a pleasure. Edward's cock was sweet and salty and fit perfectly into his mouth. This way Lee could pleasure Ed and respond to the pleasure Ed was giving him at the same time. Lee ran his hands over Ed's fine ass and ran his fingertips over the younger man's asshole. Feeling Ed sighing at the contact, Lee felt a twinge of regret that he was just too tired to fuck him that night. "Maybe in the morning..." Lee thought.

For his part, Ed was just so glad to be having sex with Lee, flesh and blood and pre-cum honest-to-God real Lee that he felt like crying. It was heaven working Lee's dick down his throat, nuzzling his wiry pubic hair and fondling his balls. Bravely, Ed let his fingers wander a little too far beyond Lee's scrotum and over his anus and got growled at. Lee! On his cock! Growling at him! "Mmmm, too wonderful, too wonderful," Ed moaned around Lee's shaft.

Because Lee didn't deep throat, he usually came first. The one time he'd brought Edward off first, his lover's jaws had twitched pretty badly in orgasm and Lee had been bitten. And once bitten...That night he took his mouth off Edward's sex and buried his face in Edward's silky pubic thatch as his lover's throat and hands coalesced his whole being into his groin and Lee's mind filled with blinding white light. Panting, Lee held tight to Edward's thighs as Edward eased his limp cock out of his mouth. The sound of Edward licking his lips was sweet to him, and Lee licked around the head of Ed's cock before taking it into his mouth. Lee wrapped his hand around the base of Edward's shaft and pumped and sucked him in the same rhythm. It wasn't very long before Edward was making strangled noises and Lee reflexively swallowed his come. He crawled up beside the still shuddering Edward and reached across him for the bottle of Evian Edward always kept on the nightstand. "Ah, s'good to be home," he said taking a swig and offering the bottle to Edward. He curled up on Edward's shoulder while Edward took a drink of water.

"It's so good to have you home," Ed said softly. He put the bottle down and put his arms around Lee, who was already fast asleep.

The lawn service woke them. When the mower went off under their bedroom window, Ed pulled a pillow over head, but Lee got up to survey the state of their lawn. He was pleased, very pleased to see it in good condition. "Hey, the lawn guy is hot," he said over his shoulder to Ed.

"Is he?" Ed asked, figuring sleep was no longer an option. He joined Lee at the window and expected to see his idol, Ramon.

It wasn't Ramon, it was another Latino guy. A hot Latino guy, as Lee had observed, but not Ramon. "Oh, he's okay," Ed said, trying to brush off his disappointment and concern. Ramon's whereabouts were none of his business. He could just hear LaGonda shouting this at him, so there was no need to call her. He closed the window and the curtain. The mower noise was cut in half. Lee was close by so he kissed him.

Lee pulled him tightly into his arms. "Let's go back to bed."

Humu Humu

Lene Taylor

Everyone said it was Paradise, but Ian Hewison knew he'd gone to Hell. First there was the heat, which was unremitting: the temperature was over 26C every day. What was that in American? Eighty degrees? Having to convert everything in his head was a minor annoyance, though, compared to the bright sun...and the humidity.

So he was hot all the time, and hungry, because he was scared to eat anything but Pot Noodle. There was fresh fruit every day, but how could he eat things he'd never heard of? Guava? What the hell was that? At least he knew what pineapple was, though the ones he'd tasted at home were always kind of bland or bitter.

Then there was the ocean.

And the fact that he hadn't gotten laid in *months*, not at home in England since he'd broken up with Andrew the Dick-Man, as he'd come to think of his ex, and not here in Hawaii, where the only people he knew were the other visiting scholars, who were mostly crazy.

"Hewison, come to the fucking beach with us today," Mórag said, grabbing a pink soda out of the communal fridge in the break room. He loved her deep, soft New Zealand accent, but he wished she wouldn't sprinkle so many varieties of "fuck" on her sentences, like salt.

"Can't. Busy. I'm waiting for the last round of comparisons to print out."

"That's fucking crap. You can look at them tomorrow." She fixed him with a glare. "I'm tired of organizing these trips and having you miss out."

"OK. I don't like the sea. And I don't like getting sand in my clothes. And I don't want to get sunburned–" He stopped short when she started laughing.

"Ian, my love, you are a world-class coward," she crowed, throwing her arms around him. "Maybe it's the price you pay for your looks and that gorgeous hair. Well, you must come next time. Tom was asking if you were ever going to join us." She picked up her soda and a bag of chips and left.

Tom was asking about him?

Since he was alone, Ian allowed himself a minute to think about Tom Boyd: short, blond, frighteningly smart, with an easy smile and the ability to surf, which seemed otherwordly to Ian, who couldn't even ride a bike. He was here at Mauna Kea from Caltech; they had time on the instrument Keck observatory, along with the University of California. Tom was as protective of his research as he was open about his gayness.

Ian was lucky to get the time he did, thanks to his grant, but it would be enough to finish his astrophysics degree at the University of Sussex. He could collect his data on zodiacal light and get back to England, where the temperature was normal and you could get a decent cup of tea. And he could go back to pining after boys he couldn't have, just as he was doing with Tom...

He stood up abruptly and went to collect his printouts, and brood.

Next day he found a note slipped under the door of his rented room in Kamuela, where all the observatory folks lived, including the transients like him.

Hope you had a lovely time sulking. I missed you and so did Tom. Next time, fucking come with us. M.

He smiled at that. And he kept smiling all the way to the shuttle bus stop. He squinted in the bright light of the afternoon and for the first time realized he was the only person not wearing sunglasses. He could just make out the bus coming, a moving bulk in the waves of heat on the street.

"Hey, Ian," Tom greeted him, and gave him a light touch on the shoulder. "You have time on the scope tonight? Cool, so do I. Another day in paradise, huh? Did you forget your sunglasses?"

"Yes, I left them on the shelf in the store in London. It didn't seem possible that I would actually need them. One never believes the reports of tourists to mythic lands." Ian was pleased to see Tom smile.

"You've been here for a month without sunglasses? Dude, you're insane. Especially for someone with green eyes—the sun must be killing you. Come on, there's a great store just around the corner. We need to fix you up." He pulled firmly Ian by the arm.

"But the bus..." he protested.

"Buses are like men. There's another one coming every five minutes."

An hour later Ian was sitting alone at his favorite terminal, staring at the sunglasses Tom had picked out for him (because of their "high coolness factor"). They'd talked and joked the whole way up on the bus

16

and Ian had been so bold as to suggest they have breakfast together after that night's work.

"Only if I can pick the place," Tom said. Ian agreed; he didn't think there was any place that could screw up tea and toast.

"Try it. Just put it in your mouth," Tom instructed him. Ian wished he'd stop smirking.

"In another context, that line perhaps might work. However, eating *goat* cheese for breakfast is not what I had in mind for today, thank you." He looked at the little round ball of cheese that Tom was holding out for him on a spoon.

"It's awesome. And I've never seen you eat any real food. There's attractively slim and then there's *thin*." He leaned across the little table, so close that Ian could smell him. And he smelled good. "C'mon, Ian. It's good for you."

Ian looked from Tom's very blue eyes to the tanned hand holding the spoon. Backing out now was not a possibility, especially not with the owner of this little cafe watching from behind the counter. He sighed.

Tom grinned and tipped the spoon into his mouth. And then he closed his eyes, because the taste was so good and so overwhelming that he didn't want anything to distract him from it: creamier than anything he'd ever tasted, even cream, and mixed throughout was the gentle accent of *fine herbs* and a tiny hint of olive oil. It melted slowly on his tongue and made him feel full when he'd swallowed it.

"Explain to me how this comes from a goat," he demanded, while he slid the dish, which held three more green-flecked cheese ping pong balls sitting in a little pool of sunny yellow oil, over to his side of the table. It was the best food he'd ever had and made him wonder if English goats were lacking in some cheese-producing ability. Certainly he'd never tasted goat cheese like this at home.

"They're Hawaiian goats. I think they surf. Um, you can have the rest," Tom laughed. "Seriously, Ian, I'm glad you like it. You wanna try something else radical today? How about a walk in the sunshine? I want to go down to the bookstore and pick up some magazines."

Ian was trying hard to resist the urge to cram the rest of the cheese into his mouth all at once. He took a drink of water to buy time. "I don't really fancy a sunburn."

"I have sunscreen." Tom pulled it out of his shoulder bag triumphantly. Ian mentally put a black star next to Mórag's name, until it occurred to him that perhaps Tom could be the one rubbing sun lotion on his back, at which point he changed it to two gold stars.

"Yes," he said, and gave Tom a genuine smile. "I would like that very much."

By early afternoon Ian was ready to fall over; working through the nights and sleeping odd hours was seriously wrecking his body clock. Plus he wasn't hungry for the first time in weeks; he could still taste the coconut ice cream they'd had on the walk back to his room. Tom was real; Tom was funny; Tom asked a lot of questions and Ian was tired of being interrogated.

"I must get some sleep," he said, suppressing a yawn.

"Me too. Are you observing tonight?"

"No. I've got miles of stuff to go through so I think I shall stay in and commune with my laptop. My next night is Wednesday."

"I've got Tuesday off too. You wanna hang out?" Ian guessed that "hang out" was American for "if we like each other, it's a date, and if we don't, we'll pretend it never happened".

"Sounds great. As long as you pick the restaurant," he laughed.

"No problemo. Um, Ian, can I ask you something?" Tom took a step closer.

"I suppose. You won't ask me if I've accepted Jesus as my personal savior, will you?"

"No way! What I really wanted to ask was...is this really the way your hair is?" He reached up and gently touched Ian's mop of black curls. Ian knew he had great hair; he carried his mother's Celtic genes and wore his glossy Botticelli spirals long, down to his shoulders. It gave a lover something to hold on to. He smiled at Tom.

"Yes, that's really the way it is. Stays curly even when wet."

"Awesome." Tom let his hand fall with a sigh. "See you Tuesday, dude. Bus stop at 6?"

Ian nodded. Ten minutes later he was jacking off in the shower, imagining Tom pulling his hair hard as he fucked the living daylights out of him.

Ian pushed back his very empty bowl. After getting to know the wonder that was saimin—noodles and fish and onions and God knew what else in perfectly seasoned broth—he knew he was off Pot Noodle for good.

"Tom, I must say, you do know how to eat." It was definitely a date.

"I'm American. It's what we do best, besides offending the rest of the world. I apologize for that." Tom finished his beer in one gulp. "And you need to eat more. You want to go down to the beach? Best place to wait for it to get dark."

Ian hated the sudden tension that filled him. "Well, actually, I think I'd rather stay closer to town, if you don't mind." Tom's disappointment was obvious, which only made Ian feel worse. "It's just—I don't have a good relationship with the sea. I wouldn't be able to relax. And I want to relax...with you."

"OK. It's weird, but the only place I really feel relaxed is in the water. I grew up surfing and swimming in the Pacific, but the ocean here is like...it's perfect. It's the most perfect water I ever swam in. Jeez, Ian, you live on an island yourself—you should dig the water."

"Your water and my water are two very different waters." Tom laughed at that and they got up to leave.

They found an empty bench on the small park at the edge of town and sat, quite close together, watching the cloudless sky turn from orange to red to purple and then to deep deep blue, with stars like confetti scattered in its bowl. They talked shop—or rather, Ian talked and Tom asked questions.

"That's why I got interested in zodiacal light—it wasn't a major research area and I thought I'd have it mostly to myself. Not a lot has been done in the last thirty years, but now, you know, everyone's looking at dust clouds around other stars, so they're taking another look at ours. Look, there's a satellite." Ian pointed at the tiny dot of light moving fast through Cygnus. "Now it's your turn. What are you looking for?"

Tom slid closer and put his arm around Ian's narrow shoulders. "Oh, someone to laugh at my jokes, who can talk scopes with me, who has green eyes...ow!" He rubbed the spot on his leg where Ian had punched him. "Listen. I don't like talking about it because I'm tired of wise-ass cracks. Everybody wants to find a new planet now—it's the hot sexy thing. Measuring the wobble around other stars, now that's brilliant—tells you what's pulling on that star. But—fuck! How many stars are there? You gotta know where to look." He was staring up into the sky, eyes shining.

"And you do?" Ian hoped Tom didn't think his hard-on was for a new planet. Their thighs were pressed tight together; he let his hand wander to Tom's knee.

"Yeah. Well, yeah, I think I do. The ones most like ours. I think that's the best bet. So I'm looking. And I sure as hell better find one soon, or I'm not going to have a thesis. But I am cautiously optimistic." He glanced down at Ian's hand. "You want to continue this somewhere else? Or keep looking at the stars?"

Ian leaned close and put his lips to Tom's ear. "I've been looking at the stars all my life. I haven't seen enough of you." And he kissed the spot just below that ear.

"My place?" Tom gasped.

"Yes, please."

Ian couldn't get there fast enough. Once they were in Tom's room (in his apartment, roommates watching TV in the living room, or something; he was too frantic to notice anything except the blessed air conditioning), he pulled Tom down on the bed and kissed him hungrily, grinding against him and getting a gratifying moan in response. Shirts came off without too much trouble, and even in the dim light Ian was thrilled to see the whiteness of his hands against Tom's brown chest while Tom's rough fingers worked his nipples. Tom's mouth tasted of salt; he was salty all over and Ian realized he must have been swimming in the ocean that day, and strangely, that didn't bother him.

"You're so white. The whitest white guy I ever met," Tom laughed as he slid his hands into Ian's pants to squeeze his ass.

"I come from the land of whiteness, " Ian replied, and added "Dude," which sounded so ridiculous coming out of his middle-class English mouth that they both broke up laughing. It only made Ian more impatient to get fucked. He covered Tom's mouth with his own and grabbed his cock with both hands; the air conditioning wasn't helping him now and he could feel the sweat on his face and between his shoulder blades. Tom's strong arms had him trapped in an embrace he'd been longing for. He couldn't wait any longer.

"I'm so sorry, but I simply can't wait any longer," Ian said, his voice husky. Tom threw him on his back and licked a line from his belly to his jaw.

"Ian..." he whispered. "Can't wait for what? Tell me..." Ian writhed beneath him, delirious with desire.

"Bloody hell! I want you in me, now, now..." and there was lube and a condom and then Tom pushed into him and the night dissolved into hot breath and hard thrusts and sweet friction. Tom fucked him hard, because he wanted it that way, and he held out as long as he could before he came in a rush, flushed and tingling. Tom slowed his pace but only for a moment; then he closed his eyes and finished fast and Ian loved the way his lower lip trembled when he came.

They lay for a while in silence till Tom said, "Good?"

"Stellar. First rate. May I have some more, please?"

And he did, until far into the night.

When Mórag asked him to the next beach party three days later, Ian knew he'd have to go. So he put on swim shorts (borrowed from Tom, since he didn't have any), a pound of sun block (applied by Tom's hands, as he'd hoped), and his cool new sunglasses, and squeezed into the minivan driven by Aloka, the senior research assistant at the remote observation station (Tom had left earlier on his bike). The heat made him stick to the seat.

When they got to the beach, he quickly parked himself on a bamboo mat and waited for Tom to show up. What he didn't expect was that Tom would rise up out of the ocean and stride over the hot sand, dripping, and greet him with a salty kiss.

"You're going to make me do this, aren't you?" Ian asked, hoping he looked pitiful.

"Totally. You need to. Come swimming with me, Ian," he said, holding out his hand. Ian sighed.

"All right. I'll do it, but I won't like it." The night before, lying in each other's arms after fucking on Ian's desk, they'd talked seriously about childhoods, jobs, schools, why Tom was afraid of having his research stolen, and why Ian didn't want to go in the sea. This was the story he told:

At 16 his parents had taken him for a summer trip to Ibiza. It was probably the worst time they could have chosen; a growth spurt had left him at his adult height of six feet but hadn't added any weight, so he looked like a coat rack with hair. And he'd just begun to come to grips with the fact that he liked boys—and further, that there were some boys who liked him back. But on the beach in Spain he felt lonely, clumsy, and terribly frustrated by all the beautiful men, who he assumed couldn't possibly be interested in a gangly chalk-white teenager.

"I bet you were beautiful. I bet they were interested," Tom interrupted.

"No and yes, but I didn't know that then. May I finish?"

"Sorry. But do you have any pictures of yourself when you were 16? Maybe in a bathing suit?" Ian put his hand over Tom's mouth and continued.

So he'd spent the first day under an umbrella on the beach, sweating. The second day he decided the ocean water might help his hard-on go down, so he'd ventured in, surprised that it was so warm. It was rocky, so he picked his way with care to where he could stand waist deep and look back towards shore. He stayed that way for a while, feeling the sun beating down in his skinny shoulders and wishing he could swim. The waves rippled around him.

"Never turn your back on the ocean, dude," Tom said around Ian's hand.

"Yes, I'm getting to that, please stuff it for now."

He really didn't remember when the wave hit him, because it all turned into dark water and sand in his eyes, nose, mouth, ears until he struggled up, gasping for air, just as another wave hit him and he fell face first, tumbling over and over in the shallow water. When he finally got right side up again, a couple of strangers offered him helping hands and words of concern, which at that age he'd interpreted as pity and condescension. He was shaking, but managed to pull himself together to walk, not crawl, out of the water—and immediately stepped on something (he never knew what) extremely sharp, and emerged miserable and bloody. He'd had to get stitches and spent the rest of the holiday inside, reading Tolkien. He'd gotten over the pain and shock, but the humiliation still stung.

"That sucks. I got hit in the head with my board once, coming back in. Not fun." He kissed Ian's fingers.

"I suppose I should get over it." He waited a moment. "Aren't you going to tell me that I must confront my fear?"

"Um, no, actually, I was going to say that the best part about swimming in the ocean is swimming naked. Maybe we could go to a clothing-optional beach one day." He kissed his way up Ian's arm and buried his face in his armpit, inhaling deeply. "Mmmm. Ian sweat."

So now they were here and Ian stood on the edge of the water, which was very calm and clear. He could even see schools of tiny fish darting around in just a few inches of water. Tom took his hand and pulled him forward.

"What are those fish? Are they going to bite me?" Ian asked, resisting a little.

"I don't know, they're like zebra fish or something. I call them ankle fish, cause they're always around your ankles. Nothing will bite you. Come on." A little wave washed over his feet. Further down the beach the other Keck geeks were splashing and whooping it up.

"Fuck it," Ian muttered and took a few steps in. "Oh my God, it's warm. Really warm! It's like bath water!"

"Bath water with fish and turtles. Come in a little deeper." The sand was soft under his tentative steps and the fish were indeed swirling around his ankles. He waded forward until the water was at his waist.

"All right, that's enough for now." Tom held both his hands, steadying him in the constant push and pull of the waves that broke gently on the shore. "What should I do?" he asked anxiously.

"Just...relax. Look around. Look how blue the sky is. Look up at the volcano. Look at me." Tom's eyes sparkled. "Bend your knees—there you go—till you're all the way in—and just...float." Salt water would make him more buoyant, of course, but he hadn't expected it to feel quite so liberating. This was nothing like being in an indoor pool full of chlorine; this was...primal. Fish swam around his legs, their passing like breezes in the water as they went on to the coral reef only a few yards away. Back on shore, Mórag and a few of the others saw him and waved, shouting encouragement.

"Well done, Hewison! Oh, well done," Mórag called. "Now you've got to learn to fucking surf!"

"I am not going to fucking surf," Ian said to Tom.

"Not today. But come here, I'll hold you," Tom replied, and in a few minutes, with Tom supporting him, Ian was floating on his back and actually enjoying the feeling of the sun on his face.

"I'm not hot. Being in the water makes it seem less hot. This is amazing," Ian said in mock amazement. "Another myth confirmed."

"No duh. Try going under." And Ian did and that was fine, and Tom showed him how to jump with the waves rather than fighting them, and eventually he got curious enough to put on some goggles and stick his head under the water by the reef.

They stayed till sunset, finishing up the last of the pineapple (which Ian was convinced was processed sugar in fruit form—who cared, it was delicious) and the bread. Tom was still in the water; they planned to meet later for ice cream. Ian walked up the beach to the van, and his last image was of Tom diving and moving swiftly through the darkening water, like a dolphin at play in the ocean fields. Ian was going back to England in a week and a half.

Tom shaved his balls, and Ian wondered if that was standard American practice, or just for him. Another novel experience, and one that he liked as much as mango ice cream. Tom was sprawled on the bed in front of him, his legs spread wide, his erection wet from Ian's attentions. Ian really did love sucking cock, and Tom's was a treasure: it fit in his hand perfectly, its color changed from reddish gold to almost scarlet as he got closer to coming, and it jumped and pulsed under Ian's expert tongue. And his come was the sweetest Ian had ever tasted.

Ian envied the graceful way Tom inhabited his muscular body, the ease with which he could move them both into a better position, or hold them steady when sex got really rough. It hadn't taken them long to find their groove and Ian was grateful that they'd skipped a lot of the awkwardness and fumbling around of newly paired lovers. They had used a *lot* of condoms.

Now Ian went back to work, licking and sucking slowly while he pressed two fingers deeper into Tom's ass, then picking up the rhythm, taking as much cock into his mouth as he could and sucking hard, feeling Tom start to tremble; Ian paused for a moment, letting his teeth graze the head of Tom's cock, and that was enough to push him over the edge and he came with a loud happy groan.

"Oh my God, you're so hot, you're so fucking hot, Ian," Tom panted. His cheeks were flushed a lovely rose under his tan and he was grinning.

Ian crawled up to kiss him and whispered, "Turn over, dude."

Yet another condom and more lube and Ian pushed smoothly into Tom, thrilling to the tightness of his ass, caressing those firm, round ass cheeks, pale as the rest of his body was tan. Tom laughed with pleasure and pushed back to meet him. Fast, then slow and gentle, Tom with him at every stroke; Ian's orgasm was building fast so he decided to run with it and finished in six hard thrusts that left him sweaty and tingling all over. Ian stayed where he was, feeling himself softening even as Tom clenched around him a few times and practically purred with delight. He ran his hands over Tom's broad back and kissed the line of his spine.

"Shall we just stay here for a few days, or perhaps a year?" Ian asked. Tom turned his head on the pillow and smiled, eyes shining.

"Yeah, but you have to go get us more ice cream."

In that last week there was more swimming and fruit and fucking, including one especially memorable event in the men's room in the remote observation station at three in the morning. They'd carefully avoided talking about what would happen when Ian left.

Three days and counting. Tom shot rubber bands up to the ceiling in the computer room as he watched Ian burning data to DVDs. Ian felt like they'd been joined at the hip lately, which he liked very much; better to get it all while you could, rather than pretend it didn't matter. Either way, saying good bye would be hell.

"What will you do when you finish?" Tom asked at last. Ian sighed.

"Sleep for a year. I don't know. I'm not very keen on teaching. I think I'd much rather have a research position somewhere." In truth, he'd been so focused on finishing the damn thesis he hadn't made any definite plans. He'd just assumed something would turn up.

"NASA's always hiring," Tom said.

"You must be joking, mate. They want people like you. Planet guys. They're not interested in my area."

"Actually, they are. I have some friends there and I asked. With all the cutbacks in exploration, they're putting a lot more money into Earth-based observing, trying to figure out how to deal with the local dust. Not too many people are experts in that area. Dude." Ian didn't reply. He was thinking hard.

"You found that out for me?" Ian asked.

"Well, for me too. That's where I want to work. All the people at NASA are paranoid fuckers, just like me. If I can find a planet, it increases my chances of getting a position there like a zillion percent."

"If only. Have you researched that percentage?"

"I mean it, Ian. Come and work at NASA with me," Tom said, as if Ian had only to accept his offer to make it come true.

Ian put the last disk in his bag and gestured for Tom to sit in his lap (not as ridiculous as it might have been a month ago—Ian had definitely put on some weight and maybe even some muscle). "Do you think I could simply move to California? What would I do there?"

"Well, there's me..." Tom said, and kissed him long and lovingly.

"Fucking hell, get a room," Mórag said as she passed by the door.

Ian insisted that Tom not go to the airport with him. So they sat in his room, arms around each other, saying very little, until the taxi arrived. The last kiss was equal parts hope and tears.

It had been a long warm summer in England and even September was positively balmy. Everyone commented on his tan, but Ian felt chilled to the bone.

Of course it was good to see his family and friends; of course it was good to go to the pub and eat greasy food and catch up on gossip. But it seemed insubstantial and unreal now, after the vivid extremes of Hawaii, as if he was falling back to sleep again.

He and Tom traded email as soon as he got back. Tom had another three weeks at Keck and was stressed about his lack of progress, though he tried to hide it. Ian told him that he'd put some British perseverance in a box and FedEx it to him. Just seeing the email in his inbox produced a pang of longing that he'd never experienced before, and made the coming semester—tutoring, writing, attending discussion groups—seem like drudgery, instead of the exciting final run up to his degree.

A fortnight went by in a haze of boredom and willful laziness. But once he got it together to sit down and review his work, he realized that he was nearly done: he'd gotten a lot more done in Hawaii than he had expected. He started making notes and soon was convinced that he could be done by Christmas, if the thesis was accepted and he passed the oral examination. Which he would, no question—the observations were sound, the numbers were fine, and his solid and completely unremarkable hypothesis was confirmed. "And then I'll be free," he said to the paper, happily.

Free? Where had that come from?

Just then his mobile jumped on the table, startling him so much he dropped his pencil. One text message, from a California number, short and to the point.

Found it.

Ian laughed and knew just where he wanted to be. By Christmas, he'd be free to go. He hit "reply" and typed:

I knew you would. Done in Dec. See you in the new year.

Then he put his phone in his pocket and went to ask his advisor how to apply for a job at NASA.

Nul Gravity

Valessa Smith

Rob Miller didn't hesitate. It was instinct: when he saw the back of a mop of brown hair vanishing under a tangle of brawling limbs, he didn't think, he just piled in. Before he'd had time to consciously review his motives, someone had yelled, "Squad!", the attackers had fled and he was lying on the sidewalk next to the man he'd intended to help.

Who wasn't Jiminez.

The hair still looked right, and the black pants that had added to the general impression of Jiminez-ness were indeed black, but they clung to well-toned thighs like a second skin. The boots were fashion items, not uniform—knee high, with impractically stacked heels, and more "buccaneer" than DSquad.

Miller's nose was about six inches from all this. He picked himself up and shook the street-dust off his uniform. Then he reached out a hand to the stranger.

Since his leave had only just started, two hours late, Miller hadn't yet accustomed himself to the traditional masks worn by local "pleasure" workers. This person was wearing a beaded example, and a beaded jacket to match. The little pieces of jet glinted in the sunlight.

"Is there a problem?"

It was most disorientating, having someone's eyes removed from the picture. Miller was absolutely certain one moment that this *was* Jiminez, but the next moment, as his gaze fell on the excessive tightness of the pants, the expensive sparkle of the jewels in among the jet beads...

...the way the words "is there a problem" sounded accented, but at the same time, could just be colored by the cosmopolitan cadence of yet another space port.

"No...uh..."

"I remind you of someone?" The stranger took a step closer to the patrolman, as if inviting closer scrutiny.

"Maybe," Miller answered defensively, declining to take a corresponding step backwards, into the gutter.

"You have only just arrived?"

Now that *definitely* sounded like Jiminez...if you closed your eyes so you didn't see the three diamond studs piercing the guy's left earlobe, and didn't inhale the aroma of syntheremones, legal here, but only if a DSquad patrolman was prepared to spend most of last month's paycheck buying it, and then scrub to operating theater standards before returning to his unit.

Miller realized he was taking deeper breaths than were entirely prudent.

"Yes. I'm meeting some friends in a bar just along here, so..."

So just why, Miller asked himself sternly, was this masked stranger making him feel so nervous?

"My apologies." The person gave a chivalrous half bow.

"For what?" It occurred to Miller that the brawl might have been staged, and his hand flew to his belt to check if he still had his wallet. He should have thought of that earlier.

The stranger smiled knowingly. "According to statute 621.5, section 21.8, subparagraph 3, volume 16, revision 2 of the current edition of the Sex Commerce Code, I am supposed to explain myself before I confuse anyone. I am the latest, Mark 4, recreational holodroid. Whoever you want me to be..." the holodroid threw his arms wide, like a drag queen launching into the final chorus of a torch song medley. "I am."

Miller frowned. "I don't remember wanting you to be anyone in particular."

"But you mistook me for someone, I think. That was enough to start the process, and now that is who I am. Until you move out of range. Which bar?"

"The...uh...the...the Fountain."

"Oh." The droid's face fell.

"Is that a problem?"

"No. Except...you probably can't afford me."

"You're expensive?"

The droid nodded. "In absolute terms, very expensive, but if you consider what I am offering you, the chance to interact in whatever way you wish with the person of your choice, I would imagine that I represent something of a bargain."

Telling himself that he could drink with his shipmates whenever he wished, but that he rarely had the opportunity to discuss demand-side economics with an android, Miller gave in to his curiosity. "How much?"

"For how long?"

It was hard to answer that without thinking about what one might do in the time available. "An hour," Miller suggested, "for example."

The droid named a figure that would have looked reasonable pasted to the viewscreen of a nearly new two person flitter in excellent condition, one careful owner.

Miller gave a low, shocked whistle of disbelief.

The droid tipped his head on one side. "Although, you did come to my rescue just now. And it is early in the evening. I probably will not pick up another client for some time..." He halved his original price.

Miller shook his head and turned away towards the Fountain.

"I would not still look like him if you were not interested," the droid said softly.

"I'm not interested. I just thought I saw a friend in trouble..."

"Of course. And the DSquad pays so badly..."

"It's not that," Miller corrected him. "I'm really not interested. I'm sorry."

"I understand."

"No hard feelings," Miller said helplessly, wondering why the hell he was having such difficulty giving this piece of technology the brush off.

"The problem is..." the droid started.

"Yes?"

"This is not your fault. But I was so certain that you *were* interested..."

"Yes?" Miller prompted again.

"I have a subroutine, because I am sensitive to the wishes of anyone who comes within range, I have to be careful not to react inappropriately. I...locked onto this persona prematurely, and now..."

Miller frowned. "You mean...you're stuck looking like this until...until..."

"Until I...uh..." The droid blushed, Miller would have sworn, to the exact shade that Jiminez would have colored in the same circumstances. "...complete the contract."

Miller shook his head and tried not to laugh. "He's not a bad-looking guy. If you drop your price a little...well, quite a lot...you should find someone to help you out."

The droid took a moment to consider this idea. Miller was worried for a moment that it would be offended, but this didn't seem to be a problem. It nodded. "You say your friends are in the Fountain?"

"Yes...hold on a moment!" Miller quickly caught up to the droid, taking hold of its arm to stop its progress toward the bar. He was startled by how real it felt, under the cool scratchiness of the jet beads. "Where are you..."

"I am designed to operate interactively. I am not sure I would be capable of sex with a stranger. That is, with someone who thought I was a stranger. If you follow me."

Miller shut his mouth and scratched one ear thoughtfully. "You can't go in there," he said after a moment. "He's in there."

"You don't wish him to know that you are attracted to him?" the droid asked.

"I'm not," Miller said quickly, "but that isn't the point. I mean...none of his friends are going to... Well, what I mean is, they might find him attractive, but he might feel a little...well, weird, if any of them wanted to pay to go off with you, rather than..."

"Sleeping with him on a noncommercial basis."

"Uh...something like that. It's...it's just not straightforward."

The droid's mouth pursed into a most Jiminez-like expression of puzzlement.

"With friends, and colleagues...it can be difficult to adjust when you realize that you're beginning to think of someone as...more than just a friend. Or colleague." Miller sought for an analogy that the droid might appreciate. "It's just too complicated, you see. Imagine if you realized you'd fallen in love with a client..."

"That is most unlikely to happen," the droid said.. "I am a holodroid. However, I understand the concept. I shall report to the service bureau. Probably one of the technicians can correct this malfunction. An adjustment to my operating parameters should prevent any repetition of the problem."

"That sounds like a good idea," Miller said reassuringly.

"Will you do likewise?"

"Huh?"

"You appear to be inappropriately programmed. You demonstrate attraction to your 'friend', yet you deny it. I..." The droid smiled shyly. "...I think that you are afraid he will feel 'weird' if you offer to sleep with him on a noncommercial basis."

"Damn right he will," Miller said, more sincerely than was perhaps wise.

The droid sidled closer to the officer. "If I report to the service bureau, I am likely to be inactive for at least the rest of the night. It would be in my interests to charge you the union minimum in order to secure this engagement. I could then return to work more quickly, and arrange to be serviced swiftly during normal office hours."

Miller frowned, wondering why there was a union minimum for holodroids.

"Among the varied justifications I have been given by those who use my services is a desire to get it out of their system," the droid continued confidentially. He leaned a little closer to Miller. "Since you are helping me with my problem, I should be most willing to assist you with yours."

Miller blinked. The droid sounded just the way Jiminez did when he was trying swap an inconvenient duty. "It's...it's not just the money," he confessed. "You see...well, like I said, if he knew I'd deliberately gone with you because you looked like him..." and sounded like him, and *moved* like him, Miller added to himself.

"But he will not know," the droid said.

Miller shrugged. It still seemed...

"And in fact," the droid continued. "I really do not look very much like him. The technology is not yet sufficiently advanced. The mask encourages you to convince yourself that the resemblance exists."

"It does?" Miller looked curiously at the creature. Perhaps it wasn't really so very like Jiminez after all. Not quite the same height for a start...

The droid took a small step forward in its buccaneer boots and kissed the startled officer on the lips.

"How much is the union minimum?" Miller asked breathlessly, a long moment later.

The droid named a figure that wouldn't cause Miller's bank to start issuing warnings. "That hotel is clean and inexpensive," it said, gesturing toward a low, white building.

Since he was saving several thousand credits already, Miller decided not to quibble. He allowed himself to be led across the street and into the lobby, where a bored native stood by as Miller typed his account number into the computer.

"Do I pay you before, or after?" Miller asked, his mind not really on the answer. Their room had white carpet three inches deep, an archway through to a marble and gold bathroom, and the bed...the bed was a nul-gravity model. A discreet grey dotted line on the floor, walls and ceiling marked the limits of the zone. Elastic filaments crisscrossed the chamber, like cat's cradle.

Miller swallowed. He hadn't looked at the details he was being asked to authorize. He'd just gone ahead and keyed in his number. Damned syntheremones.

"I'm sorry. I can't afford this." He turned to look at the rest of the room, the video wall, the champagne cooling in a small glacier of ice, the oysters sitting in their open shells, glistening invitingly.

"It's only a two hour reservation," the droid said. "And I have an arrangement with the management."

"Oh, well," Miller told himself. He'd always wanted to try nul grav sex and financial ruin; he might as well get three impractical desires out of the way in a single act of madness. He could sort out how he was going to pay it off in the morning. He smiled. Jiminez was always good for a loan.

The droid knelt down and unlaced its boots. The beaded jacket was thrown over a chair while the pants parted along their side seams and fell to the floor in a black silk pool.

When the droid straightened, its arousal bobbed proudly perpendicular to its washboard abdomen.

Within his uniform, Miller felt his own response fighting to get loose.

"Slow down," he told himself. "If these two hours are going to cost you two years' salary, the main feature better last more than just two minutes." He turned away from the immediate visual stimulus and busied himself pouring champagne. When he turned back with the glasses, his companion was standing right behind him, one hand outstretched for the beverage.

"Can you drink?" Miller asked.

The droid looked puzzled for a moment. "Oh, yes. I can simulate all human appetites."

"And what...should I call you?"

At that, the droid shrugged. "What do you call 'him'?"

"Jiminez." Miller shrugged too. "Or Frank, if we're...off duty, after a few drinks, you know."

"Frank."

The way the droid said it, it was immediately apparent to Miller that it wasn't quite right. He dredged his memory. "Francesco. Today, I'd like to call you Francesco."

The droid nodded, satisfied. "And what shall I call you?"

Miller thought for a moment, and then a smile curved his mouth. After all, this was costing him a small fortune. He might as well have *exactly* what he wanted. "I'd like you to call me...*sir*."

Behind the mask, the droid's eyebrows rose slightly. It upended its glass, tossing back the champagne like a tequila shot. "Shall I undress you, sir?"

"Yes."

Getting out of Squad fatigues just wasn't a sensual experience, but the droid removed the one-piece with graceful efficiency, ending up conveniently on its knees at his feet.

It bowed its head. "Sir?"

Fighting the urge to lean forward and unfasten the ribbon that held the mask in place, Miller considered.

Nul Gravity

Nul gravity was an interesting novelty, but it was one he could experience any time, once he was back on friendly terms with his bank.

What he really wanted, or the nearest he would ever come to it, was right here in front of him.

"I'd like you to..."

The droid opened its mouth.

The droid showered and left first. By the time Miller remembered he hadn't paid, it was too late to chase after it. And anyway, he wasn't even sure who to look for. It might by now have the bright pink antennae and engorged mammary glands of a local female in estrus.

He walked cautiously out of the hotel lobby, into the bright afternoon sunshine, half expecting everything to look different. His knees kept threatening to give way. Nul-grav sex, when they'd gotten round to it, turned out to demand muscle control in unexpected places.

"Miller! Hey, over here!" Ellis, beer bottle in hand, was advancing down the street. "Now where have you been? I can't believe the captain kept the both of you back for so long. Or did you...*'hic!*...distract each other?" The tech giggled and took another swig from his beer.

"What are you talking about, Ellis?"

"It's only a five hour leave, m'boy. Jiminez only turned up five minutes ago, and now you come waltzing along with barely an hour left to enjoy yourself. Unless...*'hic!*...you've been enjoying yourselves already an' not letting on to your friends... Lemme get you a beer, Miller m'boy. Lemme get you a beer." Ellis glanced from one side of the street to the other in search of hospitality. Eventually he managed to focus on the tables outside the Fountain Bar, and taking Miller's arm, led him unsteadily in that direction. Half a dozen officers and patrolmen, including Jiminez and Gordano, the unit's paramedic, were seated around three tables pushed together under the shade of a parasol.

Miller felt an embarrassing warmth creep into his face. "Hi," he said vaguely to the whole party. "I had to finish a report..."

Gordano frowned and glanced at Jiminez. "The same report...?"

"Mine was for Supply," Jiminez said.

"Fascists," Gordano said. He thumped the only empty chair in the group. Miller took it, thus finding himself sitting next to Jiminez without really meaning to. The patrolman was drinking orange juice. The beer Ellis had noisily ordered arrived, and Miller sat back in his chair, trying to remember how he'd used to sit before he'd paid a small fortune to simulate having sex with his best friend in a nul-grav suite. (He'd caught sight of the hotel's tariff on the way out, and reckoned that, morally, he didn't owe the droid a cent. Particularly as it had eaten more than its fair share of the oysters.)

"Probably I'd have leaned back like this," he thought, tipping the chair back into contact with the wall of the building, "and I might have crossed my ankles like this in a nonchalant kind of way..."

One of the chair's back legs buckled. He grabbed at Jiminez's arm and pulled himself up just before he was dumped on the ground, but not before he'd felt the crunch of jet beads.

The Accompanist

Amy Throck*-Smythe

Early in the third year of his more-or-less voluntary celibacy, Vron Kaeli found himself being courted by a much younger man. As flattering as that was, Vron found himself somewhat at a loss as to how to respond.

Two years before, he'd finally broken off with his on-again/off-again married lover and decided a period of celibacy, housekeeping, and clean living was in order. After a year of such virtue, he'd looked around for someone new to devote himself to and been appalled by the available men near his age. They were either players or losers or both; it was most disheartening to a respectable middle-aged queer like Vron, so he retreated back into his workshop to reconsider his celibate state, which was looking better and better to him.

Vron's workshop was a delightful place full of strange micro-tonal instruments in various stages of commission, the odd keyboard or percussion instrument for repair. A pair of concert grand pianos, long ago abandoned by their cash-strapped owners mid-restoration, still needed their cases refinished, but were otherwise flawlessly tuned and maintained, and acted as a screen for his meager parlor and kitchen. He'd begun a career as a simple piano tuner and repairman, but early on, his musical saw-playing boyfriend had asked him if he could microtune a set of eight saws and mount them in ascending order on a wooden frame. This was easily done and the ensuing, and rather bizarre, concert was a huge and outrageous success. Based on this success, his boyfriend accepted an offer to work in another town and Vron never saw him again. Not that Vron really noticed because he was flooded with orders for saws, percussion instruments, and strangely tuned lute-like instruments. Occasionally, he got orders from *Star Trek* fans to replicate a Vulcan lyre. And, of course, there were piano tuning and repair jobs, so even though Vron lost his boyfriend, he gained a career he loved.

Never lucky in love, Vron meandered from romance to romance until he discovered the lover to whom he'd finally surrendered his heart was committed to someone else. In addition to feeling devastated, he felt stupid. In a fit of pique one night, Vron wrote in the margin of *Fugue No.*

19: A Major from The Well-Tempered Clavier, Book I, "Never trust a man who only lets you call him on his cell phone."

He kept busy; there was his work and when there wasn't work, there were brilliant compositions from the gigantic piano repertory to play on one or the other of his inherited grand pianos. He was working his way through Lutoslawski at the moment. Vron was not an inspired musician, but he was a thorough and diligent one. Early in his studies, he had realized this and, also realizing there was a glut of genius pianists competing for the same work, he decided not to add another mediocre one to the pyre. That didn't keep him from playing and loving the instrument; it did, however, keep him sane, centered, and realistic about his role in music and perhaps in life.

Levelheaded, he also knew his looks were not god-like, but he wasn't repulsive either. Due to his lank jet hair framing his long soulful face with full lips below mellow more-gray-than-blue-gray eyes, a lover had once compared him to a young Anthony Zerbe. Vron never saw the resemblance, but he took it as a compliment nevertheless. He was loyal, pleasant, reliable, and pretty good in bed, but none of that was getting any exercise because he couldn't find anyone to exercise it on. Worse, upon discovering how much he enjoyed his own company, not to mention the company of his right hand, he was becoming a recluse.

And into his peaceful, if somewhat lonely existence, had bounded the brash, young Harold Wyse. They had met at Vron's friend Marcin's choir practice. Vron and Marcin had been at music school together and, because they'd never been lovers, they'd remained very good friends. Marcin was choir director for one of the larger Protestant congregations in town and although it was not the most exciting or creative job in the world, musically it suited Marcin down to the ground. In the privacy of his own home and in all the concerts he could find, Marcin listened to nothing but the atonal masterpieces of the mid-20th century and whatever was new and exciting in atonal music. This so wore him out that he could only stand the hymns and simple harmonies of accepted and very conservative church music in his professional career. He usually invaded Vron's lair with deeply weird music arranged for two pianos and demanded Vron sight-read these horrors with him.

On one particular evening Marcin arrived without a portfolio of music under his arm, but with a look of grim determination on his face. He accused Vron of being a tenor.

"Guilty as charged," Vron said dourly. "What of it?"

"I need you!" Marcin clutched at Vron's threadbare t-shirt.

"And I always need you, Marcin, but what's being a tenor got to do with it?"

It turned out that Marcin's choir was down to one tenor and that this was a desperate and intolerable situation for the choirmaster.

"I don't see how two tenors are going to help you, Marcin; who's going to hear us over your screeching soprano section?" Vron teased.

"You're not the only one I'm recruiting," Marcin said darkly. "And it would only be for a month until school starts and my usual tenor section is back from vacation. I can also kidnap a few young tenors from the conservatory then, may God help them."

Vron said he was very flattered, but he was very busy, and–

"I can't take no for an answer," Marcin said. "I'll play soft rock until you agree." He sat at one of the grands and played "Don't Go Changing" over and over, and with certain Webernian improvements, until Vron caved in like rotten fruit. "Excellent!" Marcin played a IV-I "Amen" cadence and leapt to his feet. "We rehearse on Thursday nights from seven to nine and perform on Sundays at eleven. I've got your music in the car. I'll go get it."

It took Vron the rest of the night and playing Satie's "Gymnopédies" over and over to get "Don't Go Changing" out of his head.

On Thursday, Vron arrived at the rehearsal a few minutes early and found Marcin stomping around in a snit.

"Is there some universal law that requires everyone in and associated with my choir to leave town in August?" he asked Vron, or maybe Heaven itself. He introduced Vron to Mike, another tenor conscript.

"I know a pianist who could come. He's at the conservatory with me," Mike offered. "Does it pay?" he asked shyly.

"Not as well as crime, but, yes, the pianist does get paid," Marcin said through his clenched teeth and named a paltry sum.

Mike went to the pastor's office to use the phone. While he was gone, Vron offered to play if no one could be found, and Marcin growled something about needing his tenor. He pulled himself together and introduced Vron to the other tenor, who was a regular member of the congregation and glad to have company in the tenor section.

"Okay, Harold can play for you," Mike said upon his return. "And I found you another tenor. His name is Louis. They're both on their way."

"You're an angel, Mike," Marcin said, clapping him on the shoulder. "If only you were a better sight-reader."

Vron retreated into the choir stalls to look over his music and get over being nervous. He hadn't sung in a choir since he'd sung next to Marcin in their conservatory days. The other choir members ambled in and took their places around him. Marcin frowned at his watch and ran the choir through some warm up vocalise. This was soothing to Vron and reminded him of his youth.

Next to him, Mike waved at two scrawny, shaggy-haired young men rushing down the center aisle. Vron would have spotted them as Conservatory students by their lack of haircuts alone; the t-shirts and jeans on their underfed frames made it a certainty. The young men exchanged hasty greetings with Marcin. One of them sat down at the piano and the other joined the tenor section. Mike whispered, "Hi, Louis," so Vron assumed the pianist must be Harold.

Ably accompanied by Harold and conducted by Marcin, the choir finished their warm up and launched into the repertory. Louis and Mike were strong singers; Vron thought they'd probably end up in opera choirs or regional opera companies because there's a glut of genius tenors in the world, too. With Vron and the member of the congregation, the four of them managed to represent their section tolerably well.

Harold seemed very in tune with Marcin's direction, which indicated to Vron that he was well trained and polite, even if he didn't seem terribly interested in what he was playing. He did seem interested in watching Vron, repeatedly making eye contact. Vron found this disconcerting, so he paid even closer attention to his tenor part. Musically, it was pretty straightforward stuff and Marcin was such a good choirmaster, he had most of it drilled into them and polished by 8:45. Marcin was smart, too; he recorded the last pass and let the choir hear how good they sounded. They sounded very good and everyone went home happy.

Vron was halfway out the door when Mike caught him and dragged him back to introduce him to Harold.

Harold said, "Hi."

Vron said, "Hi." And there was silence.

"I, um, like the way you sing," Harold said at last.

"You can hear me over the whole choir?" Vron asked, not sure what to make of all this. He was trying hard not to be distracted by Harold's big brown eyes and warm, but scratchy, voice. He cast a puzzled look at Marcin, who'd joined them, making it an all-male quartet.

"Well, no...but, um, you look like I'd like the way you sing," Harold said in a clumsy rush, blushing. "Or something."

"Oh...um..." Vron stammered, trying to figure out what the words and the blush meant. His face was heating, he might be blushing himself, which, for a man his age, was really embarrassing.

"Oh, look! There's the caretaker!" Marcin said gaily, waving frantically at a middle-aged man in overalls. "And we must go! Good night, lads! Thank you ever so, see you on Sunday! Come, Vron, our chariot awaits!" And he dragged the unresisting and still puzzled piano

The Accompanist

tuner to his car and roared out of the parking lot. "Thank heavens I was there, Vron! That young man was making advances to you!"

"I must really be out of practice," Vron sighed, patting his cooling cheeks. "I was confused."

"You had to see it from the side to actually see it," Marcin said cryptically. "He is kind of cute."

"They're all cute at that age, Marcin. Even we were cute at that age," Vron said.

Marcin thought about this for a moment and then said, "We're still cute. And it wasn't all that long ago we were that age."

"I'm sure you're right," Vron said, feeling a peculiar postvocal weariness he'd forgotten about. All that deep breathing; not unlike the postcoital, fully oxygenated stupor.

"Beer?" Marcin asked at a stop light.

"Nah. Sleep," Vron replied. "How about lunch on Sunday? You buy, you owe me."

"I'd be delighted." Marcin dropped him at his studio and, ever the gentleman, waited until Vron was inside before he drove off.

"He's even cuter all dressed up," Marcin observed over lunch the following Sunday after church.

"Harold? I thought his tie was a little loud," Vron said with a smile. He had noticed how cute Harold was, had thought about him once or twice since Thursday, and knew that the fastest way to shut Marcin up was to agree with him.

"He likes you," Marcin said flatly.

"Does he? I'm not sure he's gay, Marcin; he seemed to be with a girl today." At least they had seemed together to Vron, but it might have been wishful thinking.

"For a gay man, you have no gaydar, Vron," Marcin informed him.

"And for a straight man, you have too much. Why are you so interested in getting me into bed with Harold?" Vron asked, glancing up at the waitress next to him.

"More coffee?" she asked deadpan.

"Yes, please." Vron smiled up at her, hoping to cover Marcin's profound blush on the other side of the table.

"I'm not trying–" Marcin began in an undertone.

"But that is where two men who are so inclined end up and very quickly, too, if they are so inclined," Vron said, equally quietly. "We're more direct than you hets, Marcin, we usually don't waste time on elaborate courtships. Harold is cute and he's on the make, as even you noticed. It's not that I wouldn't jump him in a second, it's that I don't

39

have the time or energy to deal with the aftermath of a wham-grr-thank-you-sir one night stand with someone who's too young for me in the first place."

"I just...you seem lonely, Vron," Marcin said seriously. "And he's cute."

"I've grown a little more prudent in my old age, Marcin. I'd rather suffer a little from loneliness than a lot from drama," Vron admitted. "But he is cute."

"Are we old? I'm only forty and you're younger than me." Marcin gestured for the check.

"We're not old, but I feel old right now," Vron said, "Compared to Harold, I feel ancient."

"Hm, speak of the devil..." Marcin mused at a point beyond Vron's left shoulder. "No, don't look, he might not see us...ah, too late."

Harold appeared at their table, he nodded to Marcin and then turned to Vron. "Oh, hello, I meant to ask you to join us for lunch but you left so quickly."

"I wouldn't want to intrude on you and your girlfriend, Harold," Vron said, slightly disconcerted by this directness.

"She's my sister." He smiled fraternally in her direction.

"Oh...um..."

"Well, Harold, I liked the way you played this morning," Marcin said, coming to Vron's rescue once again. "We'll see you on Thursday night." He took Vron's arm and made to leave.

"Maybe we could go out afterwards," Harold suggested.

"Um..."

"I'll have to see how I feel, Harold," Marcin said briskly. "Those rehearsals, they so wear me out."

"I was asking Vron," Harold said.

Vron knew when he was cornered and his manners, if not wits, finally kicked in. He smiled and nodded at Harold's sister, who was looking on with amused interest. "We'll see, Harold," he said. "Until then," he added, and led Marcin out of the restaurant.

"I could fire him between now and Thursday," Marcin volunteered as he drove to Vron's studio.

"Nah, I can handle this situation...and you need a pianist on Thursday," Vron said grimly. "Oh, Marcin, I was wondering..."

"What?! You need me!"

"I always need you, Marcin," Vron said, recovering a little of his good humor. "But I'd like you to play six to eight glasses in a glass harmonica I've been asked to make in a few weeks. It pays the same as the tenor job I'm doing for you."

"Oh, touché, Vron," Marcin drawled. "I'd love to, if the rehearsals don't conflict blah blah blah."

"Not Thursday night, not Sunday morning. I'm sure it can be managed." He got out of the car and went into his studio.

The after-rehearsal-going-out-with-Harold turned into a group affair when Harold, due to nerves or manners, decided to invite all the tenors and Marcin. They wound up in a quiet bar called The Grebe and Vron decided to rustle up a few more glass harmonica players. Except for Harold, who said yes immediately, the music students consulted their calendars and said they could do the rehearsal and the performance, no problem. No, it didn't pay, but that was all right; it would look good on their resumes.

"Who is this for anyway?" Marcin asked.

"Carmenson."

"'That bitch, Carmenson,' as you dubbed her? Didn't you say you were never going to work for her again?" Marcin asked.

"She's a bitch when she doesn't pay me for eight tin garbage cans tuned in thirds and fourths," Vron said dryly. "But she's one of the major composers of her generation when she pays in advance."

"What are you doing for her?" Harold asked. He'd maneuvered Vron into the same side of the booth as himself, so he almost said it into the older man's ear.

"I'm determining how much water goes in how many champagne flutes for this weird piece of music she brought me," he said. "She actually is brilliant, Marcin, even if her work is so weird that *you* like it," he added.

"It's challenging music, not weird," Marcin said pedantically.

"Whatever you say, Marcin."

Because Mike and Louis had day jobs during the August vacation, the party broke up at a reasonable hour. Vron accepted a ride home from Harold.

"Come in for a moment," Vron said, when it was obvious Harold was parking the car in front of his studio. "I can give you your music for the glass harmonica."

Although Vron was used to it, the first sight of his studio was disconcerting to the uninitiated. While Harold was getting his bearings in the forest of tools, pianos scattered about in various stages of restoration, assorted gongs and bells hanging from the rafters, workbenches piled high with keys, hammers, strings, tuning pegs, mallets, saws, and drills, Vron rifled through a stack of manuscript on a workbench full of crystal glasses and bottles of distilled water. "Oh, here it is," Vron said, turning and finding Harold practically on top of him.

This close, Vron realized that Harold was a little taller than him and needed a shave. "I...um..." Harold's brown eyes were magnificent this near.

"Thank you," Harold said softly, taking the papers and putting them on the workbench again. "I'd like to kiss you now."

"Hm...okay," Vron said, and let himself be impressed. "I never catch on the first date," he said, coming up for air.

"I have condoms," Harold assured him.

"You're very confident, Harold," Vron said, easing out of the younger man's arms. "Want a drink?"

"We just had drinks," Harold said, impatiently. "I want–"

"Are we on a schedule?" Vron asked with an edge in his voice. After all his years of celibacy he wasn't about to be rushed into bed with anyone. He walked around to the other side of the workbench.

"No, no," Harold said, somewhat petulantly, but more politely. "I just...want to make love to you. I think you're amazing."

"How can you tell?" Vron asked. "We've just met and–"

"I knew it the moment I saw you," Harold said. He strolled around the workbench and got very close to Vron. "You were so serious about the music, but you were enjoying it, too. I could tell how much you love music. That's what I saw and why I wanted to, y'know, get to know you."

"Like sexually? Get to, y'know, know me?" Vron asked playfully, brushing some shaggy brown hair out of Harold's eyes.

"Well, excuse me for finding you hot," Harold said. He started to move back but Vron held fast to one of his forelocks.

"How old are you, Harold?"

"Twenty-two."

"I could be your father," Vron said, letting go of Harold's hair.

"But you're not," Harold said, moving closer. He leaned on Vron's broad chest and pressed his lips to Vron's and didn't move.

After a split second of debate, Vron turned his head ever so slightly to the left and relaxed his lips enough to encourage Harold to run the tip of his tongue over them and then inside. He wrapped his arms around the younger man and held him tight. Vron smoothed his hands over Harold's back and down to his ass. "Harold," Vron whispered when his lips were free. "You really should eat more. You're too thin."

"It's genetic," Harold whispered back. "So see?" He patted Vron's burly shoulders. "You couldn't be my dad." He nipped at Vron's ear as Vron laughed softly at that. "And as for eating more..."

"Brat," thought Vron. "Listen to me, Harold," he said, looking him in the eye. "I haven't had sex in a while."

"How long?"

"Well, it doesn't matter how long, I–"

"Don't worry," Harold said, nuzzling his ear. "I'll be gentle." He looked around the workshop. "Um, do you have a bed?" he asked, looking speculatively at the workbench. "Or a couch even?"

Vron nodded and led him in through the kitchen and into the bedroom beyond it. A somewhat cramped space: the large bed took up most of it, but that meant the books and scores lining the walls were all in easy reach. There was a small bookcase that doubled as a nightstand for the current reading materials and a cabinet that doubled as a headboard. There was almost enough moonlight to see from the big window set high in the north-facing wall, but Vron turned on the bedside reading light so Harold could momentarily be distracted by his rather impressive library. He sat patiently on the bed while Harold emitted the occasional squeak of surprise or approval at one or other of the titles.

"Wow, you have Stravinsky's *Poetics of Music*," Harold said with awe in his voice. He turned his beautiful eyes on Vron. "Can I borrow it?"

"No." Vron was very much hoping that Harold wouldn't open the book and see the mushy inscription from an old boyfriend on the face page. He was considerably relieved when Harold pouted and put the unopened book back in its place.

"You're mean," Harold said, sitting next to him and burying his face in his neck.

"Get it from the library," Vron said, rubbing his back.

Harold merely said, "Mmmm," as he kissed him. Vron ran his fingers through Harold's hair in appreciation. The first time in bed was always a little awkward for Vron. Whether it was nerves or just newness, there was a certain amount of fumbling and embarrassment. But Harold really had some moves, so he and Vron were out of their clothes with Vron hardly noticing. Vron did notice that Harold had a nice dick as he gently stroked it.

"Hey, careful," Harold said, pushing his hand away. "I won't last long if you keep doing that."

"Oh? Are you that intent on fucking me?" Vron asked playfully. He got a firm "Yes," and was pushed onto his back. "Harold–"

"Do you have lube?" Harold asked, digging a string of condoms out of his jeans.

"You have condoms, but no lube? Vron asked.

"I have lube in my backpack, which is in my car," Harold leaned back, looking very sexy. "Want me to go out into the–"

"No, I don't," Vron said, reaching into a cabinet over the bed and rummaging around. "Oh here it is." He waved a nearly new tube of water-based personal lubricant at Harold. "Does this stuff expire?" he asked, looking for a "sell by" date.

"How long has it been, Vron?" Harold asked quietly. He took the tube from Vron and set it on top of the condoms between them.

"Over two years."

"Oh...well, they say it's like riding a bicycle," Harold said.

"Ah, then let's find out," Vron said, reaching for him.

Vron couldn't compare it to riding a bike because sex was more about being in tune with another unpredictable human, not a set of gears and wheels. There was a balance that reminded him of bike riding; the gentle give and take and shifting of weights to keep things in motion. Harold was a little awkward and Vron had to be twice as relaxed because the slightest tensing on his part startled Harold and made him hesitate. Vron didn't encourage him, that would have been too embarrassing, but he had to be a little more passive than he normally liked to be. "Nerves and youth," he thought as Harold gently tapped his lubed, condom-sheathed cockhead just behind Vron's scrotum. Vron titled unnoticeably forward and hoped Harold wouldn't plunge in too hard. Nothing of the sort, Harold hesitated, pressed forward, and finding resistance, leaned down to gently kiss Vron. This was enough distraction for the younger man to press the head past Vron's tight ring. Vron gasped, but not so much in pain as in awe of the complex collection of sensations he'd almost forgotten in his long celibacy. He could intellectually remember them, but the real thing was quite wonderfully different. He relaxed a little more and Harold pressed all the way in and smiled smugly down at him as he began to move. Vron mentally frowned a little at that smug smile, but he was soon caught up in Harold's rhythm and was thrusting up to meet him. He forgot about Harold's smirk, which was soon replaced with a lustful grimace, probably matching his own pleasured face. Vron was overwhelmed and swept away and liked it very much.

But all good things come to an end eventually, and Harold was young and hot, so things ended a little sooner than Vron might have liked. Harold came with a cross between a whimper and choked-off scream. He collapsed for a moment on Vron's sweaty chest before he rolled off and headed for the bathroom. "Okay, now I can relax," he said when he got back from disposing of the condom.

"Hm?" Vron asked, adjusted his half-mast erection on his belly. He wondered if he should take a cold shower before he threw Harold out on his ear, or jack off in the privacy of his bathroom before he threw Harold out on his ear. "Relax? You want to relax?" What would Miss Manners have him do in this situation, he wondered.

"Yeah, relax...And blow you," Harold said, leaping on him and devouring him.

"What did you mean?" Vron asked when he recovered from an intense orgasm.

"When?" Harold asked, wiping his lips with the back of his hand.

"When you said you could relax."

"Oh, I'm always nervous the first time, I never know if I'm going to be any good or not. But once the first time is out of the way, I get better after that," he said, yawning.

"That's one way of handling it," Vron thought wryly. His breathing was getting back to normal and he was starting to doze off.

"Can I sleep here?" Harold asked.

"Sure," Vron said and pulled the covers around them. "We're half asleep as it is," he thought and nodded off himself.

Not too long after that night, Harold more or less moved in with Vron. He kept paying rent at the one-bedroom apartment he shared with three guys, but, after spending one night at Harold's place, Vron no longer objected to having him underfoot in his workshop/home space, so Harold was spending all his nights there. Harold had odd jobs over the summer, so he wasn't constantly around, and Vron could get his own work done. However, when Harold was there he was either studying, practicing on one of the grand pianos, or making Vron as happy as if they had good sense. They became a couple, and were the couple that music lovers noticed at the concerts and parties they went to. August was dead in their medium-sized town, but those marooned there managed to have quite a bit of fun in spite of it. Harold and Vron were invited everywhere there was anything going on. It amused Vron greatly to be able say they met at church choir practice. They were very happy, which is always an asset to any party, but another plus was that they could hold a decent conversation as long as it was about music.

Harold was specializing in the Classical and Romantic repertoire, especially Brahms, and he could talk at great length about that music. Vron was more of a Baroque and then Impressionists-to-the-present kind of person. But they never talked to each other about music because they had so many other things to do when they were together that didn't require many words.

"How's it going with Harold?" Marcin asked one evening, seated at Vron's tiny kitchen table. He'd been observing from a discreet distance, so as not to spook Vron, but had decided Vron could handle his old friend's curiosity, even if it was killing Marcin.

"Fine," Vron said. "He should be here for dinner in a few minutes."

"Really? I didn't know you invited him."

Vron looked up from the sauce he was stirring. "He has a standing invitation for meals here like you do, Marcin," he said. "However, I was expecting him, you just showed up."

"Yes! And lucky me! Dinner smells great!" And to forestall being thrown out, he sat at one of the scuffed-up but impeccably tuned grand pianos and began to play strange, but well-organized music.

Vron shrugged and set the table for three. He'd been evasive with Marcin about Harold, and, though Marcin had been very patient for Marcin, he'd gone on the offensive to find out what was going on. To the untrained eye this might seem nosy, and it was, but in addition to being nosy, Marcin was fond and protective of Vron.

Harold let himself in accompanied by streams of tone rows pouring from Vron's studio. He waved at Marcin as he went past to discreetly hug Vron. His entrances and greetings were usually more effusive, and if the bulge in his pants was anything to go by, he'd probably have dragged Vron off to bed for an hour before dinner if Marcin hadn't been there.

"What was that?" Harold asked when they sat down to eat.

"Some new etudes by that bitch Carmenson," Marcin said, piling his plate with spaghetti. "She should write more piano music and Vron should cook more often."

"I agree with the last part," Harold said. "I'm a Brahms man myself, can't stand much after Liszt or Chopin either."

The older men exchanged mildly shocked glances. Vron had suspected Harold had very narrow tastes in music, but had never heard him express it so bluntly. Marcin, on the other hand, had no idea what a Brahms snob Harold was.

"I'm sorry, Marcin," Harold said quickly. "I didn't mean to insult your taste in music, I–"

"Oh, it's not that, Harold." Marcin cut him off. "I just think you're missing out on a lot. I love watching a composer grow and evolve, decline and decay. Brahms holds no surprises for anyone anymore."

"Then it's up to the player to find new nuances in his work," Harold said loftily.

"But it's all been done," Vron said, and immediately regretted it.

"Not by me."

"No, of course not, Harold," Vron said quickly. "I–"

"But most of it's been done," Marcin said. "I mean, even if you decided to make a run at the concert scene, the big Brahms interpreters are all young or middle-aged and not dying anytime soon."

"I've decided to do exactly that." Harold was starting to sound defensive.

"Then I salute you and wish you good luck, Harold," Marcin said, sounding like he was offering condolences. "Are you still playing on that very living bitch Carmenson's very modern glass harmonica composition or was that just a ruse to nail Vron here?"

"Well, both, but I do have a great deal of respect for the Maestra, even if she is still living," Harold said, and winked at Vron. "And I'd perform a Philip Glass composition if it meant getting closer to Vron."

They laughed, the tension dissipated, but a small sadness lingered in the back of Vron's mind that his new lover was about to throw himself onto the rocks of the classical music scene.

Based on what he'd heard Harold play in his workshop, Vron thought he was a fine pianist; much better than the usual crop produced by the second-rank conservatory he was attending. But even the great pianists from the great conservatories were struggling because there were simply too many great pianists in the world at the moment.

In his pessimistic moments, which were many when it came to the classical music rat race, Vron felt that music and musical training were a luxury. And that the world was affluent enough to produce so many well-trained, often inspired, technically brilliant pianists (and cellists, for some reason, too), said something very good or very bad about the world. Why couldn't ninety percent of these musicians become doctors and work on a cure for cancer?

And Brahms! Brahms had been dead for a long time, there would never be any new Brahms ever, and Harold's ambition to find new meaning in old work...It was too horrible to think about. "He'll be eaten alive," Vron thought over dessert.

From that night on, Vron made sure there was some genius playing Brahms on the CD player whenever Harold was in the room. This was a huge sacrifice on Vron's part; he wasn't much of a Brahms fan, he was more of an Erik Satie kind of person.

And it was a waste because all Harold did was point out how he would play this or that passage better than, oh, say, Arthur Rubinstein. Although Vron admired his lover's confidence, he was hard pressed to hide how that arrogance shocked him a little. Harold didn't notice, or seemed not to notice.

Several weeks later, the performance of that bitch Carmenson's astonishingly good composition for glass harmonica was a smashing success. As had become usual, Harold went home with Vron, but didn't come in. "You don't think I'm good enough," he said quietly.

"What? I thought you played your glasses beau–"

"No, I mean as a pianist."

Vron sighed and looked him right in the eye. "It's not that you're not a wonderful pianist, Harold," he said as gently as he could. "It's that there are so many pianists already out there, with careers launched, that are...are better."

Harold got in his car and left without saying a word.

"Shit." Vron went into his suddenly very empty home and played Bartok's "Mikrokosmos" in a vain effort to wear himself out so he'd sleep. Partly he thought Harold should grow up and face facts, but the part that almost loved him was furious that he'd stepped on the dreams of the man he almost loved.

"Oh, what a bunch of bullshit!" he said, and banged his fist on the keyboard.

"What is?" Harold asked from the shadows by the door.

Vron jumped. He'd not noticed Harold come back and let himself in. Face to face with the man he almost loved, whom he'd recently wounded, Vron was suddenly very annoyed. "Us, Harold, you and I. We're doomed."

"We are? Why?"

"Because I don't think there's anything left to say about Brahms and you do," Vron said wearily. "It's like one of us not believing in God or Bach or something."

"Which Bach?"

"JS, of course."

"Oh well, we can at least agree on God and Bach then." Harold joined him on the piano bench and put his arms around him. "Because I love you, I thought about what you said."

Vron almost hid his surprise. "I love you, too, it's the classical music scene I have issues with."

"I have to try, Vron."

"And so you should, Harold," Vron said. He wondered if all the pianists under contract with all the symphonies and record companies could mysteriously decide to join the Trappists or move to India to study yoga or...

"But I might not have to try in New York," Harold broke into his thoughts. "I don't think the New York Phil or RCA is going to put me under contract, but I could tour the regions with ensembles, maybe teach a little..."

48

"Harold, you don't have to give up your dreams because of what I said." Vron brushed a stray lock out of Harold's eyes.

"I'm not giving up my dreams, I'm just adding you to them because I know damn well you're not moving to New York, Vron," Harold said. "Where would you put all this stuff?" he asked, waving at the jammed studio.

Vron hugged him tight. "Yeah, good thing you don't have much stuff, Harold."

"At least I'll have nice pianos to play," Harold laughed. "And home cooking and good lovin' and–"

"And all of that, Harold, and all of that."

Jewel of My House

Colleen Wylie

Cadet Brian John Lee stood watch just inside the closed steel shutters that isolated Station Four-One-Nine's control hub from the network of corridors where maintenance teams had been working through the last two shifts. They'd fixed the scorch marks, the dented panels, the trunking where power and communication channels had been ripped out like multi colored entrails. And once the alarms had stopped shrilling, they'd mopped up the blood and sprayed pastel colors over the lines gouged in the decor by steel blades and, seemingly, even harder talons.

The violence had never reached the control hub. Nor had it touched Cadet Lee. He wasn't sorry for that. He was a tech specialist trainee, not an infantryman. He had no desire, or aptitude, to be a hero.

Once everything was quiet, and while the infantrymen caught up on their sleep and R&R, a tech specialist could be allowed to hold a stun gun, so long as he was on the inside of three layers of vacuum grade bulkhead.

Four-One-Nine had been attacked seventy two hours earlier, by pirates. Herrenvorst traders had put out a vessel to assist the station to defend itself. It ended up that pirates and traders disabled each other's ships, taking to the station to finish the fight. The Regal was the nearest available help. It was only an old Supreme Class cruiser, but it outgunned both sides by an order of magnitude, and because it was on a training cruise, it pretty much had two crews aboard.

The infantrymen from the Regal, trainees and troopers alike, kept the peace. They isolated the warring parties at opposite ends of the station, kept life support running to both sides and waited for the Herrenvorst fleet to turn up and sort it out. It was pretty much an anticlimax. Brian was rostered as an emergency medic, and spent twenty-four frustrating hours in sickbay, drinking coffee and failing to summon up the courage to ask one of the nurses for a date.

Being transferred to guard duty should, he reckoned, improve his chances: "Hi, I'm Brian. I was fighting aliens on Station Four-One-Nine last week. Can I buy you drink?"

The station's anti-grav units were next door to the cargo bays where the pirates had been corralled. The way the station was constructed, "haphazardly" according to the Regal's tactical officer, the pirates couldn't be kept away from vital atmospheric scrubbers without keeping them away from food synthesizers, sanitary facilities and a length of corridor in which to exercise. Captain Campbell had suggested to the pirate's leader, a seven foot repto-mammalian hybrid whose name seemed to be "Chugin," that his warriors could either do without food, sanitation and exercise, or they could disarm and allow Campbell's officers to stand guard over the machinery.

In Chugin's opinion, his followers were not pirates. They had responded to a distress call from the station, helped to control a potential meltdown in the power core and then been ambushed by the Herrenvorst scout. There was no reason why they should disarm. If Campbell wished to avoid further confrontations, he should repair Chugin's ship and allow him to leave.

The Herrenvorst captain, on the other hand, argued that Chugin was probably responsible for the meltdown, certainly belonged to a race of pirates who habitually preyed on Herrenvorst ships and stations, and should now be in a Herrenvorst holding cell, court and execution chamber, preferably with minimal delay along the way. If Campbell allowed Chugin's People back on their ship, the Herrenvorst claimed, the pirates would simply bring their weapons online and blow up Four-One-Nine and everyone on it.

Campbell had done the neutral thing. He'd keep the peace, he said, maintain the status quo and await the arrival of the legitimate authorities. He wouldn't repair ships. He said that he didn't have the capability to repair ships, but Brian reckoned that was probably untrue.

The pirates elected to keep their laser weapons, also their cutlasses. No one thought to ask them to cut their toenails, although they probably could have ripped the throats out of the infantrymen, let alone a mere tech specialist, with those.

So now Brian found himself here, only three meteor-proof bulkheads away from armed pirates. He should work the story up ready for their next shoreleave. It was only ten days away. Maybe news of their clash with pirates would get to 16 Tauri ahead of them. Women would be lining up in the starport bars to buy him drinks. Beautiful women. Sophisticated, experienced women. Maybe even alien women...

"Are you actually awake there, Mr. Lee?"

Brian started back to attention, only to find himself face to face with Captain Campbell.

"Yes, Captain, Sir!"

"Good. Keep it that way."

He sucked in his gut and squared his shoulders, but Campbell had turned away in response to the urgent chirp of the station comm system.

A moment later, the quiet of the past four hours had given way to a flurry of anxious activity. Orders were flying back and forth. Brian maintained an attentive silence, as he pieced together a picture of what was happening from overlapping reports.

Keeping the hostile parties apart had worked for a while, but now something had happened to upset the balance. The pirates were sick and Chugin was being brought in to see Campbell.

The pirate captain was just short enough not to need to bow his head anywhere on the station. He swept past Brian, into the control hub, flashing iridescent scales wherever he wasn't wearing jeweled leather body armor or padded silk. His toe talons clicked on the deck plating. Whatever species, or mixture of species, they belonged to, these pirates were actually very humanoid indeed, even if they did have scales rather than hair. Their faces were flat, oval and expressive, and their eyes, apart from the way they blinked a third lid across every minute or so in slow motion, could have been human eyes behind their chainmail and leather masks.

Chugin had brought an escort.

"Dychu, my second in command."

This pirate was taller than his leader, and more battle scarred where armor revealed bare flesh. He looked as if he'd go out, get drunk, and pick a fight just for the hell of it, but at the same time, he was less alarming than Chugin. Chugin had that driven look, like he was a Moses, or maybe an Alexander.

The second companion was the odd one out among the pirates. Brian had heard about him through the grapevine. He, or maybe she, was pint-sized. An immature individual perhaps. No one knew anything about the family structures of these beings, and they didn't seem to want to answer questions, so there was plenty of speculation. It had been noted that "Little Chugin" was never far from the pirate leader, and that had led to suggestions that "he" was the pirate's heir, or perhaps that "she" was the pirate's mate.

"And this is Nichu, my beloved."

During these introductions, Nichu clenched a gloved fist around the pommel of a cutlass and glanced everywhere but at Chugin and Captain Campbell. For a brief moment, the little pirate's gaze met Brian's, then moved on.

"What can I do for you, Chugin?" Campbell asked.

"My people are dying. My healers cannot arrest this illness without access to those facilities which you are denying us."

"I can't..."

"I will not draw the talons of my warriors."

Brian, standing rigidly at attention, could not help his eyes moving to those lethal appendages. Chugin's talons were three-inch-long curved knives. He probably had to wear chainmail bedsocks. Even Little Chugin looked like he'd need a cutting laser to trim his toenails.

"But I can offer you hostages. My second in command, and my Nichu, my most precious."

It was Campbell's turn now to look at Nichu. "Your...son?" he guessed.

"Yes, my son."

"And...will they disarm?"

"Yes."

Dychu slipped his cutlass out of its scabbard and laid it on the deck. He then pulled his laser weapon out of the holster that formed part of his padded silk vest and, quite without warning, sliced off his own toes.

Chugin nodded to his son. "Nichu..."

"No!" Campbell stepped forward, between the youngster and his father. "Hold on!" He gestured at the bloody talons on the deck. "There's no need for this."

"Don't be concerned." Chugin nodded again. Nichu bent down and pulled his boots off. Beneath, he had white, humanoid toes with sensibly clipped nails.

Brian barely swallowed the desire to laugh. Campbell's face was a rigid mask. The boy's boots, complete with fake talons, were placed alongside his cutlass, a toy compared to Dychu's, and his laser, full sized.

"You will return them to me when the disease has been controlled."

"Yes."

Chugin placed his heel of his palms ritually over the eyes of the maimed Dychu, then walked over to his son. He held out his arms as if to invite Nichu into a hug, but the youngster took a step back and raised his head. The pirates had scales on their necks that flushed red when they were fighting. Such a gesture, the Xenobiology department had theorized, was a warning display to a potential opponent, or a family member who was overstepping his proper place. The Regal's trainees knew to back away from it. But Nichu had a pale, vulnerable neck. With a soft chuckle, Chugin covered Nichu's eyes for a long moment, muttering something too quiet for the translators to catch.

"Is it agreed?" he asked Campbell.

Brian thought he should have checked that agreement had been reached before Dychu sliced the ends off his feet. Campbell looked as if he felt he'd been bounced into agreeing, but agree he did, with the proviso that guards would be placed around the scrubbers.

Chugin gathered up the weapons and left, as magisterially as he'd arrived. Campbell called guards to escort the hostages to quarters on the Regal. As they waited, both he and Brian found their eyes wandering to Nichu's bare feet. They both looked up at the same time. Brian took a deep breath and went back to being the perfect guardsman, but Campbell beckoned to him.

"D'you think he's human, Cadet?"

"I don't know, sir."

"Well, we can be pretty sure he's not Chugin's natural son. So what do you think, booty? A slave?"

"I don't know, sir."

"Those look like young toes, don't they?"

Brian smiled uncertainly. "I think so, sir."

"Go with him. Get that mask off him and find out what you can. At some point, we're going to have to make decisions about Chugin. I'd like to know a little more about what kind of...hybrid thing he is."

Nichu moved silently as a cat on his bare feet. His left hand stayed at his side, but he walked with his right hand raised to his chest, as all the pirates did. His mask extended over his entire head, and could have covered a skull crest, or even antennae. Brian watched the white-pink digits flexing on the deck plates while they waited for the station's airlock to cycle and wondered if all the blue and grey and purple races of the galaxy had pink toes. He wondered, too, if the tension the movement betrayed stemmed from fear or from being poised to fight. Ahead of them, the Regal's security chief turned back and gestured at Dychu. "This one's going to the brig, Cadet, once he's been to sickbay. He's too big to run around loose. You shouldn't have any trouble with that one, but you know what to do if I'm wrong. We won't crowd you, but we're ten seconds away, max."

Brian was still watching the toes. They were on the short side, as toes go, very straight, and ended level with each other. Not the kind of toes that would happily fit into fancy shoes, Brian reflected. The nails were well-kept and clean.

"Cadet?"

"Sir? Oh yes." Brian knew exactly what to do. He had a low power stun weapon, keyed to his own thumbprint and locked on a setting that scrambled a target's thinking, not their flesh. He knew half a dozen code words that the computers would pick out if he even whispered them in his sleep. And if all else failed, there were reassuring red buttons on every comm point and data terminal in the ship. "Right. Yes, Sir. Nichu, you'd better come with me." He patted the weapon on his belt and gestured along the companionway. Nichu kept abreast of him, padding silently, small movements of his head showing that he was glancing through open doorways and down branching corridors through the vertical oval eye slits of his jeweled mask.

There was a moment of near panic when they walked into the mess, but the off-duty cadets recovered, and laughed at themselves, and went back to their meals and games. Brian pointed to an empty table in a quiet corner. "Are you hungry?"

"No."

"Thirsty?"

"Yes. Some water, please."

He went off to the dispenser, and came back with the water, and with orange juice, several kinds of fruit and a selection of cookies. He put them all in the middle of the table. "We're going to have to feed you sooner or later, so..."

Nichu took the glass of water. He was wearing gloves. Brian couldn't tell if they included fake talons, like the boots, or if the pirate's own fingernails had been grown long and studded with magnetite and amethyst. The mask moved elastically with the muscles below it. When Nichu closed his own mouth, the mask seemed to have no mouth at all.

"It's...uh, it's not polite to eat among humans with...with armor on."

Nichu took a long sip from the glass, the dark eye slits fixed on Brian carefully all the time. "You are humans?"

"Yes."

The pirate picked up an apple, turned it on its axis a couple of times, and opened his mouth wide enough to bite it, then hesitated. Brian now knew that the inside of Nichu's mouth was human pink, with a full set of human teeth. "And...I'm guessing that you're human too."

Nichu snapped his mouth closed. "I am one of Chugin's People."

"But...biologically..."

"I am one of Chugin's People."

Brian didn't argue the point. Nichu kept his armor on, including the mask. Brian watched, frustrated, as Nichu cut one apple and then another, uncored and unpeeled, into small, even slices and ate them impolitely, his armor in place.

"Human, but probably not Terran, not recently," Doctor Shavitz said, gazing at his readouts. "Wrong carbon isotope readings." Nichu was sitting on a scanner bed on the opposite side of sickbay. It had taken Shavitz some effort to talk Nichu out of both his armor and his clothes, but the pirate had finally accepted the sense of letting the ship's computer have a baseline reading of his normal functions. "But I am not sick," he had repeated insistently. He had short, raggedly cut, dark brown hair and his body was speckled with jewels, somehow embedded in his skin. They looked entirely natural, as if human flesh was designed to sprout opals and garnets. The jewels were placed like a partial exoskeleton, everywhere from his ankles to his cheekbones. They flashed the readout lights back at Brian. When Nichu peeled off his gloves, he withdrew gem-studded fingernails through openings in the fine knit silk. Someone had worked hard on the human's costume.

"And he's right, he's not sick. Whatever virus his friends have picked up, he's not susceptible. His age...well, that's tricky, not knowing what planet he's supposed to be from. Male, sexually mature, and he's had an exciting life, judging by the scars on him."

"Are there any...uh..."

"What?"

"Captain Campbell wants me to find out about Chugin, not just about this one, Doctor. He wondered if Nichu might be a captive, a slave even. Is there any evidence of...of any..."

"Of any kind of abuse? I'd say—I'm guessing, but I'm pretty sure—that these are sword cuts, or look here, four parallel cuts, see? Talons did that, don't you think? I don't see the kind of damage that comes from beatings, or any kind of deprivation. He hasn't been overfed, and he's extremely fit—pushing at the limits, I'd say. There's some of the metabolic...well, I won't say damage, but if he was an athlete, I'd tell his coach to ease up a little. But all these wounds have been treated, kept clean, that kind of thing. Guessing again, I suspect whoever treated them could have prevented scars forming at all. They may be a status symbol of some kind. So no, no evidence of abuse, Cadet, but that doesn't mean anything. Abuse can be psychological. He hasn't been used for hard labour, he hasn't been severely beaten or malnourished. Normally I wouldn't pass comment, but if he's the pirate's personal plaything, there's no damage to show for it. Was that what you wanted to know?"

"Yes, sir. What about the jewels though?"

"Hmm. What do you want, a medical opinion or a valuation? They're not natural, no way. They've induced something like a...like a nailbed, I guess. Yes. Maybe modified hair follicles. The jewels are just sitting there, surrounded by a lip of chitin..." Shavitz was peering at a scanned enlargement of the anatomical oddity as he spoke. "See?"

"Well, isn't that a kind of abuse?"

"I think you'll get a more accurate idea of his status by talking to him than by asking me, and I expect that's why Captain Campbell chose you for the job, right?"

"Yes, sir."

"It's a neat way to display the contents of your jewel box, though, isn't it? Not only is he walking around showing them off, but I imagine he'd give a thief a hard time." He wandered over and patted the young man on the shoulder, then switched the translator on again. "Okay, you can get dressed now."

Nichu put his clothes back on. He stopped at the point where only his armored vest and mask lay on the chair and looked around. After a moment, he breathed out slowly and picked up the armor, laying it carefully over his arm. "I am ready."

Nichu was given a bunk in Brian's cabin. The cadet's usual bunkmate was offloaded to a four-man cabin on E-Deck. Jolson frowned when Brian buzzed him on the station to tell him. "Check my closet's locked. And you'd better buzz Jeanie too. I don't want her getting into bed with some pirate reptile and thinking he's me."

"It's a mistake anyone could make."

Brian was glad that Nichu was using, or at least investigating, the bathroom while these conversations happened. The translators made life easier, but they had a habit of picking up things you thought you'd said privately. Brian bundled up Jolson's belongings and dumped them in the closet, recycled the bedlinen, requisitioned more and wondered what to do next with his new roomie. Jeanie d'Abo solved the problem for him. She appeared at the door. "I left my...Oh, you must be Nichu. Pleased to meet you." She took the pirate's hand with a fine disregard for alien sensitivities, and released it reluctantly. "*Very* pleased to meet you. What beautiful hands you have."

Nichu nodded gravely, looking uncannily like his "father." "Excuse me. Mr. Lee, where may I put my belongings?"

"Sure, um...here, I'll clear one of my lockers." Brian threw his displaced belongings in with Jolson's. He kept an eye on d'Abo as he did so. She sat down on Jolson's bunk and smiled sweetly at the pirate reptile, who had just finished hanging his mask and vest in Brian's locker. "What are you doing here on the Regal, Mr. uh...?"

"My name is Nichu. I am a hostage. If Chugin does not keep his word, which of course he will, your captain will kill me."

She opened her mouth, and then realized that she had no idea what to say. Her eyes slid across to Brian, seeking a prompt. He scowled at her from behind Nichu's shoulder. She stood. "I expect you want some time to...to settle in. I'll see you later. I could give you a tour of the ship. Or the gym. Or...or the observation lounge. That's amazing..."

"He's seen the stars, Jeanie." Brian pointed to the door.

"Later," she repeated, and shook the captive's hand again before sidling out.

"Better count your fingers," Brian suggested.

Nichu hesitated for a moment, confused. "What species was that being?" he asked. "Is it dangerous?"

Brian grinned as he realized that there might be more new experiences in store for Nichu than just apples. "Human, and not dangerous, well, not much. Just female. Haven't you ever..."

"I have not seen a human female before."

"Sure you have. There were female guards on duty on the station, and at least one of the nurses in sickbay was female."

"I did not notice."

Brian chuckled. "Oh. Well, Jeanie makes herself noticed. Do you have female...what do you call yourselves?"

"Chugin's People."

"Oh, yes. Are there females...on your ship?"

"Many."

"See, I hadn't noticed. I suppose I just can't tell the difference."

"Dychu is female."

"Right. I can't tell the difference." He felt suddenly sick at the memory of Dychu sacrificing her toes. His own toes curled involuntarily in his boots. He shifted his weight from foot to foot, thinking about what had happened, thinking about how this new information was changing the way the pieces seemed to fit together.

"I'll be back in a moment." He stepped out into the corridor and walked a few metres to a comm point. "Cadet Lee here. I need to speak to Captain Campbell."

"Lee? Problems?"

"No. I just thought you should know, Chugin might have given us those two to keep them safe from the virus, rather than to provide us with hostages. Dychu is female, according to Nichu."

"Yeah, Shavitz told me. But maybe the exact opposite is true. Maybe he couldn't give a damn for a female and a slave. Well, there's no trouble here right now, but you were right to tell me. Either way, we need to stay alert. And that applies to you, too. Campbell out."

Brian returned to his cabin, where Nichu had found a token row of books. He turned to his host apologetically, a Bible open in his hand. "I was curious. What are these?"

"That's okay. Go ahead and look. They contain information in a visually encoded format. But those aren't much good to you, the data's too inflexible to feed into our translators without special equipment. Look, you can get pictures rather than text on here." Brian flicked the computer on, moving aside the little succulent that loved the glow of a computer screen so much, that he had to turn it daily to stop it growing lopsided, "and we can probably find the text of that book for you, but I wouldn't recommend it for a beginner."

Nichu took only a few minutes to master the computer interface. He located star charts of the region around the station, and didn't seem to hear anything Brian said for a while as he keyed from screen to screen. Brian leaned over his shoulder, momentarily anxious that his visitor would rip the membrane on the keypad with his talons.

"You've been to all those planets?" he asked. Nichu had opened images of ten or fifteen Earth-like worlds and was looking at them all, spinning them and moving from one to another.

Then Nichu raised a finger to the screen, as if to touch more than point. The very tip of the nail was smooth, like the point of a human's canine tooth. "Yes. I think I was born here."

Brian leaned in again, more openly, to look at the beautiful, blue-green world. "What did you call it?"

Nichu shrugged. "I don't know."

He sat, motionless, for a moment.

Like a lizard, sunning itself, Brian thought. "Have you always lived with...I mean, have you always been one of Chugin's People?"

Nichu blinked slowly, just like Chugin, then laughed. "Of course not."

"Then where did you come from?"

"Chugin found me."

"We think you're human."

The young pirate nodded. "I think I am."

"But you weren't sure whether Jeanie was human. Haven't you ever met other humans, before now, really?"

Nichu shook his head. He was, Brian suddenly realized, adopting human gestures like they were going out of fashion. The too vigorous shake made the pirate's hair fly about and end up in a disorderly fringe over his eyes. He peered at Brian from under it. "No. There are no humans in this sector until now. Except me."

"Was that why Chugin never tried to take you home? Or contact your family?"

"Chugin's People are my family. And his ship is my home."

Jewel of My House

The door chimed. Brian frowned in annoyance. He was tired. He'd worked more than sixteen of the last twenty-four hours, and his inner clock was protesting. He'd thought Nichu was tired too, but when Jeanie d'Abo slid past the opening door and into the cabin, Nichu was suddenly completely alert. He rose to his feet, making Brian wonder if he saw Jeanie as a potential mate, or a threat. Jeanie responded with a big smile. "Hi. I hope I'm not interrupting anything. I wondered if you'd like a break, Brian? I could take care of Nichu for you. I asked, and Xenobiology okayed it."

"That's..."

"I was just going to the crew lounge for a coffee. Would you like to come along, Nichu? Coffee's a drink."

"I have to stay with him, d'Abo."

"No sweat," she said brightly. "I guess you can come too."

"Yes, please, I am thirsty." Nichu glanced at Brian, his expression eager.

Brian felt a pang of concern. Nichu had eaten nothing more than two apples in the last two or three hours, and might not have eaten for some time before that. And just because it was late evening for Brian, that didn't stop it being lunchtime for someone else.

"Of course. Let's go."

Nichu stepped over to the locker, but didn't open it.

"Problem?"

"No." He put his hand on the catch, but didn't press it.

"Go on. If you don't feel properly dressed, or something..."

"I should have my weapons, and my mask." Still with his back to Brian, the pirate set his shoulders square. "Are you armed?"

"Yes. I have a stun weapon. It's locked to my finger print. No one is going to attack you, but it's my job to protect you if that turns out to be necessary." Brian was rather pleased that he'd managed to put that so positively, but Nichu seemed unimpressed.

"Are you armed?" he asked d'Abo earnestly.

"Do I need to be, Nichu?"

Brian took his prisoner firmly by the arm. "No, she isn't. And no one you're going to meet out there this evening is going to be armed. We're just going out to have a drink, maybe watch some sport, maybe talk. There are armed security guards on the ship, and they probably know where you are every second, but you're not going to meet one unless you make trouble."

Nichu looked at Brian's hand where it gripped his bicep. He reached out with his gloved right hand and touched one of his mentor's blunt, square nails with the tip of a sparkling talon. "I am not going to make trouble, Brian."

"Come on then."

The crew lounge was a little more homey than the mess hall, with chairs of the kind you could curl up in arranged around low tables, and a big viewscreen that didn't prioritize ship's business over entertainment.

"What can I get you, Brian?" d'Abo asked, cutting between him and the food synthesizers, steering Nichu along beside her with a hand on his shoulder.

"Coffee," he said. What he wanted was a beer, but it didn't seem sensible to introduce Nichu to alcohol. "Black coffee..."

D'Abo wasn't paying him any attention. She was helping Nichu to scroll down the menu. It seemed odd for a moment that Nichu should accept d'Abo's guidance so passively. Then Brian recalled that a succession of people had been ordering the young man around all day, and when his foster father had handed him over as a hostage neither father nor son seemed to question Chugin's absolute right to use another person like a chess piece.

Brian sat down, reflecting that Nichu was lucky he'd fallen into the hands of humans, rather than one of the more aggressive and acquisitive races in the area. He sipped his coffee, with milk, which he disliked, but at least D'Abo hadn't seen fit to lace it with sugar, and turned his attention to the viewscreen. A rugby game was just starting. "What is this?" Nichu had wandered over, with a beer bottle in his hand, his eyes fixed on the screen. "A battle?"

Brian scowled at d'Abo. "Do you think that's a good idea?" he demanded, nodding at the bottle. "No, Nichu, it's a game. The players have to kick the ball into the opposite team's goal, there, see, over the bar between those posts."

"Teams?" Nichu, imitating d'Abo, raised the bottle to his lips and took a careful swig. He sputtered. It obviously didn't taste as he'd expected. He held the bottle away at arms length and looked carefully at the contents and label, but Brian could tell that he still had half an eye on the screen.

"Sides. Like in a battle, but no one gets hurt...usually..." Two players had just collided. A groan went up from the spectators, on screen and in the lounge.

"A game." Nichu nodded seriously. He'd repeated the same word Brian had used, so the translator obviously hadn't found an equivalent in his own language.

Brian grinned. He could tell Nichu was another ball-game-watching human male, however he'd been raised. D'Abo, obviously realizing the same thing, sighed. "Men!" She slid a bowl of chips onto the table in front of Brian. "Sit down, Nichu."

He focused on her. "I am sorry."

"Sweetheart," she said, taking his arm and pulling him down onto the seat next to hers. "You can watch if you like."

"Thank you."

His tone was so honestly grateful, Brian couldn't help laughing. Maybe among Chugin's People, the women set the agenda. He took a seat himself and continued to watch as the camera angle changed to track the ball.

"Brian..."

"Yes?"

Nichu pointed at the screen, where a black-clad referee had just brought the game to a halt. The crowd grumbled. "Three teams?"

"The...oh. No! That's the referee. She's making sure everyone keeps the rules."

Nichu gave him an extremely sceptical look. "I don't understand why humans are fighting each other."

"They're not. It's sport. It's for fun," Brian said. Play was recommencing. Nichu settled back into Jeanie d'Abo's arms and picked up his beer bottle again. "*Notsi*," he said contemptuously.

The translator made the helpless noise it usually produced when there wasn't an exact English equivalent, then offered, "Fifty percent certainty: aliens."

"Notsi?" Brian repeated.

Nichu looked at him. "Chugin's People do not fight among themselves."

"It's a game," Brian protested.

"Give up, Brian," d'Abo suggested. "Half the human race doesn't understand boys chasing balls. The rest of the galaxy sure isn't going to."

"Half those players are female!"

"I know." She licked beer off her lips and put her bottle on the table before leaning around Nichu's embrace to grin at Brian. "They're on the pitch because that's where all the men are looking." As she leaned back, she paused and looked at the jewels on Nichu's face. "Hey, can I touch?" she asked.

"Touch what?"

"Your scales."

"Yes."

When the doors slid open a couple of minutes later, Brian silently crossed his fingers and prayed that the new arrival wouldn't be Jolson, or anyone who'd feel obligated to keep the engineering cadet informed of his girlfriend's activities. Fortunately, it turned out to be a handful of senior cadets who'd just come off duty. They told d'Abo to get a room, and managed not to look startled when a bejeweled pirate emerged, blinking, from underneath her.

"I think it's time we turned in," Brian said brightly to his charge. "Get some sleep."

"Yes." Nichu straightened his shirt, picked up his beer bottle, and said, "Good night," politely to the astonished seniors. D'Abo held out her hand so he could help her up off the couch, but he didn't seem to notice. He followed Brian out of the lounge, still carrying the beer.

Back in Brian's cabin, the pirate yawned extravagantly, much to Brian's relief. He lifted the beer bottle and drained another quarter of it, still imitating d'Abo's drinking style.

"I am beginning to like it," he said.

"It's alcohol," Brian said warningly. "You do know what alcohol is?"

"A hydrocarbon." Nichu sounded rather insulted.

"Do Chugin's People drink alcohol?"

"I don't think so." He took another swig. "I have never tasted anything like it."

"Yeah, well, you're not tasting the alcohol as such. That stuff is probably only three per cent alcohol by volume. The taste comes from the other ingredients. But the alcohol...well, I think if you were in the habit of drinking alcohol, you'd know about it. It's a drug. It has a depressant effect on the brain, but for some reason, it feels like the exact opposite. Humans use it as a social drug, a social lubricant. It makes people feel like they're getting along better."

"Better than what?"

"Better than they really are." Brian shrugged.

"I like it." Nichu finally upended the bottle and drained it. He wiped his mouth, just as d'Abo had done earlier, and placed the bottle on Brian's desk. "I feel like we are getting along better. Do we sleep now?"

"Well, sure. Do you want to bathe? The shower's only sonic. I'll show you how it..." He stopped. Nichu had started to undress. Chugin's People sure had efficient clothes, Brian thought, distractedly. However they were fastened, once Nichu wanted to remove them, they fell apart at a touch.

Nichu straightened up, unconcerned by his nakedness. He'd certainly relaxed since the exam in sickbay earlier in the day. "Sonic? Of course. How else do you clean yourselves?"

"Water. When we have the resources, humans like to bathe in water."

"Water? We take dust baths." Nichu smiled, obviously recalling some happy dust bath in his past. "On suitable planets. On our ship we use sonics. Dust is bad for the ship's systems."

"Right. So is water. Tomorrow, I'll see if I can talk someone into letting you take a proper, wet shower. You'll like it."

"In water?" The pirate seemed unconvinced. "Is that safe?"

"Of course it is. It's...it's just like rain. Warm rain."

"You bathe in the rain?"

Brian laughed. "Don't worry about it. Try it tomorrow. You'll see. For now, you can take a sonic shower. Here, I'll set it for you. Just step in to the cubicle, and stay as long as you want to. Don't worry about turning it off. I'll be in right after you."

He turned back from the humming shower and watched the pirate look up at the cabin's ceiling before entering the cubicle. "Something wrong?"

"I am checking for rain clouds." Nichu gave him a teasing grin and then stepped inside. He didn't seem to realize that the cubicle had a door. He stood there, rolling his shoulders, looking as if, like a reptile, he was basking in the gentle radiant heat that accompanied the sonics.

It was no wonder that d'Abo had taken a shine to him, Brian thought. Then the pirate turned his back and stretched his arms up over his head. Brian felt a warm glow of appreciation in the pit of his stomach. He wasn't often strongly attracted to other men, but he had to admit that Nichu could have been one of the occasional exceptions. It was a pity the shower was only sonic. Those jewels would have looked even more irresistible covered in rivulets of water. He shook the thought out of his head and stripped off his own uniform, replacing it with a robe but leaving the belt untied. He didn't want Nichu to think that he'd done something inappropriate by shedding his own clothes so freely. He was just turning down the covers on Jolson's bed, when a voice spoke in his ear. "Brian?"

Startled, he spun around and had to grab Nichu's bare shoulder to stop himself losing his balance. The pirate was standing so close to him that Brian barely had room to shift his feet and regain some stability.

"May I ask you a question?" Nichu asked.

"Yes."

Nichu cleared his throat. "Was the female in season?"

"Jeanie? Well. Human females are...are slightly unusual, because they're potentially receptive all the time. So, if they think they've found the right man...an attractive male..."

"So, she was...displaying to me?"

"No, well...not exactly. They're not always receptive. And humans don't just mate in order to conceive. They mate for...for social reasons. And they flirt."

"Flirt?" Once again, the translator betrayed that this was a concept Chugin's People had no word for.

"Display, without intending to mate. I think that was what Jeanie was doing."

When Nichu was thinking hard about something, he seemed to stop blinking for lengths of time that made Brian's eyes begin to sting. "Why?" he asked eventually.

"Well...to look out for potential mates, without committing until they've found out more about them. Because the interest that the males show makes them feel good about themselves, um, and it makes other males interested...it's complicated." Brian carefully disentangled himself from Nichu and sat down on his bed. The pirate followed his example and sat opposite. Brian placed his palms flat on his thighs, and then watched as, a moment later, Nichu followed suit. He cleared his throat. "It's hard to know how to tell you all this, not knowing what you're used to. The females on your ship, they display when they're in season, and fertile?"

"And at other times. They are not fertile for the first few seasons," Nichu corrected. "Receptive, but not fertile."

"Good system," Brian said, with an approving nod. "So, the females display, and...do the males display? Do they compete for females?"

"We fight."

"You fight? I mean, have you done that, fought for a female?"

Nichu scowled at Brian's apparent scepticism. "Yes. Of course. Don't you fight for females?"

"No. Well...we...we compete, but...that game we were watching? Human males compete by playing games better than their rivals, or...or by being stronger, or...or more amusing, or more intelligent. Not by fighting. We don't fight over females." He laughed awkwardly. "Most of the females I know, if I broke another guy's nose fighting over them, they'd take him off to sickbay and fall in love with him on the way there."

Nichu looked blank.

"What I mean is, they wouldn't let two men settle who was going to have them by fighting. They'd make up their own mind, and their reasons might have nothing to do with the ability to win fights."

Jewel of My House

"Our system is better," Nichu said complacently.

"Oh? Is that how you got those scars?"

Nichu glanced down at his side, and smoothed a hand over the pale flank, marked by several sets of silver-white parallel scars. He nodded. "Here, I fought with Maki for Diagu's sister."

"So you can..." Brian stopped. This was getting a little personal, but Nichu answered his question anyway.

"I can mate with Chugin's People, but..." His mouth twisted into a smile. "Probably not fertile."

"And did you win? When you fought Maki?"

Nichu shook his head and Brian relaxed inwardly at the confirmation that the fights weren't, or not always, to the death. "It must be a disadvantage, being smaller than everyone else."

"No." Again, that shake of the head, and a little smile.

"Because you're faster?"

Nichu's smile broadened. "I'm better at what comes after the fight."

"Right! So the females do get to choose!"

"No." The smile faded, as if Nichu was beginning to suspect that Brian was teasing him. "I'm a better fuck than the females." He frowned, and then spelled it out for this ignorant alien. "When Maki knocked me down, he fucked me, and when he fell asleep, I fucked with Diagu's sister."

"Oh. Right. I see." Brian clamped his jaw shut before it could open too far. He guessed there were tropical fish, or something, on Earth, that employed similar tactics, but no examples sprang to mind. "I see," he repeated, thinking that Nichu had a nerve, calling humans dirty aliens, or whatever *notsi* amounted to, just for playing football. "Didn't you...didn't you object?"

Nichu laughed out loud. He pointed to his own penis. "Maki has a little cock like a..." He glanced around the room for comparisons, and finally gestured at the finger-sized succulent on Brian's desk. "Like that. I didn't even notice him."

"And the females...they don't mind that you're..." Brian found he couldn't take his eyes of Nichu's penis as he spoke. It was responding, either to Nichu's recollection of these amorous adventures, or maybe to the simple fact that Brian was looking at it. "Bigger than their males?"

"I'm very careful. It's not good to injure a female."

"No," Brian said, wondering if this was chivalry or...

"Their sisters will rip your skin off."

...Or self defence. It suddenly struck Brian that, biologically alien or not, Nichu was the first real alien he'd met, the first being who hadn't read the guide book before arriving on Earth. He, Brian Lee, was sitting

67

in his cabin with only a fold of terry toweling between himself and a naked, jewel-encrusted pirate prince, scarred by mating fights, light on his bare feet as a stalking leopard, and very definitely aroused, and getting more so by the minute.

As if they had both become aware, in the same moment, of what was happening between them, the cadet and the pirate looked up and their eyes met.

"So..."

"If..."

Brian laughed. "Go ahead. Your turn to ask a question."

Nichu, however, didn't ask a question. He reached out his hand and slid it under the hem of Brian's robe, lifting the fabric and folding it back on itself. Brian didn't let himself protest. He took a deep breath and put his hands behind him on the bed, leaning back to give the pirate a clear view of his genitalia. Nichu trailed his fingertips up the inside of Brian's thigh, turning his hand so that the pointed tips of his nails tickled the sensitive skin.

"These." He stopped short of the cadet's testicles. "Chugin's People don't have these."

Brian sucked in a breath and responded with a factual, "Probably because they have a lower body temperature than we do. These sacs hold the glands where the sperm are formed and stored. Too high a temperature lowers fertility, and increases genetic damage."

Nichu slid to his knees at Brian's feet. "This is pleasant for you?" His cool hands were palpating Brian's testicles.

"Yes, that...that feels good. That's...that's certainly pleasant."

"Do humans..."

"What? Go on, ask."

"Do humans swallow their ejaculate?"

When Brian didn't answer, Nichu sat back on his heels, increasing the distance between them, as if concerned that he might have overstepped an undefined boundary.

"Well...some of them...um, some of us do."

"Chugin's People...say that human ejaculate tastes...unpleasant."

"Well, some girls have said that to me too." Brian's answer was merely flippant, and then it occurred to him that if you were uncomfortably big for conventional intercourse, alarmingly big, oral sex might be the only thing on offer. "Hey...Nichu...That might just be a biological thing, different chemistry." The pirate looked up at him, wide-eyed. Brian noticed for the first time that there was a tiny glittering black stone set in the lid of each of his eyes, just at the outer corner.

"How frequently do you mate?" Nichu continued.

"Um, me personally, or humans in general?"
"You."
"It depends. If I have a girlfriend, maybe every night, if I'm not studying like crazy for a test, or on night exercises. If I don't have a girlfriend, like now, then...not so often."
"Girlfriend?"
"A regular partner."
"A mate."
"Not exactly. A mate for a while, not permanent."
"What about..." Nichu gestured at the bunk behind him.
"Jolson? No way! We're just roommates. Nichu...get up off the floor." Brian reached out with both hands to help the pirate to his feet. Nichu shook his head. His erection had firmed up. He ran a fingertip up the underside of Brian's cock, making it jump and swell to matching firmness.
"Nichu...this isn't a great idea..."
"Why not? Don't you like to fuck?"
"Well, yeah, but..."
Nichu dropped his hands to his sides, sighing. "I am sorry..."
"No. Don't be. You didn't do anything wrong. It's just...I think maybe Chugin's People are a little more...unrestrained, about sex, than humans. You should take it slowly. I'm not offended, but...you're moving a little fast here."
The pirate blinked slowly. "The female..."
"She was being stupid. She has a boyfriend...a mate. She was flirting with you, and expecting you to flirt back. That's all. And don't let Jolson catch her doing it. He'll kill you." Nichu continued to sit on his heels, watching Brian. For a moment, Brian just sat and looked back. The unwavering stare was hypnotic. He broke it, folding his robe round himself again and knotting the belt. "I'm going to shower." He hadn't taken two steps toward his bathroom before Nichu was blocking his path.
"Brian..." The pirate hesitated for a moment, then ducked his head. "You can fuck me."
"Look." Brian pulled the knot in his belt a little tighter. "I like you, but I'm not sure I want to fuck you. I prefer to...to fuck females. Generally."
"Always?" Nichu looked slightly surprised.
"No, not always. It's more that...if I have the choice between a good-looking guy and a good looking girl...I'll probably be looking at the girl."
Nichu craned his head around. He smiled. "I can't see any good-looking girl in here."

Brian woke to the fretful wail of his alarm. He turned, and almost cursed aloud as his muscles reminded him of the previous night's exertions. That prompted him to look over at the pirate hostage, who seemed oblivious to both the alarm and the gradual rise in the intensity of light in the cabin. He had shed his cover and lay spread-eagled on the bed, arms and legs at crazy angles, face half buried in his pillow. The river of jewels down his torso gleamed and sparkled as his breathing shifted them. Utterly alien jewels. Utterly human eyelashes stroked his cheek. He sighed, as if he was dreaming pleasantly.

Brian bit at his lip. This morning, sleeping, Nichu looked just a little young for last night's adventures. Still, everyone looked younger when they were lying down. It was something to do with relaxation, and the effect of gravity on your face. Last night, he sure hadn't acted like a kid.

The com bleeped and Brian hit it before it could rouse his guest.

"Brian? This is Barnum, in Xenobiology. D'you want us to give Nichu breakfast? Let you take a breather?"

"Oh. Sure. Thanks."

"I'll come by for him."

"Give him five minutes to get dressed." Brian grabbed for the cover and threw it over the naked pirate, as if Barnum had been about to burst in through the door. "Nichu, uh...Nichu?"

Nichu yawned extravagantly, without opening his eyes. Then he blinked and focused. "Brian."

"Yeah, that's right. Someone's coming by in a moment or two to take you for breakfast. You'll have to get dressed."

"Mmmm." Like a young human roused from bed for school, the pirate seemed incapable of getting any speed up. He stretched first one arm and then the other. Then he swung himself up to sitting and looked around the cabin. "My clothes..."

"You left them in the bathroom. But...I'm sorry. I should have put them in the fresher overnight. Can I get you a clean outfit?"

Nichu blinked, more awake by the second. "From my ship?"

"Oh. No. I didn't mean that. I can lend you something. If you want me to."

The pirate, having braved human food and sexual intercourse, seemed uninterested in human clothes. "Yes."

"Not a cadet uniform, of course, but..."

"Yes. Clean clothes. Please."

Brian stood up and remembered his own nakedness for the first time. He grabbed his robe from the deck as casually as he could and wrapped it round himself as he crossed to his locker. He pulled out a pair of black pants and a grey-blue tunic, civilian gear that he hadn't yet had any opportunity to wear on this trip. "Those should fit you."

"Thank you."

"You want boots?"

"Boots?" Nichu laughed. "Can I have my own boots?"

"I don't think..."

"No boots then."

"Are you going to shower?"

Nichu did his wide-eyed surprised look. "I smell of you," he said, and sniffed his open palm. "It's good."

Brian's gut fluttered anxiously. "Um. Well, humans are sort of...funny, about smelling each other. You should shower. We...uh, we worked up quite a sweat last night."

"Then I will shower," Nichu agreed, with a hint of muted rebellion in his voice.

"Nichu..." The buzz of the sonics wasn't loud enough to stop the pirate hearing him, but Brian still followed him into the bathroom, suddenly panicked at the thought of Nichu cheerfully telling everyone exactly how he'd spent the previous night. "There's a lot you don't know about humans yet. Like...we don't talk about who we sleep with, not specifics. We don't..."

"You have a mate? Am I in danger?" Nichu gazed at him for a moment, then continued fluffing his hair under the sonic beam. "Is Jolson going to kill me?"

The nervous flutter became sour and nauseous. "No, not Jolson. I mean, even if I did...I wouldn't tell everyone about it. We don't talk about sex, not in specific terms. We don't..."

Nichu stood in the shower, looking blank.

"You're doing this deliberately," Brian thought.

Nichu leaned forward and kissed him on the nose. Chugin's People, Brian had learned the previous evening, didn't kiss in quite the way that humans did. Nichu found kissing ridiculous at first, and then, apparently, irresistible.

"Don't!" Brian took a deep breath. "I'm just saying...because you don't know how we..."

"I understand."

"It's not because it's a secret, or anything like that. We just don't..."

"Talk about it," Nichu finished for him. He shrugged and stepped out of the shower. "You must shower too. Or I won't need to talk for everyone to know. You smell..." he paused to check on his facts, "...wonderful." He left the bathroom, jewels gleaming. Brian stepped into the shower and turned it up to full intensity. He rubbed at his face and

71

ran his hands under his arms and through his hair, to speed the shedding of old skin and dried-on sweat and acute embarrassment.

Then he stepped out of the shower and wrapped a towel round himself, throwing his robe into the 'fresher. Nichu was dressed and seated at the computer. From the back, he looked utterly human. The clothes Brian had lent him added to the overall effect of an ordinary young human. Brian resolved to buy something a little smarter at the next opportunity. Clothes that could make Nichu look ordinary must be seriously dull.

"Nichu..."

"I agreed. I won't say anything." He was scrolling through an article on terraforming, illustrated with examples from the current Venus project. "What is this?"

"That? It's the biggest planetary transformation humanity has ever tried. We need to reduce the atmospheric pressure three hundred times, bring the temperature down by a couple of thousand degrees..."

"Why?" Nichu asked. "If you need a planet, surely it would be easier to take one that was already habitable?" He didn't look away from the screen.

Brian suspected that Nichu wasn't really interested, but the question, coming from a pirate, was too contentious to be ignored. "We don't do that."

"Well," Nichu said, "why not?" He turned and looked at Brian. It felt like a challenge, but before Brian could respond, Nichu changed the subject. "I must speak to Dychu. I want to tell her we fucked."

Brian stared at him. "I thought you agreed..."

"We agreed humans don't talk about it."

"Yes, but...if you tell Dychu, everyone in Security will know. And then everyone will know. Why do you have to tell her?"

"Because...it's important."

"Important? In what way is it important? I mean...I'm not trying to say it wasn't good, but...important?"

The door chimed. Brian raised a fist in frustration, then shook it open. "Look, I'll try to arrange something. Just keep quiet for now." He opened the door, frowning.

"Where's..." Barnum had stopped in the doorway, looking confused. "Good grief. I thought for a moment, he'd given us the slip."

Nichu laughed. "No, this is me."

"Well, good morning, Nichu. Did you sleep okay?"

"Very well, thank you. Yes." Nichu addressed these words demurely to the deck, but Brian could see he was smiling. "I slept very well."

"That's good. Well...you can have some breakfast now, and then we need to plan what you're going to do today."

"I will return to Chugin."

"You will?" Barnum said. "No one told me." He glanced at Brian for confirmation. "What's he talking about, Lee?"

Brian could only shrug. "I don't know."

"Maybe it's a twenty-four-hour bug those guys caught," Barnum theorised. He looked at Nichu, but the pirate simply looked blankly back at him. "Well, we'll get breakfast, and then we'll...we'll see what the situation is." He stepped through the doorway. "C'mon, Nichu."

Nichu still hesitated. "I don't have to tell Dychu," he said uncertainly. "Not now. But I must tell Chugin's People."

"Fine. Tell them," Brian snapped back.

The door closed on the two men and Brian sank down into the chair at his desk and glanced at the screen. It still showed a simulation of the terraformed Venus that lay four or five years in the future. It looked beautiful, and not at all alien, like Nichu in his borrowed clothes. In a sudden burst of frustration, Brian ordered the screen to shut down and began stripping the sheets off Jolson's bunk. Last night, he'd made love to a pirate. Moreover, last night, for the first time, he'd let another man fuck him. He wasn't sure why. He'd had some idea in the back of his mind that he was reassuring Nichu that he wasn't some kind of out-sized physical freak, but once they'd started, he hadn't really needed any motive but lust, and Nichu hadn't seemed in need of any kind of reassurance.

He picked up the pirate's clothes from the bathroom floor, meaning to toss them after the sheets into the recycler, then turned to place them on the bed, realizing that Xenobiology would want them to analyze and catalogue. A creased sheet of plastic fell from the folds. Brian picked it up without thinking. It bore uneven characters of a language he couldn't read, written manually, he guessed, but the diagrams of positions and techniques, even though they were roughly drawn, were perfectly understandable. It helped that he'd explored several of them with Nichu the night before.

"You planned it," he said aloud to the departed pirate. "You planned the whole damn thing." He spread the sheet flat and held it up to the vision sensor of his terminal, taut between two clenched fists. "Translate," he told the computer. The following appeared slowly as the screen brightened and the computer struggled with the handwritten symbols:

"'My Jewel: This is what Dychu has discovered. Prove yourself, my son, with someone for whom the proving will bring pleasure, and not pain. Then you can take your place as a man of our people. You will truly be the jewel of my house.'"

"I've been had," Brian thought. "In more ways than one."

A message icon popped up on the screen and Brian automatically activated it, even before he noticed it was from Barnum.

"Hi Brian. Nichu was right. He's gone back to Chugin and those pirates are on their way. But...well, you know we have shoreleave coming up? I was telling him about that. I wasn't really thinking. The problem is, he said to tell you he'd see you at 16 Tauri. I thought I should warn you, or something."

Brian stared at the screen. "Of all the aliens in all the galaxy I had to meet you, didn't I?" he whispered. Then he flicked the message closed and looked down at his desk, at the crumpled plastic sheet, and the drawings. That one, and that one...but not that one...and certainly not that one, not yet. "Nichu..." He could feel a broad smile pasting itself on his face. "Oh, Nichu, you'd better believe you'll see me at 16 Tauri."

Mage Vows

Kathryn L. Ramage

In all the civilized world, only four universities boasted having a College of Magic: Wittenberg, Edinburgh, Padua, and Maryesfont. In truth, these were sufficient for the needs of those who studied the craft, and any more would be ridiculous. There weren't many independent students of magic. The few great wizards took the most talented youth as their apprentices, and the rest sought lesser magicians—the aged, long past their zenith, or the young and not-yet-established—to teach them. The universities accepted those who could find no more prestigious education, as well as scholars of magical lore who were not magicians themselves.

Mikha was the only magician at Maryesfont. Though still in his early twenties, he showed some remarkable powers and was considered a most promising talent, even if he was the son of a town merchant and had never found a mentor to train him.

The university at Maryesfont had begun as a convent school for the benefit of women in the dark days when such higher education was not available for females, but in these modern times, male students were also admitted provisionally if they were of good reputation and impeccable moral character. The rules of conduct within the university were exacting: students could be expelled for sexual impropriety, for drunkenness, blasphemy, obscenity, impudence, or irregular attendance of chapel, lectures, or tutorials—all evils that the Sisters of St. Mary, Font of Wisdom, were inclined to believe young men more vulnerable to.

Mikha, however, was just the sort of student they welcomed. In addition to being a serious scholar and a true magician, he had already begun the third purification phase of his mage's training before he'd entered the university. This phase was a seven-year period during which a young magician lived under strict vows of abstinence: he lived chaste, drank no wine and ate no blooded meats, fasted and kept sleepless on certain days of the year, and performed rituals on certain nights. A mage might as well be a priest, and there were several of those among the university faculty.

He had been given rooms to himself above the College of Magic's library. This arrangement gave him privacy and ready access to all the magical resources the university possessed so that he could concentrate on his studies at any hour. In return, he occasionally aided the university's other students of magic, who knew the collection less well, in finding books, and helped the librarian keep the collection in good order.

In this cloistered and monkish life, Mikha passed the first four years of his education with relative ease. His mage vows weighed lightly upon him, for he rarely felt tempted to break them.

Then, late one evening as he wandered the long rows of tall shelves on the upper floors of the library, returning any books that had been removed to their proper places, he discovered a little student asleep at a table, head pillowed on the soft parchment leaves of the original manuscript of *The Source of Human Magic* by Uillod of Orkeney, complete with notes of revisions and marginalia.

Mikha couldn't see the student's face, for the hood of the shapeless brown scholar's robe was up over the head. Girl or boy? He stepped forward to lean over the sleeping figure, and caught sight of the pink tip of a nose, a long lock of fair hair that had escaped from beneath the hood to fall over the young person's cheek, and a down of ginger-colored fuzz on a dimpled chin. Gently, he shook the student by the shoulder.

The student awoke. "Oh, I'm sorry! I must have fallen asleep."

"Old Uillod can be dry reading," Mikha said, "especially for a beginner." He thought he was acquainted with all the students of magic at Maryesfont, but this one must be new.

As the youth sat upright and twisted to look up at the mage, his hood fell back to show his face—the face of an angel. Mikha was not poetic; this was simply what he thought in that first astonishing moment. He knew that he spoke to a boy, but the youth's beauty came as a surprise. The boy looked like the angels in the stained glass windows of the chapel. In the light of the single candle he held in his hand, the boy's flushed face, still soft with sleep, was rosy and childlike; his mouth opened slightly in wonderment was like an angel's in silent song, and his fair hair was lit to fiery gold.

"Who are you?" Mikha asked him.

"Andemyon Lightesblood."

This was the oddest name Mikha had ever heard. He could not imagine what the family name meant. Was this a noble youth? Mikha had never seen a nobleman before, but they were popular figures in the comedies and romances performed in the city theaters; those foppish creatures with their dandified clothes and ridiculously elaborate manners looked nothing like this boy.

"Are you the librarian?" the boy asked in return, then looked him over, taking in the long, black robe the young man wore. "No, you have magician's robes. I was told a mage lived in the library. Are you he?"

"Yes, that's right. Mikha is my name."

"Is the library shut?" Andemyon turned again to look out of the narrow window above his table. "It's after dark. I must've been sleeping for hours. What time is it?"

"It was just ten o' the clock when I shut the library doors."

"Ten! It's past curfew. I'll be terribly late." He rose and tried to dart past the mage, who unintentionally blocked his exit.

Mikha stepped back, but took the youth by an arm. "Wait," he offered. "I'll accompany you."

Being out past curfew was not by itself enough of a breach to warrant expulsion, but the boy would be in for at least a scolding from the dean of his college and some severe penalties, such as being limited to his room except for meals, chapel, and classes, for up to a month. Mikha hated to see that happen. This was, after all, an accident. Andemyon had been up to no mischief. Besides, there were so few other young men in the university, and he didn't like to see any one of them be caught and punished. If he couldn't help Andemyon sneak into his room unnoticed, perhaps he could speak on the boy's behalf? His position and mage state gave him certain privileges that other students, male and female, were not allowed.

They went down the stairwell together, to the library entrance on the ground floor. A large white moth was battering its wings frantically on the tall, mullioned window above the turn of the stairs; the light of the candle Mikha was carrying, reflected multiple times on the numerous small panes of glass, seemed to dazzle and confuse it.

"Poor thing! It will fly into the flame in another moment and be burnt to an ash." Andemyon stood on tiptoe to reach up and carefully capture the moth under the palm of a cupped hand, then reached out with his other hand to unlatch the window and push open the casement. "I don't like to see anything needlessly killed, and especially not a moth," he explained as he brushed the fluttering insect outside. "Have you heard the old myth that moths are truly dead souls lost? People thought so in the old days, when this part of the world was wild."

Mikha had heard this myth, but such pagan tales were not generally known among the common folk. Scholars might learn of them, but the Church did not encourage them among the unlearned who might confuse them with accepted doctrine. "Where did you read that?"

"Father told me." Andemyon turned back to look up at Mikha, who stood several steps behind and above him. "I really must go."

They swiftly crossed the lawns and gardens of the university to reach St. Ambrose's College, one of the smaller and older buildings on campus. They were met at the door by the college Dean. Mikha, surprised that they were caught so quickly, made ready some excuse—any excuse—for the boy's being out so late, but Andemyon spoke first:

"'Tis nothing to fret for, Auntie. I'm sorry if I worried you. I fell asleep in the library of magic. This is my friend Mikha—he's a mage."

The dean, who knew Mikha by sight, nodded and thanked him for showing Andemyon safely home.

As he returned to the library alone, Mikha was filled with an inexplicable burst of joyous energy; like a boy at play, he lifted his robe to his knees and raced across the grass, bounding over bushes and flower beds, leaping up to snatch at the leaves on low-slung branches of the trees above the path. He ran up the stairs two and three at a time, his heart light. He did not realize that he had left Uillod's book lying out where Andemyon had been reading it until the librarian asked him about it the next afternoon.

He did not sleep well that night. Andemyon's voice repeated again and again in his head: "This is my friend Mikha—he's a mage"—until the words lost all sense. He turned restlessly, and his dreams, when they finally came, were more confused than his waking thoughts, and were filled with moths and golden-haired angels.

In the morning, he rose early and went back to St. Ambrose's. He stood for ten minutes, twenty, on the dew-damp lawn of the quad before Andemyon emerged. The boy smiled at the sight of him; Mikha felt as if he had waited all night.

"Your aunt—the Dean—she isn't angry with you?"

"Oh, no. She couldn't be. Aunt Pacia was only afraid that I'd come to some harm. She was greatly relieved when she saw I was with you."

"You haven't been punished?"

Andemyon shook his head.

"Do you have a class now?" Mikha persisted.

"A meeting with my tutor."

"May I walk with you?"

While they walked to the tutor's rooms, Andemyon told his new friend more about himself. The Dean of St. Ambrose's was his mother's aunt, and Andemyon was under her protection while he was a student here at the university. Mikha had no reason to disbelieve this, but then Andemyon went on to tell him some absurd and fantastical tales: he claimed that his father was Lord Yryd Lightmaster, the premiere wizard in the Norman Empire. He had spent his childhood in the wizard's castle on the cliffs over the sea at the very tip of Greenwaters Island and had been educated among his father's apprentices and his magically talented elder brother and sister, but he possessed no magic abilities of his own. At fourteen, he'd been sent to the Duke's court at Pendaunzel to be a herald, and had become a favorite of Duke Dafythe himself. Now that he was eighteen, he had left the court to begin his formal education at Maryesfont.

As he listened to these incredible stories, Mikha thought that this angelic boy must either be an accomplished and imaginative liar or completely mad. In time, he discovered that Andemyon had only spoken the truth.

This was their beginning. In the months that followed, their friendship grew swiftly. On other days, they took walks around the university grounds or on paths along the river beyond the city walls. Andemyon talked about his father and his family, and what it had been like to serve at the Duke's court. In turn, Mikha told Andemyon about his childhood as the younger son of a respectably prosperous merchant family in the city of Storm Port, and how his family had reacted when he'd first shown signs of being magical. While the peasantry and common folk might be superstitious about magic and cross themselves when they spoke of a wizard's power, among the merchant classes magic was considered to be in questionable taste. Mikha's family had been at pains to suppress his burgeoning talents, just as they would if he'd shown a fondness for writing poetry or a desire to run off with a troupe of actors. Once he'd reached an age to decide for himself, Mikha had left home to seek his own education.

They spent long hours discussing magic. Andemyon asked question upon question: What did it feel like to cast a spell? How did Mikha *do* it? Andemyon could speak the same incantations, make the same gestures with his hands, and it would come to nothing. Could Mikha form a cloud from a cup of water? Could he light a candle's wick? Could he move this book across that table without touching it? Where did this power come from? The Church claimed that magic was a gift from God, or a tool of Satan, depending on the use it was put to, but was there also a physical source to it? Were there any other magicians in Mikha's family?

He took an interest in Mikha's studies, and Mikha was astonished by how much Andemyon had already read. That foray into Uillod of Orkeney at their meeting had not been the first time Andemyon had opened this book. It seemed odd to Mikha that this angelic boy with no magic of his own should know as much of wizard craft as the most promising adept apprentice, but Andemyon had been reading the books on his father's shelves since he was too small to understand them.

"I grew up among magicians. All of my family are magical, save myself," Andemyon explained. "But I've always wondered—why I am not too? Why am I different?"

He meant to find the answer. He often observed Mikha while spells were being cast. Could he place his hand over Mikha's while he made the requisite gestures? He wanted to see if the power were transmitted through the fingers. Could he touch Mikha's chest to feel if his heartbeat changed?

No, Mikha had no objection to these requests. The hours they spent working together were the most exciting and fascinating of his day. He felt that they were making important discoveries into the nature of magic. His own studies were the traditional course for young magicians: spellcraft, the history of wizardry, the philosophy of magic, and plenty of practice to hone his skills. Andemyon's questions and experiments, by contrast, seemed unusual and imaginative.

As a magician, Mikha sensed the natural world around him: the living energies in the leaves of the trees, the shimmering grass, the clouds of midges over the deep river water. All things, he perceived, were endowed with an individual power that might be channeled and controlled. With Andemyon, he felt the Earth begin to open its secrets to him and believed that it was all part of the same energy. The boy drew him into it. Andemyon possessed a keen intellect, immature but developing, and yet there remained an elfish strangeness in his clear blue eyes. He had a childlike wonderment at the world around him, and his ideas were often bewildering, even to a young mage. It astonished Mikha to think that such a remarkable creature as Andemyon Lightesblood was his friend. Beyond doubt, this friendship was the most important thing ever to happen to him.

He didn't understand why, until they were caught one afternoon in a rainstorm outside the city. In the sudden downpour, they fled from the open fields, pausing only briefly under trees in their dash, but never stopping long once they heard the rumbles of thunder. They slipped in the mud and slick grass as they ran, stumbled against each other, caught and dragged each other back to their feet to go on, laughing all the while. When at last they reached the city, they sought the first shelter within the university gates, the porch of a college. Andemyon reached it ahead of his friend. When Mikha caught up, Andemyon flung both arms around him and collapsed against him, breathless and soaked.

"Can't you stop a storm, Mikha?" he teased. "My father could do it. He can pull lightning out of a clear sky, and dispel a storm as quickly."

"My talent doesn't lie that way," Mikha answered. "I'm no master of rain and lightning, and I'm not so powerful a wizard as your father. Nobody is."

"Oh, but you will be, one day." Andemyon smiled at him.

"You sound more certain of that than I am."

"Of course I am. Don't I know your talents better than anyone? Haven't I watched you perform hundreds of spells? You never go wrong. I used to watch Father's apprentices at their exercises—you never miscast the way they did. You're going to be a great wizard. I know it."

Mikha was immensely gratified at this expression of confidence, but there was something in the way Andemyon was gazing up at him, something in that smile, that made him feel very odd. He released his friend in confusion. "I don't know if we can reach St. Ambrose's without getting in a worse state," he said. "It's on the far side of the campus."

"The College of Magic is much closer," Andemyon agreed, and darted away.

They went into the library and raced up the stairs to Mikha's rooms. Mikha was no master of light, but he could create a spark to set the tinder on the hearth afire. A good magician had no need of matches. When he turned to look up from this task, he found that Andemyon was already shedding his drenched clothes.

Mikha stopped in the act of shrugging off his own soggy robe. His mouth felt dry and his heart began to race. He and Andemyon had been alone together in his rooms dozens of times before, but he was aware for the first time how isolated they were at the top of this building. He heard the rain drumming down on the roof immediately overhead, and no other sound. There was no one in the library below. No one would interrupt them. No one ever had while they were up here on other afternoons, and it would be no different today.

Andemyon pulled off his shirt and hung it over the back of a chair near the fire. Drops of water ran down the long curls of his hair and onto his bare shoulders and chest, where they trickled down in tiny rivulets. One drop hung suspended for a long moment off the end of a cold-puckered nipple; Mikha couldn't take his eyes from it. He felt a shocking desire to kiss it away...before it fell.

When Andemyon shook out his hair with spread fingers, more droplets showered around him in a sparkling spray. Next, he peeled off his hose and stepped out of them. Mikha was used to thinking of his friend as a young boy, but Andemyon was nearly nineteen and no longer a child. His body was not childlike. The joints of his arms and legs, like his hands and feet, were raw-boned and outsized in proportion to the rest of his body, but the rest of him was growing rapidly to catch up. He was not yet so tall as Mikha and not so bony, nor was he as ungainly. There was little hair on his body, only a cluster of reddish curls where his legs met, darker than the hair on his head. And dangling beneath these curls, pink and flaccid...Mikha stared, then quickly averted his eyes. He was not in so blameless a condition himself.

"I'm muddy to the knees!" Andemyon laughed as he picked up his dirty hose from the floor. "I'll have to give these a wash before I can put them back on, or else go home barelegged. Auntie will be scandalized." Then he noticed that Mikha was still sitting on the hearth. "Aren't you going to get out of those wet things?"

Undressing was the last thing Mikha wished to do. He didn't dare let Andemyon see him in this embarrassing state. "I'm not so wet," he answered, and removed his mage robe to set it aside. Beneath, he wore black hose and a loose, white shirt. "I can dry myself here by the fire."

"I never saw you without your magician's robe on before!" said Andemyon. "You look quite ordinary. Almost like any other boy. Is there something else I can put on?"

"There's a spare nightshirt in the chest, over there."

Andemyon walked unselfconsciously naked to the chest of drawers to find the nightshirt. Mikha shut his eyes and tried to will his body into obedience. He had performed similar efforts of self-control countless times. He knew how to discipline his mind and flesh. During his childhood, he had suppressed his magical abilities in the face of parental disapproval. As a mage, he had fasted for days at a time and had kept sleepless vigils over many nights. He could command the rhythm of his breaths and the measure of his heartbeats. He could control *this*. He must, before Andemyon noticed.

After he had found and put on the nightshirt, Andemyon rinsed his muddy hose in the wash-basin and lay them over the back of the chair beside his shirt. He kept up a cheerful chatter about Mikha creating a spell to dry clothes more quickly, which gave Mikha time to master himself.

"When are you expected back at St. Ambrose's?" he asked once he had regained some control.

"Not for hours. Aunt Pacia knows I'm with you." Andemyon sprawled across the foot of Mikha's bed.

"Doesn't she mind that you're with me all day?"

"Oh, no. When I first came to the university, she was afraid I'd be taken up by some older lad who would want to take me out to the drinking-houses and gaming-houses, and worse places, in the town and corrupt me. She was relieved when we became friends instead." Andemyon grinned and, as his friend crossed the room to stand over him, raised his foot to poke at Mikha playfully with his toes. "A mage is as safe as a young man can be."

He had placed his foot squarely on Mikha's breastbone. Mikha gripped the bare ankle, and his head swam with a delicious haze. He was overtaken by a fantasy so vivid that he almost believed it was real: he saw his own hand moving up Andemyon's bare leg, ruffling the ginger-colored fuzz on his calf, and gently brought Andemyon's knee to his chest. Andemyon smiled up at him, waiting. Mikha leaned down and kissed him.

He shook his head, dispelling this picture, and let Andemyon's ankle go.

"I tell Auntie all about our experiments, everything we do," Andemyon went on. "She doesn't understand my interest in magic, but she says I mustn't occupy too much of your time with my silly questions. Your studies are too important. She says that the university hasn't had a graduate magician in over fifty years. They're so proud to have one now—and such a promising one! They wouldn't want anything to spoil your chances. You'll be tested soon, won't you?"

"In three years," said Mikha.

"As long as that?"

Mikha nodded. "There'll be a difficult time ahead, but once I pass into my fourth phase, I'll leave off my mage vows and become a full wizard. A minor one."

"You must have a wizard to test you." Andemyon sat up. "Shall I ask my father to do it? I want very much for you to meet him."

Mikha quailed at the idea of meeting Andemyon's father. He'd heard too many tales of the foes the Lightmaster had met in wizard-battle, and how he had vanquished them. Some still lived.

Andemyon saw his expression and laughed. "Don't be so frightened, Mikha! Father won't be hard on you. I've seen him test others, and he is fierce, but fair. Besides, you'll do wonderfully. Haven't I said so before?" He lay back again, propped on one elbow, perfectly at ease and unaware of Mikha's efforts to keep up his side of the conversation.

Mikha's heart was thumping so loudly he was surprised Andemyon couldn't hear it. His innards felt gelatinous, and his head bubbled with more wild, impulsive, delightful thoughts. He imagined lying down beside his friend, holding him in his arms. He thought about kissing Andemyon, tasting those lips, tugging aside that flimsy nightshirt to cover his body with kisses. He imagined burying his face in the puff of reddish curls.

After awhile, Andemyon looked up at the beamed ceiling above them. "The rain's stopped. I should go." He rose from the bed to feel his clothes laid out by the fire and decided they were dry enough to be put back on. In a few minutes, he had dressed. Mikha dared not watch him this time.

"Will I see you tomorrow?" the young mage asked.

"Of course! I'll come as soon as I've finished my classes. That is, if it won't inconvenience you."

"No, you're no inconvenience, Andemyon."

As he opened the door to exit, Andemyon turned to give Mikha a smile—a smile that pierced Mikha through to the core of his being. Andemyon might not be magical in the usual sense, but he certainly held some enchantment of his own. A powerful spell had been cast today.

After his friend had gone, Mikha curled up on his bed and groaned. This strange new sensation that had overwhelmed him was achingly sweet, agonizing, bewildering, wonderful, terrifying. He felt deeply shamed as if he had been caught in the act of a mortal sin, for he could not deny the nature of what he was feeling, but neither Church upbringing nor a mage's self-command could banish it. It was the very worst thing that could happen to a magician bound by a vow of celibacy. He'd fallen in love. It had happened months ago, but hadn't seen it for what it was until today. Andemyon was all he desired...and couldn't have.

The mage vows he had barely felt restrained by these last four years were suddenly unendurable. Three more years! Could he hold out for so long without facing disaster? How could he bear to have Andemyon near him? But he did not wish Andemyon to go away. No. That was worse. To see Andemyon, to think about him—that must be enough, for now. For the next three years this must be endured. At the end of that time, he would be a full wizard, free of his vows, and Andemyon would be a young man of twenty-two. He could tell Andemyon the truth then. What would Andemyon say to that? And what would they do?

Chiaroscuro

Ginger Mayerson

It was the package delivery guy at the door again.
"We're seeing a lot of you this week, Mr. Arkin." He always said that after he took off his envirosuit hood. He handed over the envirosealed grocery order and a small package. He held up the optical scanner up for ID verification and delivery confirmation.
"Yeah, I guess," Arkin mumbled, leaning forward for the scan. The luminous green grid before his eye expanded, contracted and then went dark.
"Ah, still you," the delivery guy said with a smile. He said this every time and it suited Arkin fine; it meant he didn't have to hold up his end of the conversation.
Arkin opened the package. It was the new game his employer wanted him to test and review. "Chiaroscuro" was emblazoned on the CD case. Arkin had to look it up to know it meant either the arrangement of light and dark parts in a work of art, such as a drawing or painting, whether in monochrome or in color, or the art or practice of so arranging the light and dark parts as to produce a harmonious effect.
He tossed it on his wreck of a computer desk, which was not at all arranged to produce a harmonious effect, and took the groceries into the kitchen. There was a can of tofu stew in the latest grocery delivery; it was something he was slightly less than indifferent to.
The groceries were a neat service: for a few weeks he'd entered what he wanted into their online request form and after that, the database had, based on his previous purchases, sent him a ration of whatever was consistent with those requests. Arkin didn't use the word desires because, beyond food and shelter, he didn't have any.
His job as a software tester provided for both, and made it possible for him to never have to leave his apartment. That was all right. Since the war, the global pollution levels made going out in protective gear essential.
He sat at his desk and put the CD in his computer. Usually his boss sent him a download link for such things, but he'd been told that this was

a special project. Based on his previous stellar work, Arkin had received a small promotion, a raise in pay, and better products to review. This was the first assignment of the new era and the packaging was certainly deluxe. He hoped the game would live up to his expectations.

His boss's email had also said the game was going out to several other reviewers at different companies and that there would eventually be contact with the others as the game progressed. This made Arkin a little wary of playing; he preferred to play the game, not other gamers. But if it was part of his new job, then he'd at least try. He hit the "play" button and was ushered into "Chiaroscuro", where he was informed there were two players online. He wondered if this meant him and someone else, or him and two other players.

It was a very black and white environment he lumbered around in, trying to adjust to the nonhuman game form. Arkin began to feel bored, but then caught a flash of movement to his left. He lost it, got lost, thought he saw it again.

"Always to my left," he thought, veering to his right and doubling back. He caught a glimpse of his quarry, but not a good one. It seemed to be a game creature similar to his, but somehow different. On the other hand, any other game creatures online at the moment would have a great view of him, standing on a windswept plateau, thinking things over. He scowled at his monitor and ended the game. It might be better to spend his evening reading the promotional BS that came with the CD.

Over the next few days, Arkin got better and better at the game, but so did his opponent. He was never sure if there were one or two because the game always said there were two players online. Occasionally he nearly made contact with his prey, which is how the promotional material wanted him to imagine his fellow players. The game was designed to be predator against predator. Arkin thought he was a poor choice for this game because he was more prey material than anything else. But he persevered and eventually knew the environment and his opponent well enough to lure him/her/it (he wondered) into a box canyon. It was Arkin's first good look at what he was chasing and it was beautiful. Or was beautiful until the other player logged off.

Arkin made a screen shot of the cornered creature to study and admire. He printed it out and taped it to the wall where he could see it from his bed.

The next few times he played there were more players involved, but not the one he'd become obsessed with. Late one evening, when he was about to quit the game and go to bed, he was tackled from behind by his idol. Points were calculated and the screen went black.

But he had an instant message from someone named Darcet.

darcet:: you should know better than to stand in the open like that
arkin:: how do you know it's me?
darcet:: there's a link back to all the players, don't you check who you're playing?

Arkin never really believed in "other players" and wouldn't know what to do with one if he did. It had been a long time since he'd had a social-like email, longer still for a real conversation. He could not remember the last time he'd spoken to anyone for...for...fun.

arkin:: sometimes I check
darcet:: :)
akin:: and sometimes I don't
darcet:: you there?
arkin:: yeah
darcet:: log on
arkin:: it's so late
darcet:: i won't run

Darcet's game creature was male and very gentle.

"We're seeing a lot of you this week, Mr. Arkin." He handed over the grocery order and held up the optical scanner up for ID verification and delivery confirmation.

"Yeah, I guess," Arkin mumbled, leaning forward for the scan. The luminous green grid before his eye expanded, contracted, and then went dark.

"Ah, still you," the delivery guy said, but didn't smile and didn't leave. He was studying Arkin.

Arkin cleared his throat, tried to make eye contact, but only got as far as the nameplate on his envirosuit: Bob. He'd never noticed the nameplate before. "Um... thank you... Bob," he mumbled.

"You're welcome, Mr. Arkin," Bob said cheerfully and finally left.

And not a moment too soon. All Arkin wanted now was to get back to the game and Darcet, on the game or on IM. That was all Arkin wanted now.

darcet:: where are you?
arkin:: on the coast. you?
darcet:: same, near the delta
arkin:: me, too
darcet:: oh
arkin:: yeah

darcet:: it's nice here
arkin:: yeah

They exchanged addresses and realized they were less than an hour apart. But for Arkin the game and IM were enough. For now.

"We're seeing a lot of you this week, Mr. Arkin." He handed over the grocery order and a large box. He held up the optical scanner up for ID verification and delivery confirmation.

"Yeah, I guess," Arkin mumbled, leaning forward for the scan. "Bob," he added. The luminous green grid before his eye expanded, contracted, and then went dark.

"Ah, still you," the delivery guy said, but didn't smile and didn't leave. He was studying Arkin.

"Yeah." Arkin glanced up at him. He could make eye contact, but not sustain it.

"I see this is from the EnviroSuit Company," Bob said, nodding at the box. "Going out?"

"Maybe," Arkin mumbled.

"Then maybe someday I'll come here and you'll be out, Mr. Arkin," Bob said cheerfully and finally left.

"Yeah, maybe," Arkin thought sadly. "Maybe not."

He had learned over the course of their, um, romance, that Darcet had been injured in the war and was paralyzed from the waist down. If they were ever going to meet it was Arkin who would have to leave his apartment. The idea of leaving his apartment terrified him. He'd not been able to admit this to Darcet, so he made excuses: he had the flu, he was working on a deadline, he had to stay in his building to receive a package for his neighbor, he'd sprained his ankle, and, finally something close to the truth—his envirosuit was damaged.

The complete truth was that Arkin had not been outside of his apartment for so long, he no longer owned an envirosuit.

Darcet stopped asking him to come visit, but continued to play the game and other, more personal games. They spoke on the phone; Arkin got hard just from his voice. The next day he ordered a new envirosuit.

"We're seeing a lot of you this week, Mr. Arkin." He handed over the grocery order and a small envelope. He held up the optical scanner up for ID verification and delivery confirmation.

"Yeah, I guess," Arkin mumbled, leaning forward for the scan. "Bob," he added. The luminous green grid before his eye expanded, contracted, and then went dark.

"Ah, still you," the delivery guy said, but didn't smile and didn't leave. He was studying Arkin.

"Yeah." Arkin glanced up at him.

"Have you gone out yet?" Bob asked.

"Not yet."

Bob seemed disappointed, but managed to smile professionally and finally leave.

There was a new game CD in the package. It was called Trompe d'Oeil. Arkin thought it was a boring, but well-made game.

arkin:: are you on trompe d'oeil?

darcet:: no

No... their worlds were diverging.

arkin:: i can email it to you

darcet:: i have lots of games right now

Arkin's chest got tight.

arkin:: i can

darcet:: to review

arkin:: bring it

darcet: i'm here

Arkin put on his new envirosuit and went to Darcet.

He forgot the Trompe d'Oeil CD. They did not miss it.

It was the package delivery guy at the door again.

"We're seeing a lot of you this week, Mr. Arkin." He always said that after he took off his envirosuit hood. He handed over the envirosealed grocery order and a small package. He held up the optical scanner up for ID verification and delivery confirmation.

"Yeah, I guess," Arkin mumbled, leaning forward for the scan. The luminous green grid before his eye expanded, contracted, and then went dark.

"Ah, still you," the delivery guy said with a smile. "Hello, Mr. Darcet."

Darcet looked up from his computer and waved at the delivery guy. "Wha'd we get?" he asked after Arkin closed the door.

"Chiaroscuro, version 2." He handed it to him.

Darcet pulled him onto his lap. "I wonder if it will be as fun as reality."

Arkin said he doubted it and, after a kiss, went into the kitchen to start dinner.

After dinner, Darcet installed it on their computers and they had a look around. It was familiar, but more complex than the previous version of Chiaroscuro. The landscapes were different and game characters were only people who'd succeeded in the previous version. This made the play more challenging.

Arkin found himself noticing one game character more than the others. While Darcet darted off into the game's middle distance, Arkin followed the character discreetly. It seemed to Arkin that the character was keeping the same space between them, while leading him into a secluded part of the gamescape. His guide seemed to be male in the game, but just as Arkin was getting close enough to find out, Darcet announced it was late and time to go to bed.

Arkin switched off the game and helped his lover out of his wheelchair and into their bed.

In the beginning of their relationship, Arkin had worried that his sex life was going to suffer with a lover paralyzed from the waist down. He should have realized that Darcet's imagination and sensitivity in the game would carry over into reality.

The next day, Darcet had other games to beta-test and Arkin was back in Chiaroscuro 2. He was only on for a few moments when he realized he was being stalked. He was hopeful and fearful that it was the same character from last night.

It was, and it took all of Arkin's skill to stay ahead of him. Not too far ahead, but just out of reach. Just as Arkin was about to let himself be caught, the doorbell rang and he had to sign off.

"We're seeing a lot of you this week, Mr. Arkin." He always said that after he took off his envirosuit hood. He handed over the envirosealed grocery order and a small package. He held up the optical scanner up for ID verification and delivery confirmation.

"Yes." Arkin leaned forward for the scan. The luminous green grid before his eye expanded, contracted, and then went dark.

"Ah, still you," the delivery guy said with a smile. "Hello, Mr. Darcet."

Darcet waved from his computer. He gave Arkin a funny look as his lover handed over the small package of medication. "You were kind of sharp with Bob," he said softly.

"I was in the game..."

"That's not Bob's fault."

"Yeah, I guess," Arkin mumbled. He put the groceries away and sat back down at his computer. The game was dark, but he had an instant message from someone named Tianos.

tianos:: that was sudden.

arkin:: are you...?

tianos:: yeah come back in the game.

arkin: I can't now but later is eleven tonight...?

tianos:: what time zone?

arkin:: coast.

tianos:: I'm two hours ahead of you but I'll stay up see you then.

Arkin closed the IM window and became very intent on an ad for an online game.

Darcet went into the kitchen to make lunch and Arkin glanced nervously at his back. "It's just a game," he thought.

Arkin slid carefully out of bed when he was sure Darcet was asleep. Darcet slept heavily on the pain medications he took.

He was a little early, but Tianos was where he had been earlier in the day. He was with another game character. Something surged in Arkin's blood and he chased the other character off. Then he ran Tianos down and they were rough with each other.

Sometime later a very spent Arkin crawled back into bed and went to sleep.

There was an instant message the next day.

tianos:: let me call you!

arkin:: no...we can't...

tianos:: come back in the game then.

Arkin glanced at Darcet, who smiled fondly and looked back at his own computer.

tianos:: arkin?

arkin:: later tonight...same time...tianos?

tianos:: well, all right, later then.

"You look tired, Mr. Arkin," Bob observed a few days later. He held up the optical scanner up for ID verification and delivery confirmation.

"Yeah, I guess," Arkin mumbled, leaning forward for the scan. The luminous green grid before his eye expanded, contracted, and then went dark.

"Ah, still you," the delivery guy said with a smile and, after saying hello to Darcet, left.

"You do look tired, Arkin," Darcet said sympathetically.

"I'm not sleeping very well," Arkin said, staring at the floor. "I'm...I'm seeing someone else."

Darcet looked startled. "When, Arkin? You never leave the apartment."

"After you're asleep..."

"Is someone coming here!?"

"...in the game..."

"In the game?" Darcet pointed at Arkin's monitor. "In Chiaroscuro 2?"

Arkin nodded, and looked up shamefacedly.

"Oh...well, that's okay, I guess," Darcet said quietly.

"It is?"

"Yes, I mean, it's just a game." He pulled Arkin close for a kiss. "Who is it?" he asked, logging into the game.

"That one," Arkin pointed to the sexy game character.

"Oh, Tianos..."

"You know him?"

"Oh, yes. You should schedule your trysts with Tianos earlier in the day," Darcet said with a smile. "Like I do."

Darcet didn't live very long after he was moved to the huge hospice in the center of town. So many people were dying of their wounds, pollution illnesses, radiation exposure, that soon only those too young for the war and as acclimated as possible to the new environment would survive.

Arkin was one of those, and after Darcet died, he wasn't sure he wanted to survive. He found he couldn't leave the hospice. He slept in chairs, lived off the leftovers the kitchen staff gave him, and wasted his dwindling bank account on the slow but public cyberaccess terminals. He was not the only one; there were dozens of lost souls like him in the waiting areas. Some of them moved into jobs at the hospice, which made them sympathetic to those poor bastards still stuck in their former condition. Some would stay and some would get out. There was no betting either way on Arkin; he was already a kind of ghost to everyone. They were waiting for him to leave or end up in a room and die. Either seemed imminent.

After several weeks, he finally picked up his email and found his employer had wanted to know where he was and then fired him. His and Darcet's former landlord had padlocked their door for nonpayment and then moved their things to storage. That things were being taken care of by themselves gave Arkin a great deal of comfort. But eventually he began to look for a way to leave the hospice waiting rooms.

The environment outside was as hostile as ever; even looking out the windows distressed him. He knew no one in the city he could email to fetch him. The idea of being fetched like a package was distasteful. However, after several failed attempts he screwed up his courage enough to ask a package delivery guy if he knew Bob.

"Bob who?" the guy asked, turning away from the reception desk.

Arkin gave him his old address. "The Bob who delivers there. Can you tell him Arkin is here and needs help?"

The package delivery guy looked dubious, but he must have called someone because Bob showed up later that evening.

"I was wondering where you were, Mr. Arkin," he said.

Arkin told him about Darcet's death, losing his job and apartment, and having nowhere to go.

"I'm sorry about Mr. Darcet," Bob said when Arkin had finished. "We'll be seeing a lot of you for awhile then."

"Yeah, I guess," Arkin said, and followed Bob back out into the world.

The Fall

Laura Dearlove

They should have chosen white wine; it was so cold that the red tasted brassy, metallic. Carla strolled at his side with her fingertips barely emerging from her bear-sized parka, while Adam had one hand stuffed deep in his pocket and the other gone numb around the bottle. Every now and then he took a gulp, and passed it along to Carla, who always swallowed and passed it back quickly so she didn't have to hold it for too long.

"Michael. Boatie Michael, with the...arms." Carla rowed her arms for a second to illustrate, making bulky chicken wing angles of her elbows. "I haven't slept with *him*, thank you very much. All he does is row and he smells like the Cam anyway."

"Yes you have. After that stupid toga party–"

"I didn't *shag* him, we just had a bit of a fumble." She snatched the wine back, took a slug, scowled and handed it back, and swallowed. "He practically tastes of the Cam too. And you, I never slept with you."

"Obviously."

"So not the *entire* male population of Cambridge, thank you *very* much. And what about you, anyway? You ever planning on getting laid?"

"Why does it always come back to this?"

"Because some days I think you're gonna shrivel up and drop off."

"Carla, hell–"

"What?"

"It's not always about just getting a shag and it's not like I never *have*, maybe I would just...just rather wait for the right person, okay?"

"Oh, the right person. Princess Charming. You are worse than a girl, for the record. It's not like you're unattractive or anything, you have the darkest eyes—maybe a bit of an old-fashioned haircut but I could–"

"I am not...I'm not having this conversation with you. Again."

"Again."

A couple more swigs of wine, and they walked along the river in silence for a while. It was wider out here, away from the city and the colleges, and here and there narrow boats were moored up but they seemed to be empty. Cambridge was a dark, mismatched hulk of rooftops ahead of them, the old and new built on top of each other, ancient colleges and gleaming new lecture halls all silent now and dark.

"You spend so much time in your head I wonder if you can hear your body anymore sometimes," Carla said thoughtfully. "Like, when was the last time you *wanted* someone—maybe didn't shag them but you *wanted* them so much you could taste it–"

"I don't know, I can't remember."

"You never forget that. Pass it back." A quick gulp and the bottle handed back to him again; he took another belt because, well, why not? "If the love of your life dropped into your arms–"

"Because it happens just like that."

"–you wouldn't even notice you'd be so caught up in being proper and doing the right–"

And then there was a *boom*.

Carla shrieked and Adam yelped, stumbled, the wine hit the grass and rolled away on the path, and the light burst overhead like a firework had gone off course and exploded on top of them—had exploded right behind Adam's eyelids...

The scream didn't come from either of them.

And then a second, smaller *boom* of the river as a body hit it, and the white circle of light phutted out as quickly as it had appeared. Adam stood breathless, like he'd been thumped in the chest. Carla stood silent for a stunned second and then said, "Why haven't they come up?"

"Fuck." Adam scrambled down to the bank but Carla dropped, was scrabbling at the endless laces on her boots and muttering, "Shitshitshit, Adam, I can't get 'em–"

"They haven't come up–"

"There's all sorts in there! Dumped bikes and rusty—Adam, get them *out*!"

Adam did have the time as he kicked his trainers off and shrugged off his coat to think, "If there's all sorts in there why am I jumping in?" But, like he was on an invisible line, he leapt in after the body. Just enough time between ground and water to realize quite how horrible this was going to be, and then the temperature smacked all thought and breath out of him, November river water turning his skin to numb-cold metal. He fumbled, stunned and stupid and freezing, through the slime of weeds and endless stabbing water.

His hand caught a long trail of hair, and he tightened his grip automatically. It cut into the skin of his hand, wire-sharp with cold. He reached out, blind, aching for air, and got his arms around a body, but not

The Fall

the woman's body he'd been expecting with all that hair; it was a boy's flat, skinny chest his arms caught and he kicked for the surface desperately, feet tangling in the long lazy flutter of the boy's clothes, brain a single scream for air.

It turned out the water had been practically lukewarm; the night air was as cold as knives. Adam retched breathlessly to the stars, "Fucking—Cam–"

"Here! Here, you idiot!"

Clumsy with cold and the lolling body of the boy in his arms, Adam floundered for the bank. Carla leaned down, arms open, and as Adam slung the body half onto the bank she said, "Urgh, he's all wet–"

He wanted to say something pointed but could only heave for breath and chatter incoherently. Carla rolled the boy over, scraped his wet hair from his face and tipped her cheek to his mouth, said, "He's still breathing..."

Barely the strength in his arms to heave himself out of the water, Adam lay dumb with cold on the bank but Carla poked him in the shoulder and said, "You. Call an ambulance."

Adam panted, "Tell 'em what?"

Carla, who had now wrapped the pale-lipped boy in her parka—he looked about their age, maybe a little younger after all—said, "Ah."

We were walking along drinking and then he just fell out of the sky...

"We don't have the time for this. You'll both get hypothermia. So, best way to get you both warmed up—you carry him back."

"What? People are going to call the police on *us*!"

Wrapped in Carla's bulky parka the boy was still wearing a sodden...*dress*, and at his side—no wonder such a bony body had been so heavy—hung a sword in a thick black scabbard. Adam didn't want to explain this to the A and E or the police, no. Nor did he want to lug it all the way up the hill to their rooms, though.

There was a clear winter half-moon overhead, and it lit the boy's damp cheek with a pale crescent curve of white.

"Adam! King's Chapel sprouts traffic cones! Gangs of students in pajamas hang around in pubs! Drunken Daleks patrol the streets! You think one person in this city'd look twice at us? Now get a bloody move on or I'm pushing you back in!"

Well. When she put it like that...

Carla had pushed and badgered and berated him the entire way, and Adam was warm by the time they made it back to Wychfield and up two flights of stairs to their rooms—too warm, once Carla had got him to put the boy on his bed (he didn't have the breath to say, "But that's *my* bed.") he was peeling wet clothes off himself, sticky and hot now, to just his t-shirt and raspy wet jeans.

"I'm gonna run a bath, we need to get him warmed up," Carla said. "You get him undressed."

"I—what?"

"I can't undress a strange boy, think of my reputation," she said, striding out unconcernedly.

"I am thinking of your reputation," he muttered, and looked down at the boy. He was maybe an inch taller than Adam, which had made carrying him on his back awkward, though he weighed much less. He had a hell of a lot of hair, a tangled ponytail that must have fallen to his waist, now trailing over the edge of the bed and curling on the floor, darkened with water. Must have been pale brown and very straight, when dry and combed.

And he was wearing, well, robes. And carrying a sword.

What exactly have you brought home with yourself, Adam Lawson?

Cloth belt around the boy's waist; Adam had to hike him half-upright on the bed to untie it, slip it off. Robes came off over his head. Damn it. A long shuffling peel-and-jerk upwards, eventually revealing baggy trousers underneath the robes and a slim pale chest. Boots off, socks off. Pray he's wearing underwear underneath all this get-up, and trousers off. Underwear. Relief. Even Carla wouldn't be cruel enough to ask him to de-underwear another man.

Long clumsy colt-limbs, unconscious face cheek to the pillow, wet hair in his eyes. Adam tucked it behind his ears and hiked him awkwardly into his arms again, back groaning, staggering backwards from the bed and stumbling for the door and the bathroom and warm water, and getting some blood flowing in the boy's cold limbs. He could hear raucous laughter from downstairs, drunken students having a normal Friday night in. The lucky bloody bastards.

Adam woke in dim weird dawnlight, pigeons cooing stupidly above his window, hurting like hell in a sleeping bag on his floor. The carpet felt rough and scratchy even through the sleeping bag, which smelled faintly of Carla's shampoo. His eyes ached. He sat up awkward and slow like an old man, rubbed at dark hair gone insane with water and sleep-tossing, and blinked up.

At a boy in his bed, sitting with his back to the wall, shielded by his knees and the sheets pulled almost to his chin, eyes a sea-grey in the strange dawn light focused on his and terrified.

"Uh," Adam said.

The Fall

The boy's hands were gripping the sheets tight at his knees, and shaking.

"Who are you?" he whispered.

"I'm Adam. Natsci." He cleared his throat, remembered that the entire world didn't speak Cambridge, and amended, "Natural sciences. I'm a student. Look, I know this looks weird, we found you in the river last night, we brought you back so you didn't freeze to–"

Weak and rasping, "Are you going to kill me?"

Adam's breath caught in his throat for a second.

"What? No! Why would...? No!"

His hands didn't relax on the sheets, and his eyes searched Adam's face, desperate to believe him.

"What's your name?" Adam asked, trying to make his voice soft, like talking to a wounded wild animal.

The boy stared into his face. He looked small and helpless and terrified.

"Luke," he said, and swallowed. "I'm a necromancer."

Saturday morning meant lectures still for science students, but Adam would just grab the notes off Simon when he next saw him. Carla, a feckless philosopher, hardly had any lectures at all and an almost nocturnal schedule, and would be sleeping still in her room down the hall. Adam pointed out the bathroom to his strange, mad guest, changed into some dry, clean clothes himself, and made toast.

Luke crept into the kitchen like he'd never seen one before. He stared up at the light for a long time, like it might drop on his head, then edged around it to stand beside the sink, which he gave a long, odd look to. A puzzled look to the oven, then the microwave, then back and forth a couple of times like he was trying to work out the connection between them. Then the toaster popped and he nearly leapt out of his skin. Adam gave him a long look, then plucked out the bread and began buttering it.

Luke stared at the toast. "How did it do that?"

Adam looked back at him. Either he had brought home a madman, or an extremely good actor, or else there'd been something fucking weird in that wine last night and he was living through the most realistic and yet surreal hallucination ever. He handed a piece of toast to Luke, who took it with a shy, apologetic bob of the head, and nibbled on the corner of it.

"So," Adam said, sticking more bread into the toaster. "Are you actually going to explain any of this?"

Luke swallowed his mouthful miserably and said, "Explain what?"

"You fell out of the sky into the river. And you were wearing—hell, wizard's robes and a sword, have you just been reading too much *Harry Potter* or what? What the hell..."

But Luke was just staring at him uncomprehending and scared again, so Adam forced his voice to soften. "You're a necromancer," he said, trying not to sound too skeptical.

"Not a very good one." Luke said softly. When he tipped his head forward, loose hair that didn't catch in his hair tie shielded the sides of his face a little, protecting his expression. His eyes in stronger light were incredibly blue, Adam could see now, the bluest he'd ever seen, like summer skies and happiness.

"So, what? You mean you use magic to bring back the dead?"

Luke's head shied up again. "No—how could you—? What? What's gone is gone. I just—we don't do that." He turned his piece of toast around nervously.

"Then what *do* you do?"

Luke stared at him for a second, then began looking around the kitchen. Adam finished off his own piece of toast, and when the toaster popped again Luke gave a little yelp. Adam rolled his eyes, began buttering again, and Luke pushed a couple of pans aside on the windowsill behind the sink, swallowed the end of his own toast, picked up something and came back to Adam with cupped hands.

Inside them was a dead moth, a brown shriveled flower petal. Luke was looking down at it with a sort of tender grief, before he closed his hands, closed his eyes, and Adam paused in buttering to watch him.

Mad, or a really good actor, or...

Luke whispered underneath his breath and opened his hands. And the moth's body still lay there like a piece of ash but above it fluttered...

Like a silver spark drawn off a fire, like a firefly trailing a moonlight-colored fizz of electricity, *another* moth, a moth that blew left and right and out of Luke's hands, circled the tiny kitchen in crazy bounces, almost invisible in the stronger light than its own body generated when it flew past the window and then up to the electric light in the ceiling. Adam couldn't see it at all against that brighter light but he could hear it, bumping its tiny frail body against the casing.

He was a scientist, after all. He felt dizzy with disbelief.

"Its...soul?"

"No," Luke said, closing his hands again around that tiny dead body. "It would be cruel to bring its soul back just to... an echo, that's all. An echo of its life."

The echo bounced off grubby plastic, eager for the light.

"You're a necromancer." Adam repeated, dully, dumbly.

The Fall

"I'm not a very good one," Luke said again, and Adam sat down with a scrape in one of the plastic chairs, and stared at the ghost bumping around the light, and couldn't even think.

"So how did you end up here?"

He'd loaned Luke a green t-shirt of his that hung off his skinnier frame like a parachute, and a pair of jeans with the belt as tight as it could go. At least he was tall enough that they fitted, instead of dragging off the ground a little as they did for Adam. Luke sat on his bed, arms wrapped around his knees, while Adam sat in his desk chair with a cup of oh-god-needed coffee, trying to make this make sense.

"They...my college got attacked." His hands had tightened on his knees. "I had to get out."

"Attacked by who?"

Luke's lips tightened, he shook his head. "They hate necromancers. They hate us. Because we wear grey and we don't hate death–"

"Who?"

"They wear white and they're scared of death." And Luke made a little noise that could have been a laugh, breathless and terrified behind his knees. "They're scared of their *own* deaths. They were running with red before they'd got halfway through the college, and everyone was screaming–"

Luke was eighteen, he'd told Adam. And Adam, a wise old second year now and nineteen, thought, "A fresher," but Luke had been in that "college" most of his life, like a monastery, like an orphanage. But still—a college. He tried to imagine it in his own college, ancient brick and golden stone and pretty gardens, and people in white robes walking in and beginning to butcher students. Screaming and confusion and terror, and blood.

"–and the little ones are only kids and everyone was panicking, the teachers were fighting and the magic was—it was like trying to walk through an earthquake—trying to run for the vaults and in the dormitories the blood was up the walls and–"

His breath choked and his arms shook and tightened around his knees and still shook, and Adam realized that he was crying.

"Hey," he said softly, but Luke just shook his head and his voice was a rising wail and then a sobbing moan as he lost control of it.

"Couldn't do anything, killed Nico and Seven and couldn't do anything, trying to run the kids down to the vaults but they were screaming and crying and I couldn't, I—couldn't do anything once we'd locked ourselves in, Marley holding the doors and yelling at us to do some magic but they were only children and didn't know enough and I'm just no *good* and I wasn't working a spell I was praying—please don't let us die please don't let us die not yet not yet there's no balance for them they're *children* not yet please please not yet–"

He lost his voice into his knees, hid his face there and his shoulders shook. "Hey," Adam said again, awkwardly. He got up, walked over, felt too uncomfortable for this, began rubbing Luke's shoulder because he didn't know what else to do. Hard round bone under his hand, jerking with Luke's sobs.

"I don't know what I did, don't know what anyone did, there was light and then—I don't *know*, I woke up here—and I'm not even on my world anymore, am I? You don't even know what magic is, this is— where am I? And I can't—even if I could get back, get back, get back to *what*? A building full of blood and no one even left to scream anymore–"

"Hey, hey." And Adam didn't know what possessed him to squeeze harder at Luke's shoulder and say, "It's alright. It will be alright. You're safe here. You can stay here."

Luke looked up with wet red eyes and hair sticking to the tears on his face. "But," he said.

"You can stay here." Adam said again, and part of him wondered what the hell he was thinking, but all he was really aware of was Luke's helplessness, Luke's terrified, hopeless eyes, Luke's wobbly sobbing breath and the fact that he didn't have anyone else in this world.

Carla listened to the story from over a can of breakfast Coke, dark red hair left messy, grey eyes darkened with kohl. Luke was sleeping some more in Adam's bed, exhausted with fear and misery and confusion. They were sitting on the bed in Carla's room, because the other students in their block had already realized that *something* was going on, that there was an extra presence amongst them, and longed for gossip. They wanted to know who Adam had brought home with him last night, and Adam didn't know how to tell them "a necromancer"...

"Poor kid," Carla murmured.

"He's hardly any younger than us to be a 'kid'."

"That's what I mean. Can you imagine living through...? Hell. That sucks. 'Sucks' doesn't even..."

Carla had taken some convincing to get here. In some ways she was more skeptical even than Adam; Adam required the evidence of his senses to believe in something, but Carla needed an irrefutable argument, and "he made a ghost-moth in the kitchen" took a while to swing her. She was also, in her own weird way, infinitely more practical than Adam.

"We're not even allowed to keep pets, how are you just gonna keep him here?"

"Where else can he go? If we hand him over to the police they'll have him sectioned."

"Or men in black will come take him to some hidden Government lab." Carla sighed, rubbed her hair. "If the bedders spot him they'll tell the porters, and the porters will go nuts. We're meant to sign in every guest, remember?"

"I can think of something. I will think of something. I can't just send him out into the streets, he doesn't have anywhere to go and he doesn't understand how anything *works*. He nearly screamed when I turned the light on. He thinks the computer's alive. He's scared of everything, he needs–"

Was Adam really going to finish that sentence with "me"?

"He stands out too much himself, I guess." Carla took a thoughtful slug of Coke. "All that hair, boys just don't wear it like that, he'd have to've been growing it since he was a kid. And he's got no clothes except those robes, and that sword... and he's insanely pretty too, pop star pretty, he's gonna stand out on any street."

Adam checked her eyes, and scowled at the smirk there.

"Carla, for God's sake, you're not serious."

"Maybe he needs some love and–"

"He's post-traumatic and terrified. Leave him alone."

"I wasn't suggesting *I* offer the love," Carla said, airily, and tipped her can back again, and Adam was just confused. She swallowed her grin. "Look, you're right even though you're wrong. It's gonna be *insanely* difficult to keep him hidden here. But we can't just leave him to wander the streets, clueless pretty boy who's probably never seen a car before... he could end up killed or mixed up in anything. We have to keep an eye on him."

How hard could that be?

"I'm in your bed," Luke said guiltily.

Adam, climbing into the sleeping bag again, felt something harden in his throat and didn't know what. He coughed and said, "It doesn't matter, Carla gave me the sleeping bag. It's fine."

"But it's your bed." Luke wriggled. "I shouldn't drop into your life and push you out of your bed, you're already giving me somewhere to stay–"

"I don't mind."

"But I do, I'd be more comfortable if–"

"I really don't mind."

"–stealing your bed from you, and it's not like it's big enough to share–"

A little pause, during which Luke went pale and then bafflingly red, and his voice came out in a stumbling sprint. "And I mean, the floor would be more like the beds in the dormitories so it's not like I'd mind but you must be used to this so you should have this and I should just–"

"Luke. Shut up. Go to sleep."

A long pause.

Luke whispered, "Thank you."

Every morning the bedders came to empty the bins, to clean the bathrooms and the kitchen. Adam had no idea how to keep Luke hidden from them; Luke just looked puzzled at his confusion and said, "I don't see the problem. I can just go invisible until they leave."

...and Adam was beginning to come to the state of mind where he didn't even need to say, "You can just go *what*?"

They were new to each other's worlds, and equally fascinated. Adam really should have been working this weekend; instead he was explaining the modern world in baby words for a boy who thought that electricity was a breed of magic, while Luke explained necromancy to him, explained magic to him, in the same faltering thought-through infant talk.

"You don't—reanimate bodies," Luke said, face twisted with disgust and horror. "What does that have to do with necromancy? We...deal with the borders between life and death, not the seriously, seriously dead... there's not much really heavy magic involved in the day to day, only in those few times when it's the heaviest magic of all. We learn a lot of healing. We walk people along the border and keep them at this side of the wall when it shouldn't be their time yet, if we can. But we accept that everyone and everything crosses that wall. That's all life is, the time before you cross it. You have to accept that. Accept the balance, don't hate the dark half of it, you may as well just hate the night."

And accepting that balance had got them hunted down and murdered, and thinking of that made Luke go quiet again, and scared.

And Luke was half a child still when faced with almost everything. Television made him shriek like a little boy, eyes alight with joy, bubbling with it. He found the whole experience—well—magical. And the delight came off him like an aura, infected Adam too, he'd never laughed so hard at *Buffy* before. It was only afterwards that he realized that it was a bad choice of program, that now he had to explain to Luke that there weren't actually any vampires in the world, there weren't actually any witches like that who could help him.

That weekend, the other students became used to Luke's presence—a *friend from home* Adam told them, doing most of the talking, praying Luke didn't say anything to give them away. Don't tell the bedders, he's just going to be staying for a while, okay? And odd laws of student loyalty made it a done deal from the start, they'd all hidden boyfriends, girlfriends, friends, stray cats and pet rats in their rooms when they really weren't meant to before.

Monday morning approached, and lectures. Adam didn't know what Luke would do, alone in his room all day. But Luke said, "This is a university, isn't it? There must be a library I can use, I could—try to find out what magic there is in this world, try to find a way to at least find out what happened at home."

"You can't just stroll into the library, Luke, you have to have permission to be there, you'd need a student card and—"

"Invisible," Luke said cheerfully, sitting cross-legged on his bed and grinning at him, wicked little boy's grin, and Adam's chest did this weird clenching thing.

The presence of magic, he supposed, and tried to ignore it.

It was hard to concentrate on chemistry when Adam knew that Luke was out there in a world he barely understood, alone and weird and innocent-slash-naive enough to tell God alone knew what to perfect strangers. Adam had dropped him off at the library this morning, a building so huge it made the bricks it was made from look like Lego blocks, and so full of books that Adam had never walked through even a third of it. Luke had kept close to his side, terrified of cars on the roads they'd crossed, startled and scared of bikes and nervous of all the people—and so delighted by all the books he was faced with that he squeezed Adam's hand inside the echoey, over-warm building, and slipped unseen close behind him through the barrier (he said he was invisible; Adam could still see him, but no one else batted an eyelid so...), squeezed his hand once more and disappeared up the stairs with his hair a long streamer behind him. Adam let himself out through the barriers again with his student card and walked to lectures, feeling oddly aware of the air all around him without Luke's presence at his side now, and very aware of his own left palm.

He met Luke for lunch in the library tearooms, where Luke was less cheerful after being buried underneath incredibly unhelpful books all morning. Adam showed him, painfully slowly, how to use the online databases to search, but he still doubted Luke would find anything of use. Did he honestly think he'd find a book of magic in here?

He'd arranged to meet Luke at half past four in the entrance hall again, but he wasn't there. Adam sat at the edge of the room, to the side of the enclosed circle of the librarians' desk, watching the comings and goings and the thumping of books onto the desk every few minutes. No Luke.

Half an hour later, still no Luke.

There had been little waves of anger and worry, but the fear had now washed out the both of them. Luke didn't have a mobile phone, Luke didn't technically exist, Adam could hardly start asking people if they'd seen him. And the University Library was...huge didn't even begin. It would take hours, *hours* to walk the entire building. If he had to check every nook and cranny for an invisible boy, *days*.

He hurried through the shelves, running up and down staircases with his heart in his throat. No sign of Luke. And it was dark outside now, and the library would close soon, and if he didn't find him, if Luke was here all night—alone in the dark, he'd be terrified, Adam couldn't bear the thought, or what if he'd left for some stupid reason and he was wandering the streets of Cambridge with no idea of how fast cars could go, no clue about anything and such wide, wounded, lost eyes–

His mobile went off. Dirty looks from a whole row of desks along the windows. Adam pulled it out and ducked back into the stairwell, checking the name. Carla. He clicked it on and tried to keep his voice low and not as terrified as it really was. "I can't find Luke, I don't know where he–"

"You have to get back here," Carla said urgently. "I can't even make him open the door, what the hell happened? Did you two have a fight or something? He looked like he was going to throw up–"

Luke didn't have a key, and Adam didn't know how he'd got himself back into their house and into his room without one. Invisible boy, of course, but what other tricks did he have?

Adam unlocked the door.

The room was dark, odd blue light streaming through the open window which Luke was leaning against—odd blue light lacing the walls with lines and runes and odd symbols, odd blue light glowing all around the door and lighting Luke's eyes as he looked back at him. Adam closed the door behind himself. It was like standing inside a model of the night sky, planet trajectories in fine lines of light and symbols he didn't know marking off stars and satellites and solar systems...

Luke whispered a few more words to the glass, which gleamed with light, and stood up with his hands shaking. "I saw one," he said hoarsely. "Through the window, outside—on the grass..."

Adam did a quick calculation; opposite the library was a newer outpost of one of the colleges, St Catherine's maybe, and—and whoever was standing on the grass *must* have been invisible, because it was almost a beheading offence to walk upon the sacred grass of the Cambridge colleges.

The Fall

"Cloaked and hooded in white and *looking for me*." Luke looked small and delicate in this weird blue light, but this weird blue light had come *from* Luke, it was his strength, it was magic in a world where magic didn't belong and it made him uniquely powerful. "They came through after me. They want to wipe us all out. Magical genocide. They're going to kill me–"

"No." It came out as a bark and Luke leapt. "No," Adam forced his voice softer, steady and hard. "They're not."

And part of him thought, "You're nineteen. Your greatest skill is not falling asleep in lectures. Exactly what are you going to do?"

Maybe he was as terrified as Luke. He couldn't let Luke see that, though.

"I'm not strong enough to fight them," Luke whispered.

"But you can hide. They don't know this world either, and you'll be safe here with me–"

"They won't find me in this room," Luke said, slowly, softly. He raised a hand to the glowing walls. "I made it safe. I don't know what else to do, I didn't... I made it safe."

"Okay. Good. That's good. So..." He felt exhausted, now. All that worry and now an uneasy nausea of real terror in his guts. If they found Luke they would kill him, and if Adam tried to stop them then they'd kill him too, and... he realized that he'd never really grasped what death *was* and couldn't imagine it properly now. "It's been a long day. I'll put a pizza in the oven. You hungry?"

Luke smiled weakly. Adam had a whole flash of thoughts he didn't understand—Luke's hand squeezing his left palm, and hugging his narrow body to himself, and Luke's little boy smile and the way the light gleamed off his wet cheek—and opened the door, letting in the obscene bright light of the electric bulbs, and waited until Luke was at his side before heading to the kitchen.

He woke in the night to a rustling noise.

He hadn't wanted to scare Luke any further, so he'd hidden the kitchen knife underneath his pillow without letting Luke get a glimpse of it, and Luke was distracted and generally clueless enough that he didn't even notice. But he'd known then that he didn't know if he could use it, and–

And there was someone moving in the room.

He sat up, snapped his mobile awake—the screen lit up and the room went green, and Luke in his mage's robes was pinned against the door. Luke screamed.

In less than two seconds Adam had dropped the handle of the knife under his pillow and had a hand hard over Luke's mouth, holding him to the door.

"Idiot, you idiot, you'll wake the whole building–" he hissed. Luke squirmed and struggled and kicked him in the shin. Adam yelped, and Luke twisted from his grip and scrabbled for the door handle, whimpering as he pulled. Adam grabbed his wrists and wrenched him back and Luke yelped, "–*go*, let *go*–"

Adam tripped over the sleeping bag and down they went, in a confusion of robes and hair and legs and sword and Luke's elbow whacked all the breath from Adam's lungs and the room spun black again when his phone went back to sleep. In the darkness Luke's breaths panted against the side of his throat, and then he rolled over and laid a warm hand over where his elbow had just stabbed like a blunt blade. He whispered, "I'm sorry—are you alright? I'm sorry–"

Adam's breath wheezed back into life. "Fine. I'm fine." His chest wracked a cough out which hacked off before he managed to snap, "What the hell were you doing?"

Luke sat up and Adam heard the rustle of his robes, pressed himself up on his arms to sit as well. In the darkness he could barely see Luke's shape, but his breathing sounded very close. "I was leaving."

"Leaving where? You don't have anywhere to go!"

"But they'll find me. They'll follow me, find me, and they'll find you and they'll kill you—you don't even have any magic, you won't even know they're there until you're dead–"

"I thought you made it so they couldn't find you in this room."

"So they couldn't find *you*! I can't stay, I can't stay in this room forever and they'll find me, they'll find me and you and you've looked after me and I know I'd be dead if it wasn't for you and I can't let them kill you there was blood up the walls and I can't let them–"

Adam reached out, caught Luke's arms. "They won't. We will think of something, they won't hurt you–"

"*Hurt*, Adam, they'll *kill* you—and I won't be able to–"

"You can't leave. Where would you go? You don't have any money, you don't even know where you are! You wouldn't last half an hour out there! You're safest here, I can look after you–"

"You don't have to! You just found me, I just dropped on you, I'm not your problem! You don't have to die just because I dropped into your life, I'm not your problem–"

"Yes, you are."

"Why? I'm making a mess of your life, I know I am–"

"I don't care. You're here now. We're both here now."

"If they kill you—"

"They won't." Adam pulled him forwards, trembling bony body in his arms, and Luke grabbed at his t-shirt despite everything he'd said.

"My fault, it'd be my—"

"And if they killed you now it'd be my fault. We're in this together." He should be terrified at what he'd gotten himself into. Instead Luke was rocking against him and Adam closed his eyes to his hair and got a sudden strong pull of his scent; he'd used Carla's shampoo, patchouli and heavier spices, and an underlying scent that was just Luke. "We're in this together now."

"It'd be my fault—"

"Only if I cared. And we're in this together." He wasn't used to soothing someone like this, but his hands rubbed down Luke's back easily, naturally now. "We're in this together, you idiot."

He should be feeling uneasy because of the deadly people with magical powers who would kill the both of them given the opportunity. He actually felt uneasy for a reason he didn't even begin to understand...

"Huh," Carla said. "I thought he screamed because...well, never mind. Scared the shit out of me, for the record. I was trying to write an essay."

"Sorry."

"Doesn't matter." Luke was taking a shower, so they had a few minutes without him there, worrying like a cross between a sheepdog and a sheep at Adam's shoulder. Carla was making soup, stabbing into a squash and snapping the top off it with a twist of the knife and a thoughtful scowl. "You ever wondered why you are looking after him, by the way?"

"What?"

"Well—I do get the impression that, you know, you were the sort of kid who took in stray cats and tried to save birds with broken wings and stuff—"

And once got beaten up, when five years old, for trying to stop some other boys from killing a mouse they'd caught. Snot and tears and humiliation and hopelessness and a bloody nose; odd how some things come back so sharp sometimes.

"—but he's not a lost dog. He's a person. And he is in some serious shit, Adam, we're not talking broken wing here, we're talking mass murder—"

"I know."

"So why haven't you handed him over to someone who could look after him better? Why didn't you just let him go? You would have if he'd been someone else."

And Adam didn't know what to say.

Yes. He probably would have let Luke go if he'd been someone else—if he'd been less clueless and naïve and clumsy, less like a lost puppy. Or maybe if he'd been less cheerful despite everything, less caring and smiling and innocently happy, maybe he'd...

He was nineteen and studying chemistry. He needed glasses to see the board in lectures and the screen at the cinema; he was allergic to bee stings. He wasn't a hero. He was so very not a hero.

When Luke had been trembling in his arms Adam would have fought down armies to make him safe.

"I can't just—*dump* him—"

"I know, I'm not suggesting it." Carla began whacking off chunks of orange flesh from the squash, with the same knife Adam had hidden underneath his pillow on the floor last night. "But don't you wonder why you've taken him in like this?"

"What exactly are you suggesting?"

She sighed, her boys-are-so-tiresome-and-stupid sigh, and picked up a heap of squash between knife and hand and dropped it into the pot. "You think it through, idiot. Otherwise I'm gonna have to sit you in front of some educational films and hope it clicks. Jesus."

Carla talked in riddles and strange prophecies. But then Luke came in with long wet hair down his back and Adam smiled for him, and Luke smiled back like he was genuinely so happy that Adam of all people in the world was there.

Adam got back from lectures and found his room in darkness, the curtains pulled, and Luke in his mage robes sitting in one circle of burnt-out candles in front of a second circle, a figure eight of dead candles on the floor. Adam could smell something burnt and thick, and Luke's eyes were lost, gazing into space over the circles of candles.

"I asked Carla to get some herbs and candles for me," he said, without yet looking to Adam. "I contacted one of my teachers. It took all day. He said he sent us all somewhere else from that vault, he made us safe. The children are out there, somewhere, on this world or another. And I ought to find them if I can, find somewhere safe for them to go and then gather them, because we're going to need our arts if those mages in white take over."

Adam watched Luke's straight back and just the side of his strained but calm face.

"Only he couldn't fight and perform that magic at once. He made us all safe, but he died." Luke breathed slow and soft. "I just spoke to his ghost."

The Fall

Adam could hear rain dotting the window. He stepped into the circle of candles, knelt and put his arms around Luke from behind. Luke pressed his face to Adam's arm but said nothing, and didn't cry, just held himself steady and strong.

"I wish I knew where to start," he whispered, and Adam did too.

It took a few days ("I'm not very good at this," Luke mumbled when attempt number two spontaneously caught fire and set the smoke alarms off and started a half-hearted panic amongst the students) but Luke made a charm, a little pouch of Adam-didn't-know-what that smelled earthy and herby and glowed softly when Adam squinted at it, which he wore on a long thread underneath his clothes. It should keep him hidden, he said. Not if one of them stood in front of him and looked him in the eye, they'd know then. But if he was just another figure on the street it should keep them from looking twice at him.

And it was Friday night again, and there was the last bop of term in their college, everyone wearing tinsel and silly hats and being absurdly happy. Still almost a full month to Christmas but Cambridge terms were weird and this was the closest to Christmas they would get in this city. Adam had to insist Luke come, pointing out by pressing a finger to his forehead between his eyes, that Luke was developing worry lines. He was young and he ought to have some fun when he could. There would be dancing, and drink, and...

Luke didn't take much convincing really, his eyes sparkled, and he would follow Adam like a puppy everywhere anyway.

The college common room lit with fairy lights and a disco ball, and Christmas pop music thumping out of the speakers. Girls in reindeer horns and boys in big beards, and it was wild, raucous, after a few drinks Adam had to keep sight of Luke by the pale t-shirt he was wearing and that immense fall of hair gleaming in the flickering on-off lights.

Carla was working a shift at the bar so she got free entry and drinks. When Adam bought another couple of drinks, trying to keep an eye on Luke's bright smile in the crowd as he talked to another girl who lived in their block, Carla leaned over the bar and murmured warm to his ear with lips painted wicked red, "You want to kiss him."

Adam nearly spilled both drinks. And looked back at Luke as Luke burst out laughing. And with it said out loud, thought about it for the first time. Carla didn't speak in riddles, Carla spoke in logically necessary imperatives...

His mouth went dry, and Carla laughed out loud at whatever expression was on his face.

Whirl of lights and the Pogues were playing, and Adam caught Luke's hand before he could lose him deeper into the crowds swaying and bellowing the words on the dance floor. Luke swung back into his body—an impromptu tango—blinked at him and smiled, happy little boy's smile, all the joy in the world.

How had he not noticed this before, what this feeling meant before?

Adam slipped a hand underneath Luke's hair and rubbed the soft skin of the back of his neck. Luke gave a tight shudder all the way down his body and stared at him, neck pressed back against his hand, mouth open. Adam couldn't remember how much he'd had to drink, how much he'd given Luke to drink. And if this ended up being a stupid thing to do then it could fuck everything up, he knew that, could end up with Luke out on his own on this world he didn't understand, could end up with Luke dead...

It didn't feel like something that could lead to a fuck up. It felt like the most simple decision in the world.

His thumb stroked down the line behind Luke's ear and the angle of his jaw. Luke closed his eyes and his breath whispered, close enough that Adam could feel it now, and then his eyes flicked to Adam's and he said, "Do you...do you mean this?"

They were clumsy together, awkward on the line between teenage boys and young men and new to this anyway. Adam's nose bumped Luke's, Luke's eyes were too needy, Adam wished he had a height advantage on Luke instead of the other way around so he could hold him closer, safe inside the angle of his own body.

"Guess I do, wouldn't've if I hadn't, I do." Adam said, and let his hand tighten a little in Luke's hair. Luke let his head bow, neck bent to Adam's hand, let his eyes close. They kissed.

It was like being drunk in the best, best way possible, it was like the world had stopped and all there was was this. Luke, and Luke's mouth, and Luke's arms settling at first unsure and then so close around his sides, the rest of the world just vague bubbling noise around them.

And then Luke's eyes again, the bluest in the world and soft, and shy, and so happy.

Adam kept hold of his hand. "Come on."

Out of the stickiness and the shouting and the closeness of the bop, into night air as cold as the stars above them. The river behind them, the gardens smelling of clean earth and the cold and these ancient brick and mellow gold buildings that had seen all this before a thousand times—two figures hurrying hand in hand and one of them laughing, long long hair a ripple of silver in the moonlight. Out of the college, underneath the grand stone arch and into the street, and Adam kissed Luke again in a safe

The Fall

corner against the wall to check he hadn't dreamed it. His stomach tried to twist inward and explode with bubbles. No, this was true...

Numb fingers twisted together and breath panting out white as steam as they ran. A long way back up the hill, through a town alive with students partying, noisy and wild with joy, the streets a carnival just for tonight, then over the bridge and into quieter streets, underneath trees muting out the rest of the world, a straight line between here and home. And bed.

Should've done this a week ago, Adam thought, his nose pressed to the side of Luke's neck and the scent of his skin and hair while he fumbled with his keys, through the door, up the stairs, to his room. Should have done this forever ago. Why did I bring you here and keep you here?

Because they were born on different worlds and were never meant to cross paths, and yet, and yet Luke had fallen out of the sky into his life...

"I thought you would never–"

"Why didn't you say anything?"

"I didn't think you–"

Adam looked at Luke's blue blue eyes as deep as the sea in the dark and thought, "Why would anyone ever say no?"

It turned out his parents had named him well after all—because Adam had been tempted between the safety of libraries and lecture halls and then the danger and the glory of falling in love with this boy, and he'd chosen to fall. But in the falling was the rush and the joy and ecstasy, in the falling he found his destiny came into his own hands—as Luke came into his hand with a cry and into the warm wet and the hard angles of his groin Adam ground, ground, ground–

Close in the afterwards, Luke's long bony body warm and thrumming beside his, Luke's fingers curled against his chest and his hair running off the side of the bed like a silent waterfall, Luke whispered, "They will come for me, you know. One day..."

Adam turned his nose to the crown of Luke's head, to the scent of his hair. Carla's shampoo and the underlying spice of Luke. "I'll be here. I'll protect you."

Luke gave a soft laugh. "You don't even have any magic."

"I'll hit them with a textbook. Luke. I'll protect you. Anyway, I thought "they" came for everyone eventually—I thought that's what your lot were all about. And... I think maybe you're right." Maybe it was because of what they'd just done, maybe it was because he very suddenly felt like a fucking superhero, but– "I'm not scared."

He wasn't a superhero. But he wasn't scared, either. "They" came for everybody, and Adam chose to face them with Luke, for Luke, not hide his life away in books and chemicals and classrooms.

For a moment, just silence and their breath.

"Thank you," Luke whispered, and shifted on the mattress, closer to Adam's side so his breath touched his throat. "Thank you."

Christmas holidays coming up; there was a complication, juggling his family and Luke who had nowhere else to go. Luke needed to find the other scattered necromancers and Adam had exams, they were worlds apart and yet...right now, right now this felt like something that would work. That had to work. Right now this felt like the biggest beginning Adam had ever faced. He'd never known he was living a grey existence until Luke handed him a whole world of color with shining bright blue eyes.

"Thank you," he mouthed in the dark to Luke's hair. "Thank..."

A long way to go. But for now, they had one narrow bed, four enclosing arms, four tangled legs, four closed eyes and nothing to do but sleep. In the morning would be another beginning. Tonight...the last thing to do...

He fell asleep, deep in the safety of Luke's magic and his embrace.

The Omega Men

Kitty Johnson

If an afternoon in Alabama ever decided to be beautiful, then its beauty would explode in long bursts of mute golden dust and an eternal dream Egyptian feeling. That was why Darrin kept gazing out the window as Wright finished his demonstration of the attic weight room.

"Well, that's it. That's the end of the grand big-welcome-howdy dorm tour for you, the little junior college rube." Then Wright looked longingly back at the weights and sighed. "So, tell me, Darrin, what's your major?"

"History," Darrin murmured. The long shadows were motionless on the college yard.

"Arrrghh," said Wright. "Me am history major. I gots lizards in my hair."

The shadows looked like history themselves, and Darrin felt very safe when he was looking at history.

"Looks like you're not much of a fighter." Wright's voice sounded neutral, disinterested.

"Um, I'm not sure that's true," Darrin said. "I mean, all battles are won by their historians."

But he found it difficult to look directly at Wright as he said this. His gift was intruding again. For as long as Darrin could remember, he had had the horrifying blessing of omniscience, so he already knew this attic weight room would be someone's undoing. And he also knew that he and Wright would be involved in the whole miserable scene. It was all as clear as the sunlight floating between the dust motes.

"Do you have a girlfriend?" Wright demanded.

Darrin felt stunned, trapped. He finally raised his head and gave Wright a sober look. "You surely know the answer to that," he said.

Then they both laughed so hard the shadowed lawn seemed to shake.

(When he made the transfer from his hometown community college to the University, Darrin had been invited to live in the men's honors assembly. As an omniscient, however, he was unsurprised to discover the "honors" part had been amended with the concept of "selective satisfactions.")

And omnisciently he also knew what Wright was going to say as they walked back down the stairs. "Well, join the club. Nobody around here ever has any sex. We're too creepy. Which is a shame considering how all the giant frat sloths get some every weekend."

That night the assembly held its first meeting of the semester. Following the proper rules of order, they voted to make the fall of 1975 different. No, not like the appalling fall of 1974, or the even more demeaning spring of 1975. This semester would be different. And to insure their success, they would elect a new officer to the assembly cabinet, one just as important as the Purgemaster or the Hootologist. They would elect themselves a Social Chairman. "That way we'll fit in really well," said Wright with a curiously intense bitterness. Then he nominated Darrin for the newly created position.

Darrin wrote "Vote Darrin for Social Chairman" on sheets of lined notebook paper and posted them around the dorm.

That night on the first-floor sign with bright turquoise ink someone wrote: "He doesn't have as many lizards in his hair as the other history majors." The note was signed, "Betty Ford."

Darrin found the graffiti the next morning. "Who did this?" he asked though, of course, he knew.

The Hootologist happened to be walking by. "It was Wright. Wright abuses all the signs around here."

By the afternoon, someone else had drawn a crude cartoon of Darrin's head with even more crudely drawn lizards standing on it. Many different handwritings had named the lizards: Dr. Hook, Savage Louis, Tittylizard.

Even so, Darrin's campaign was successful. No one was running against him, and at the next meeting he was unanimously elected Social Chairman.

As Darrin had sensed from the very beginning, Wright's power was enormous. For example, during orientation, Darrin had tacked to the door of the room he was sharing with Atwele Fonbah a picture of Charles Darwin's orangutan face which he had labeled "Darrin's Revolution of the Species." The second night of orientation, someone had held a cigarette lighter to the edge of the paper until it caught on fire.

Fair enough. Darrin expected no other fate for a dorm door sign.

On the other hand, not only did Wright have one of the very few private rooms, but the spookiest testament to his sway was that no one dared defile the image taped to *his* door, a photograph of Robert Conrad with a battery on his shoulder. The battery was not even made to spurt semen or given a name like Tittybattery.

Wright's intact door meant business.

"What do you think guys from Africa are really like?" Darrin asked Wright as they walked up to the attic. Despite Darrin's general omniscience, things weren't working out so well with Atwele.

"Oh, black. African-looking mostly. Probably slender. Black to the bone, I'd say. Now start spotting me."

The weight room had become their regular thing. Before everyone went to the cafeteria for supper, Darrin would accompany Wright to the attic to make sure no predatory tubes of steel fell on Wright's strong flushed neck. Sometimes Wright would get a hard-on as he lifted. It was kind of wonderful to see, like a twenty-dollar roll of quarters. However, Darrin's infallible omniscience held. He knew the very thing they were both being drawn towards would inevitably end badly with tears and fearful accusations and packed bags. Yet it stayed before him, a dream as irresistible as Eden.

When he was younger, Darrin's gift had tended to throw him. He would be listening to a teacher, and then the omniscience would hit and he would panic. Did, say, the Gadsden Purchase actually mean anything? Or did anything mean anything? It would appear not.

Darrin had found that the only effective antidote to his irritating omniscience was noise. There were always some big noisy extroverted girls loitering in the halls of the dorm as if it were their personal Kasbah. Darrin liked to talk to them at great length because he didn't feel so troublingly omniscient when he was with these big noisy girls. Of course, that probably meant he would marry one of them someday.

Wright wasn't omniscient. He stayed single and silent and somewhat innocent up in the weight room.

"Are all of those dog women you know coming to our party Saturday night?" he said as he lifted. Even his grunts were becoming enticingly heroic to Darrin.

"Possibly," Darrin said.

"You do know that having sex with any of them is just too ironic. No can do."

"Well, you'll have to get over it. We all have to. We must mate, or we'll end up like that Anthony Zerbe movie."

(Everyone in the dorm had gathered in the television room to watch *The Omega Man* when it came on. Of course, they were disappointed when Anthony Zerbe's zombie mutant army was defeated by huffy straight arrow Charlton Heston. They booed and threw things at the television. Only Darrin had stayed calm; he knew in advance how that movie was going to end.)

Wright set his weights down. "I guess we could have sex," he said enigmatically.

Suddenly it was raining and mysterious in the weight room, no layers of history to protect them from the rain, nothing but the ancient wood of the dorm roof and it could burn. Darrin breathed out. It was as if they were in a hidden closet like children unable to escape eager molesters who would drag them away to a specified molesting point. The very air was flavored with smoke and history and sex and danger.

Wright sat unmoving on the bed in his room, and Darrin sat down beside him so he could kiss him on the side of his mouth. Then he let his lips stay there as if they were dreaming on their own while his left arm crept around Wright's waist. "We could just lay back and talk."

Wright said nothing.

"Okay then, here we go, away with the old gym shorts." Wright stood up and let Darrin peel the shorts off to his tightywhities. Then, since Wright had not resisted, Darrin stripped down to his own tightywhities.

Wright finally breathed out. "Darrin, are you sure you're okay with this?"

"I'll just think of it as breaking the law, like when we buy dope or when the dorm seceded from the United States. I mean, it's only sex, Wright. Not a magic ointment that will change me forever."

"Hey, Anthony Zerbe became a mutant instantly. I mean just like that." Wright snapped his fingers.

"Shall I leave?"

"No," Wright said suddenly, and the word was an Elvis-animal growl, impossible to tell where in his soul it came from. Even his skin had the same animal quality; unlike the big noisy girls whose moist skin sought Darrin's flesh out and leaned into it and whose huge droopy breasts melted in his hands, Wright's skin stayed whole, kept its shape. It was extraordinarily wonderful to run his hands up and down Wright's tight-skinned back. He felt the bed could be water and Wright a safe little boat with a satisfying rudder. And Darrin handled him as he rubbed himself against that same tight skin, feeling the even pulse of Wright's blood as the safe vibration of a sturdy ship engine. Then the ecstasy came, and it was as if they had awakened, and Wright was making irrational breaths into Darrin's wet neck.

Darrin was awakened as usual, by Atwele's mysterious African morning rituals. As soon as he opened his eyes, though, he knew what had happened. He had lost his omniscience.

What would Wright do now? Darrin had no idea.

He went to the window. The sky looked as if it had been washed by the sunlight until it was bone-colored, ungiving, guarded.

What would Wright say now? What meaning did his muscles hold?

Even the oxygen seemed to hold a secret.

"The Purgemaster's mom is coming to get him."
"Why?"
"Mary Beth wanted to break up with him, so he told her he was going to slit his wrists."
"Bullshitter."
"You know how women are."
"What was Mary Beth thinking?"
"Nothing. It was just she got pinched by a frat Jethro."
"Well, that's a fucking shame."
"Maybe his mom will let him come back in the spring."

For the first time since he had started up with Wright, Darrin had a sure sluice of his old omniscience. The Purgemaster lived in a tiny town with its own little one-building junior college, sitting as snugly self-contained as a Shell gas station under the pecan trees. It was obvious that the Purgemaster's mom would make him go to the Shell Station Community College for two semesters before he could even think about coming back to the University. By then, Mary Beth would be a distant wisp of a memory riding the dust of a dream, and the Purgemaster would be a bigger misfit than ever.

"You can. I swear it, Darrin. You can fuck me. Let's do it. Let's take it to the next level. A much bigger crime than possession or secession."

They were lying tightly together on the bed naked, but Darrin felt paralyzed.

"Goddammit, Darrin, you got an insurmountably big virginity." Wright sounded outraged.

Wright was wrong. Because Darrin wanted nothing more than to be lost in Wright, although it was possible that he might not survive. He loved looking at the mannered excellence of Wright's body, but that perfection made him diffident. If he did push it into the enticing curves and pulsing paths of Wright's muscles and blood, Wright might take him in and breathe him out in small gasps, and Darrin would never be able to assemble himself again.

Yet the temptation was there. Below the waist there would be the ever-relentless liquid biology, difficult to think about and feel human, while above the waist he would be kissing the prickly hair at the back of Wright's neck, the one thing he wanted to do over and over again.

On an impulse, Darrin straddled him as if they had just been wrestling. "Wright, I have something to tell you."

"You're gay."

"I'm not gay."

"You're high."

"No, Wright. No, listen. It's just that...I know...too much to live. I'm kind of a monster mastermind."

Wright gazed up at him with an unfathomable look. "Maybe we should knock this off." His voice was kind.

Even as Darrin's omniscience surged back, he was still shocked by the tragic truth emerging from its tragic chrysalis. So now it was over. He knew it would be and there it was: just as he had foreseen.

"Wait, we can still do this," he told Wright. But he knew that, if he touched Wright's independent back, he would lose him forever, and if he didn't touch him, he would lose him forever. It was a certainty as large as the largest pyramid.

"I'm not in the mood anymore." Wright sat up and pushed him away. "It's beginning to feel too weird."

Darrin said nothing. Now no music would ever sound the same; no weather would ever breathe the same breeze.

The semester passed more slowly after that. They rarely spoke when they saw each other in the halls. Darrin's omniscience was entirely restored, more painful and paralyzing than ever.

Then there was one last assembly meeting before Christmas break, and Darrin had to stand up and make the semester social report.

"This semester, nothing got worse. Except, you know, for the Purgemaster and his fate. I always think, if things never get worse, then, under the circumstances, that can be defined as them getting better." Inwardly he was referencing history; that was the way history worked.

There was some perfunctory applause.

"We're losing Wright too," the Hootologist piped up. Some of the noisy girls were there visiting, and they began to clap and whistle. The girls had never taken to Wright's frosty disdain. "He says he's getting an apartment."

For the first time since the night the truth came out, Darrin felt compelled to go to Wright's room.

"Why are you leaving?"

Wright was sitting on the edge of his bed doing arm curls. He didn't look up. "Why do you care? You have what's-her-name."

"Kim?" Kim was the name of the noisy girl Darrin had ended up with.

"It's okay. You can have my room. Get away from Atwele for awhile."

"That doesn't matter. Atwele decided to go back to the Cameroon. I'm going to have a private room anyway."

"Look." Wright stood up. "I have a new boyfriend, okay?"

Wright had never used that important word before, and hearing it frightened Darrin as much as it thrilled him. So there was once a time when he had been a boy's boyfriend, not at all like being the boyfriend of the perpetually raucous Kim. "Wright, I just thought we were desperate for sex. I didn't know we were boyfriends."

"Oh, I think we had a pretty standard relationship. One of us was sensitive, and one of us had an erection. That's the way relationships always work, you know."

Darrin's eyes felt wet, stingy. He had not actually known that. So that was Wright's great gift to him: ignorance. Wright had the great advantage of knowing only a select number of things, which let him be the sturdy little samurai of love that he was.

Darrin, on the other hand, had the disadvantage of knowing far too much. If he had confined himself to learning about Wright and Wright only, Wright's capillaries, his uvula, his femurs and medulla, then that would be all the knowledge he would have needed.

Suddenly it was crucial to remind Wright of how important he was to Darrin. "Did you hear that I'm not majoring in history anymore?"

"Well, that's interesting." Wright was obviously lying. "Fewer scalp lizards. So what's your new major?"

"I don't know yet. I just know I want to major in stuff that nobody knows much about."

Wright nodded. "How about computers? Or snowmen, maybe?"

"I guess I could major in love."

"Oh, God. You've got to leave. Now."

"I am," Darrin said in an unsteady voice. "I'm leaving."

And he backed out of the room as Wright sat down and picked up his weights again.

Then he shut Wright's door.

It had been so long since he had visited Wright that he hadn't noticed that Robert Conrad's picture had been mutilated. The eyes were erased leaving two blank hollows, and someone had written "666" on his forehead.

Darrin supposed he should abuse the picture too; after all, he could give Robert Conrad fangs or draw antennae on his head.

Instead, he put his palm to the door as gently as if it were a part of Wright's body. He was suddenly glad he had a lot to learn.

The Dipsy Doodle Inn

Karmen Ghia

The phone rang as Clayton was on his way out to get Tyler from the hospital. Since his housemate had survived a severe asthma attack, Clayton figured he could wait a few more minutes and stopped to listen to the message.

"The boytoy again," he thought, jingling his keys. "Dipshit. Tyler was on adrenaline, valium and hooked up to an IV all last night, that's why he blew off your date."

He left before the end of the message; the stressed and pained voice bothered him more than he wanted to admit and as much as all the other messages the poor kid had left since Tyler stood him up last night.

Of course Billy—no, Gilly—didn't know why Tyler blew off his date. Tyler was keeping the kid in the dark about most things, working up through a long, slow seduction to a wham-bam-hit-and-run night in the sack. It was pure Tyler, although Clayton did wonder why it was taking so long. Something in Gilly's voice nagged at him.

It was a nice voice, but even on the phone machine the innocence was there: the hurt feelings, the confusion, the minor tones of guilt and doubt and fear, but above all the innocence. Gilly's was a heart for the breaking and if Tyler was having second thoughts, Clayton approved. But knowing Tyler's capacity for mistreating his lovers, Clayton thought it was probably just more fun for his housemate to have his lovers madly in love with him, as opposed to sort of in love, when he dumped them. Not that Clayton was an expert on gay romance, but he was an avid Tyler watcher, and Gilly sounded like yet another sacrificial victim on Tyler's altar dedicated to Tyler's ego. It wasn't exactly that Tyler was mean; he was just easily bored. He'd had his heart broken in college and never quite got over it. Clayton knew all this because Tyler had cried on his shoulder for weeks after that break up. But it was the last time Clayton had seen Tyler cry about anything.

At the hospital, he found Tyler flirting with his doctor and the floor nurse, so Clayton thought no more about it.

Tyler was looking a hundred and ten percent better. He was conscious, breathing normally, and had his waist-length blond hair pulled neatly back in a ponytail like usual. Other than the spacey drugged look softening his hard green eyes, he looked as cool and sardonic as ever. "How do you feel?" Clayton asked.

"Completely wonderful," Tyler drawled. "I've had the best care my insurance will pay for." This got a laugh.

"And drugs, too," Clayton said, easing the prescription out of Tyler's paw.

"Oh, yeah, I'll be high on prednisone for a week or so," Tyler sighed. "Small price to pay for livin'."

"It's time to go, Tyler," Clayton said, and he shepherded Tyler to the car. On the way home, Clayton very considerately stopped at the drugstore and had the prescription filled. Tyler was happily spaced out and babbling, but more importantly he was breathing, so Clayton tuned him out and drove.

Tyler's asthma attack, especially the convulsions and the turning blue, had unnerved Clayton, but the doctor and Tyler seemed to take it in stride. But, since Tyler was neither inclined nor in a position to move to the desert or the mountains, what else could they do but monitor his condition and hope someone was always around to drive him to the hospital or call the paramedics? Clayton didn't mind racing to the hospital. Even the cop that chased them right up to the Emergency Ward let him off with a compliment on his defensive driving and good wishes for Tyler's recovery. He didn't want to come home someday and find he was too late.

"Clayton! Are you listening to me?" Tyler asked, sounding exasperated.

"No. How do you feel?"

"Fine. I was supposed to go out with Gilly last night."

"Yes, I know, he called and left a message," Clayton said. "Several, actually."

"Why didn't you tell him...?"

"He is your boyfriend, Tyler," Clayton said in his trademarked "end of discussion" voice. No need to add that he didn't get involved in Tyler's love life, except when it got violent and he happened to be home to throw the guy out and bandage his housemate (if necessary), because Tyler went through men so fast, Clayton was afraid of getting to know any of them well enough to feel their pain when...

"I said, what did he say?" Tyler raised his voice a little.

"He said a lot of things..."

"Hit the high spots, Clayton, please."

"He said, 'Where were you?', 'Did I get the date wrong?', 'Are you okay?', 'Did I do something to make you angry?', 'Is there...'"

"Oh shit."

They were at a light, so Clayton looked over at him; he was frowning. It was unlike Tyler to frown over a boytoy's distress: cause it, yes, enjoy it, definitely, but frowning over it was new.

The light changed. Tyler continued to frown in silence all the rest of the way home. The phone was ringing when they walked in and Tyler practically lunged for it when he heard Gilly's voice on the machine. "No...no, honey, I'm not mad at you, no..."

Clayton hung up their coats, put Tyler's steroids by his bed, and generally ignored the conversation in progress. And failed. "Tyler, you're giving him directions to the place you lived in college," Clayton said, holding his hand out for the phone.

"Here, let Daddy give you directions, I'm on too many drugs." Tyler handed him the phone and folded his arms. "I said he could come over and watch *Buffy the Vampire Slayer* with you, I mean, us. I'm stoned enough to endure it for once."

"Tyler, Daddy is on the phone and I can only listen to one of you at time."

Tyler wandered off and found a menu for a Chinese restaurant he liked. He came back to hear the last of Clayton's excellent directions from the university to their place. "Ask him what kind of Chinese food he likes," Tyler said, engrossed in the menu and oblivious to the fact that Clayton had already hung up the phone.

"Let's just order what we like and he can eat some of that," Clayton said, taking the menu and dialing. He ordered shrimp chow mein, barbequed pork, won ton soup and white rice. "I can't believe you invited Billy, I mean Gilly, over here," he said, guiding Tyler to the couch.

"Didn't I have a sketch pad here?" Tyler asked, looking around.

Clayton had seen it in his bedroom, so he got it for him. Tyler was single-minded anyway; the drugs were just making him spacey and single-minded. "I said, I can't believe you invited Gilly–"

"Where's the pencil?" Tyler was making himself comfortable in the far right corner of the couch.

Back in Tyler's bedroom, Clayton found the pencil and brought it to him. He brought the eraser and the little knife Tyler used to sharpen the pencil, too. It was a very little knife; a bigger knife and Tyler on drugs would have concerned Clayton very much. "Anything else, Tyler?"

"No, Clayton you're wonderful," Tyler drawled shamelessly. "And I invited Gilly because he sounded suicidal."

"Oh, well as long as he doesn't kill himself during *Buffy*, I'll try to be polite to him," Clayton, the long-suffering guy, said.

"Well, that's good," Tyler said vaguely. He was adjusting the light so he could draw, and so it wouldn't glare on the TV screen. He could be a total pain in the ass, but he was fairly considerate to Clayton, who was one of the few people he liked very much. The light was perfect and he was thoroughly engrossed in his drawing by the time Clayton came back with a plate of shrimp chow mein for him. Try as he might and much as he liked shrimp chow mein, Tyler could only get half of it down. He had more success with the soup, but there'd be lots of leftovers for Gilly. He ignored the TV and did a quick sketch of the cartons on the coffee table before Clayton cleared them away. Then he switched to drawing the pile of cushions by the window seat, something that changed and stayed the same enough to keep his drawing chops up without being too much of a challenge. It was more of a challenge on drugs and he was concentrating so hard, he hardly noticed Clayton answering the door.

Clayton opened the door on a pair of big worried brown eyes that got bigger and more worried when they looked at him.

"Is Tyler...?"

"On the couch," Clayton waved him in. He watched Gilly—for it could only be he and none other—throw himself at Tyler's feet.

He had mousy brown hair brushed over dark brown eyes (eyes that would actually turn out to be hazel when Clayton got close enough to notice). He was taller, more lithe and even younger than Clayton was expecting. Tyler's taste in boytoys ran to huge, burly, muscle freaks or useless, effeminate blonds. Gilly was neither and that made Clayton a little nervous. He preferred Tyler to be predictably unkind to people who might deserve it. If that got Tyler punched out occasionally, well, it just proved there was a God. But Gilly didn't fit the pattern and that meant anything could happen, and probably would.

Tyler patted the empty couch space on his left side and Gilly got off his knees and sat next to him, not touching him, and warily watching Clayton saunter over to join them. Ever the gentleman, even on drugs, Tyler introduced them and offered Gilly some leftover Chinese food. Gilly said no to the Chinese food so graciously offered and tried to relax as Clayton made himself comfortable in his usual armchair at the end of the couch.

"Come here, sweetheart," Tyler cooed, and tugged Gilly into the curve of his left arm. Even high on prednisone, he could draw with his right hand, pet Gilly with his left and ignore the dreadful television program Clayton was putting on. Gilly was tense but Tyler did feel him relax a little when the *Buffy* came on; perhaps he liked the show or maybe he was just distracted. Tyler thought that his being in the hospital had had a very traumatic effect on Gilly, and having his attention diverted from the stress of the trauma of Tyler's hospital stay was causing him to relax and almost snuggle, really adorable almost-snuggling, too, into his arm. Tyler liked to think it was just that Gilly was so happy to be near him.

Actually, Gilly was trying to figure out who the hell Clayton was and why Tyler called him "Daddy" on the phone. It was most distressing, and even more so when Tyler put his arm around him. Wasn't this "Daddy" person jealous and was something very strange going to happen? He thought he knew Tyler well enough to trust him, but who was this huge blond guy in the chair at the end of the couch? Gilly was happy to watch *Buffy* and not think about it any more. What was going on in *Buffy* might not make much sense, but at least he could understand it.

Clayton had great peripheral vision, really amazing; in fact, he was able to watch *Buffy* and watch Gilly watching *Buffy* and glancing furtively at him at the same time. Actually, Gilly snuggled into Tyler's side was a show unto itself. Clayton found himself wondering if Tyler wasn't so drugged up, would he be such a patient human bolster pillow for Gilly? Tyler sat there serenely drawing with his right hand and petting Gilly with his left. Occasionally something happened on the TV that was almost as interesting as Tyler and Gilly on the couch, but never interesting enough to get Clayton's undivided attention.

The kid was restless, Clayton observed, probably naturally so. But Tyler never even looked away from his drawing when Gilly's rustling around for a more comfortable position got towards vigorous. He merely altered his caress and this quieted Gilly for minutes on end.

Actually Gilly looked very comfortable propped up on a couple of pillows and Tyler. If he wasn't so busy keeping an eye on Clayton, who was keeping an eye on him, he might have dozed off. He'd gotten very little sleep the night before worrying over Tyler, but now he had Clayton to worry over.

If there had been a quiz on *Buffy* that night, all three of them would have flunked it, and only Tyler would have had a good reason for having not paid the slightest attention. "Darlin', you seem exhausted, would you like to sleep here tonight?" Tyler asked, sounding tired himself.

"Can I?" Gilly asked, eyes widening.

"Of course, honey, I just invited you," Tyler drawled. "You can borrow some of my jammies and sleep out here or with me. Just don't expect a lot of company from me tonight. I'm on drugs, you know."

Gilly opted to sleep in Tyler's room and after a quick solo shower, he was curling into his host's arm again. "Who's Clayton?" he asked.

"My housemate," Tyler said sleepily.

"Your boyfriend?"

"Oh, heavens no," Tyler chuckled. "If he were my boyfriend, Gilly, you and I would never have met. I'd be too busy keeping him happy." He yawned. "No, dearie, the horizon is straight but Clayton Bob Marsh is straighter, as we used to say in college."

"Is that where you met him?"

"Yes, seems so long ago," Tyler said around another yawn. "You'll like him when you know him. He's not nearly as frightening as he seems at first because he's so big. He's an angel, really, a perfect angel, when you get to know him." He was asleep by the last word.

Gilly watched him sleep for a minute and then dropped off himself.

The only person who wasn't sleeping was Clayton, who was emailing his friend Tyndale Gottshock to find out what had happened on *Buffy* that night. He was also listening hard in the direction of Tyler's room. Clayton had superior hearing, too, but didn't really need it because his housemate was a noisy lover. It was quiet, too quiet, so Clayton assumed this really was a sleepover and not a seduction. "I hope Tyler knows what he's doing," Clayton thought, brushing his expensively-cut naturally golden hair off his forehead.

The next morning Gilly woke up and rubbed his cheek into Tyler's long tawny hair fanned out on the pillow. The morning sun shone through the white curtains bathing the room and its occupants with a creamy glow that was especially flattering to the sleeping Tyler. At least at that moment Gilly thought Tyler was the most beautiful being he'd ever seen in his life. He also thought he'd better go into the bathroom and get rid of his hard-on before Tyler woke and caught him thinking impure thoughts. Slipping out of bed and into the hallway, he also hoped he wouldn't run into Clayton before he could take a cold shower and take care of "it". Fortunately, he didn't, but he did pass the large blond man on his way back to Tyler's bed.

"Is Tyler up?" Clayton asked and then added a grouchy, "Good morning."

"Not yet," Gilly said, trying not to look as cowed as he felt standing there in Tyler's pajamas. The fact that Clayton was wearing the most magnificent suit Gilly had ever seen didn't help matters.

Clayton frowned at his watch and then frowned at Tyler's door. Then he frowned at Gilly. "If you get dressed, I'll drop you off on my way downtown," he said, buttoning his suit cuffs. He tapped on Tyler's door and then went right on in.

Gilly followed him and tried to ignore Clayton sitting on Tyler's bed, gently shaking him awake. He gathered up his clothes and went into the bathroom to change. Putting the neatly-folded pajamas on the bureau, he could not help but catch the last of their conversation.

"Here're your drugs. When are you seeing your doc again?" Clayton asked a very sleepy Tyler. "Tyler. Wake up."

"Yes, 'Mother'," Tyler snarled. "I have a three o'clock appointment with Dr. Dreamboat, if you don't mind."

"Which one...?"

"Dr. Weissbrotenian," Tyler said wearily.

"Can you get there by yourself?" Clayton asked.

"Of course."

"I mean, like actually drive a car," Clayton persisted.

"Oh...well, maybe not," Tyler conceded.

"Take a cab then. I have clients and court and won't be able to get away," Clayton said, rising and pulling his suit cuffs down.

"I can take you at two or two-thirty if you let me drive your car, Tyler," Gilly said. "I don't have any classes this afternoon."

The housemates jumped slightly; they'd forgotten he was there.

"Well, honey, I don't want to inconvenience you," Tyler drawled sweetly.

Clayton shot him an amused but disgusted look and said, "That would work for me, Gilly."

"You know, I haven't the vaguest notion what you two are so worried about." Tyler sat up and began to struggle with the top of his meds and was vanquished. Helplessly, he handed the bottle to Clayton, who opened it with one twist. "Well, maybe you should come back around two, Gilly, I'll make you a sandwich or something before we go."

"Just don't try to light the stove, please, Tyler," Clayton said. He went out and came back with a glass of water and motioned Gilly to follow him out.

Gilly bent down and kissed Tyler on the forehead and said he'd be back at two. He asked Clayton to drop him at the downtown end of the University and thanked him very nicely when they parted.

Thereafter, Clayton saw quite a bit of Gilly around the house. Tyler invited him over for dinner, or met him there before they went off and did whatever they did. Much of what they did together were things Tyler might have done alone, but was too drugged to do, like grocery shopping, sizing canvas, shopping for art supplies, and running errands. Clayton was frankly delighted to see Gilly doing these chores because it meant he was off the hook. And he noticed that Gilly never seemed to connect Tyler buying Travelers Checks and a map of Southern France with Tyler taking an actual trip.

Clayton did feel a little guilty because Gilly was such a nice kid and Tyler was probably going to rip his heart out and hand it to him. But this was none of his business, and exactly why he never wanted to know Tyler's victims too well.

Gilly came over for dinner and to watch *Buffy* again the following week. Tyler might have been distracted and stoned, but he was still one of the best cooks around and laid out a very nice meal for the three of them. As before, Tyler spent the evening drawing with his right hand and his left arm around Gilly, snuggled into his side.

Not as shy as before, Gilly made a few observations about *Buffy* that Clayton found amusing. He also refuted the occasional sarcastic remark from Tyler in a sweet and charming fashion; this also amused Clayton. Gilly spent the night again, but as far as Clayton could tell, it was another pure and quiet night in Tyler's bed. This indicated to Clayton that either Tyler's libido was flatlined from the medication he was on or that he was saving it for Fabrice d'Horlouge, the guy with whom he'd be spending the next six weeks at Villa d'Horlouge in Nice. But this was still none of Clayton's business. He was merely a passive observer of the Tyler Ray Cain Sex Show until and unless things got violent, and the star called for help.

Several days after Clayton had seen Tyler and his painting gear off at the airport, he let the machine pick up a call. "I knew it," he thought, lunging for the phone. "I just fucking knew it."

"Oh, hi Clayton! I was just calling to see if Tyler wanted go see a movie this weekend," Gilly said in his happy, cheerful voice.

"Gilly, didn't he tell you he was going to be in France for six weeks?" Clayton asked. "Guess not," he added when Gilly's silence confirmed it.

"...oh, um, I..."

"Look, Gilly, I'm going out to dinner with some people tonight," Clayton said, suddenly seeing Gilly as a useful object of his compassion and generosity. "Why don't you come along? It will be my treat."

"Could I?" Gilly asked brightly.

"Sure," Clayton said, hoping he wasn't making a mistake. "Can you get here by seven, or where can I pick you up?" he asked, cursing a certain painter, who was probably getting nicely laid in Nice at the moment.

Gilly said he'd get there by seven and was enthusiastic in his thanks. Clayton was glad he was glad and hung up, feeling a little better. Well, better than if he'd left the poor kid on his own that night. At least he thought he felt better; what he really felt was confused. He went back to reading the paper—the world was much more confused than he was at the moment—and that took his mind off his potential troubles. He was bending his policy on never getting interested in Tyler's love affairs (or whatever this thing with Gilly was), and this made him a little nervous.

On the other hand, Gilly was a godsend. Clayton usually took Tyler with him when he was dining with Clementine and Jesus Romanoff because Clem liked to flirt with pretty men and would leave him and Jesus to their conversation if she was suitably distracted. But Tyler was in the south of France, painting and living large for six weeks. Poor Gilly; but at least he'd get a nice dinner out of it.

The kid was punctual, and Clayton could not help but admire that. He also looked tidy in a black mock turtleneck sweater and black pleated pants. Clayton evaded as many questions about Tyler and his whereabouts as he could on the short drive to the restaurant.

"Clayton, what is it with you and all these beautiful men you drag around with you?" Clementine asked when they arrived.

"Is he beautiful, Clem? I hadn't noticed, but I thought you might," Clayton said, bending over her hand.

"Very much so," she said, turning Gilly in the light for a better view. Her husband, Jesus, was silent as usual, but did roll his eyes when he shook hands with Clayton. "Got a name, pretty one?" she asked in her annoying nasal drawl.

"François," Gilly said shyly. "But everyone calls me Fran."

Clayton frowned, realizing that Gilly was a nickname and he had no idea what the kid's real name was. There was no way he'd be able to finish the introduction, but fortunately, Clem didn't need him to finish it.

"Impossible," Clementine flatly stated. "Prove it."

Gilly dug out a battered wallet and handed her his student ID.

Clementine studied the front, turned it over, studied that, and handed it back. "Sexy photo," she cooed. "What's the 'GM' stand for?"

"Guillaume Marie."

"François Guillaume Marie La Farge," she chanted. "A name like a song. So much prettier than the other one Clayton brings around with that common as dirt name."

"I'll tell Tyler that when he gets back from France," Clayton said, holding up four fingers for the hostess. She waved at the sushi bar and shrugged. "Can you cope with the bar, Clem? They seem to be out of tables."

"Only if I'm allowed to sit next to François Guillaume Marie La Farge, yes."

"I'd never have it any other way." Clayton nodded at the waitress and herded his little group to the quiet end of the bar.

"Do you prefer sushi or sashimi, Fran?" Clementine asked. She'd maneuvered it so Fran, as he now would be called, was on her right,

Clayton on her left and her husband on Clayton's left, where he wouldn't distract her from flirting with Fran.

"I don't know, I've never had it before," Fran admitted shyly.

"Clayton! You angel! You've brought me someone capable of instruction!" Clementine cried, and spent the rest of the evening teaching Fran the finer points of dining at the sushi bar.

This had been Clayton's plan all along and he'd brought Gil–sorry, Fran—along to distract and amuse Clementine so he could spend some quality time with Jesus. Although he had no idea Fran was a sushi virgin, it was icing on the cake and would keep Clem out of their hair all evening.

Clayton had met Jesus when they were in law school and they'd been pretty good friends until Jesus married Clementine. She was a nice woman, but needy, pushy and grabby for attention. That would have been fine if she'd been willing to let Jesus meet his friends alone so they could talk like adults, but she never would. So it had become Clayton's policy to always bring a nice-looking guy to these dinners. Clementine would be occupied, he and Jesus would get to talk uninterrupted, and usually Jesus would pick up the check in gratitude for a few hours respite from Clem. She was rich, too, though Clayton couldn't imagine there was enough money in the world to chain himself to a creature like Clem. But it was none of his business and everyone had a nice dinner. Including Fran, who learned about sake that night as well and promptly fell asleep in Clayton's car on the way home.

Because Clayton didn't have a clue what dorm Fran lived in, he decided to take the path of least resistance and let Fran sleep it off in Tyler's bed. It was the least Tyler could do for them both. He carried the sleeper in and dumped him on the bed. Pulling off Fran's shoes was as far as Clayton went in undressing him; part of drinking too much was waking up in your clothes. Lucky for Fran, he got to wake up in Tyler's bed and not in the gutter, which was the one, true sake initiation.

The next morning, Clementine called to invite Clayton to a barbeque the next day, Sunday, if he brought François Guillaume. Clayton had had quite a bit of sake himself the previous night so it took him a second to remember who François Guillaume was. But he graciously accepted for both of them, making a mental note to ask Fran, formerly Gilly, when he came to.

That was almost immediately after he got off the phone. Tyler's door opened and Fran tottered out, one hand at his temple, and with the peculiar dazed look that is signature for a sake hangover. "Am I going to die?" he asked in hushed and pathetic tones.

"Not from a hangover, Fran," Clayton said, noting that Fran glanced up at being called that. "Come into the kitchen and I'll fix you up."

Clayton got out three aspirin, a thousand mgs of vitamin C and two B complex tablets with a high niacin content. He handed the lot to Fran with a glass of water. He then turned back to the most important part of the hangover cure:

The Prairie Oyster

1 oz. brandy

1/2 oz. worcestershire sauce

1 teaspoon tomato ketchup

1/2 oz. vinegar

1 egg yolk

pinch of pepper

He made two, one for himself and one for Fran. "Just pour it down, and don't think about it too much," he said, clinking glasses and taking his own advice.

Fran choked, but kept everything down. "Oh God, now I am going to die," he moaned.

"Sorry, kid. Too bad Tyler isn't here so you could do the other, better hangover cure," Clayton said, feeling the brandy taking the edge off his suffering.

"What's that?"

"You blow him and the protein fixes you right up." Fran blushed so hard Clayton felt almost bad for making him do so. "Oh well, never mind. Go back to bed and get some more sleep. You'll be all right in an hour or so," he added.

"Yes, Daddy," Fran said shyly and left the kitchen.

Clayton saved his smile for when he was gone. No sense letting Fran know he amused him. That could lead to being charmed by him, which always led to some serious trouble, and Clayton knew it.

He also knew he had transcripts to read for an appeal he was working on. After a long hot shower to steam the last of the sake out, Clayton sat up in bed with a bound transcript or two. A few hours later he heard Fran go into the shower and later on a tap on his door.

Fran came in wearing Tyler's frowsy around-the-house flannel robe. Except it didn't look terribly frowsy on Fran; it looked charming. "No, it doesn't." Clayton mentally slapped himself. "What can I do for you, Fran?" he asked, all business, at least he hoped so.

"I just wanted to say thank you for taking me along last night," Fran said politely.

Clayton graciously accepted his thanks and told him about the barbeque the next afternoon. "Can you make it? Clementine will hunt you down and drag you there, screaming, if you say no to me." Clayton could be on the charming side himself when necessary.

Fran nodded. "I think she would, too," he agreed. "I can go, but I won't be able to stay very late or drink very much because I have classes on Monday." He looked fetchingly at Clayton. "Would it be too rude if I didn't stay for too long?"

"No, not all," Clayton said briskly. "An hour or two should give her enough time to make all her matron friends jealous of her new 'find'."

"I thought she was very nice last night," Fran said gallantly. "What I can remember of it."

"She can be very nice, Fran," Clayton admitted. "And you'll make her very happy, however long you can stay at her party tomorrow. Be here at three, okay? We'll be fashionably late."

Fran said he would and that was the last Clayton saw of him that day. Not the last he thought about him, but at least the last he saw of him.

Predictably, Fran was a huge hit at the barbeque. One could almost say he was the "beau of the barbeque"; it was that disgusting. Poor Clayton nearly had to shoot their way out when he decided he'd had enough to eat and drink and was bored by all the Fran worship. Fran had happily doubled his two-hour stay limit, but there was still considerable gnashing of the teeth (for Fran, not Clayton) when they left.

Over the next few weeks, Clementine showed Fran off to everyone and everywhere she could. She even took him shopping, which was, Jesus reported to Clayton, one of the highlights of her year. Clem had excellent and expensive taste in clothes, so Fran was suddenly very well dressed, well shod and otherwise outfitted. As far as Jesus and Clayton could discern, her interest was purely aesthetic; Fran was an improvement project for her, that's all. A week before Tyler's return, and probably so she wouldn't have to invite him, Clem threw another huge barbeque. Clayton, who had the dubious honor of chaperoning Fran at these parties, had come to think of these events as Fran-fests, but never turned down an invitation. Clayton enjoyed himself immensely and, as usual, there was considerable despair when Fran was ready to leave. Also, as usual, Clayton had to exercise much firm diplomacy to pry the kid away from Clem's jealous friends. Of course he managed, but not before introducing Fran to Monrovia Dahlton-Rhys, III, Esq., one of the senior associates at his law firm, and the trial lawyer shark of all time. He was at Clem's party partly to celebrate his win in a long court case, which is why he'd not had the pleasure of Fran's acquaintance until that day. Clayton let Monrov get just enough Fran to want more. A lot more.

Clayton had introduced Tyler to Monrov early in his career at Morganthral Morganthral Morganthral and Barstow LLC. Those two had circled each other for a week or two before deciding they'd rather kill each other than be lovers, so they settled for being friends. They liked to dance in the rougher biker bars on the highway, most often at the Dipsy Doodle Inn, where men can dance a two-step crossed with a mosh pit brawl in a hurricane during an earthquake. Slamming your partner around the room was *de rigueur*. Clayton often accompanied them and danced with guys even bigger than himself. No one tried to pick him up, the straight vibe was too strong in him, but he sure could dance and the physicality of the dance, the noise, the heat and light were really all these crazy maybe-biker, maybe-queer, definitely-redneck males wanted. That was all Clayton wanted, too: male closeness without the threat of sex, male violence without the rage. Why it never occurred to any of these guys to take up boxing is a mystery to him to this day.

However, as long as they had the Dipsy Doodle Inn, there was a place that gave healthy guys a chance to get sweaty, be all over each other and if anyone got hard and came in the process, well, it was the just another night on the dance floor. The musicians were all gentlemen behind the chicken-wire screen designed to keep their heads and beer bottles apart; they would never tell what they saw from their unique vantage point.

Anyway, Monrov was waiting in Clayton's office when the associate attorney arrived. He wanted to know everything there was to know about Fran and said he'd clear his evenings for dinner with him that week, if not that night.

"What? No chaperone?" Clayton asked in his best lawyerly deadpan.

"If I have to feed you to get to him, I can live with it," Monrov said in his best reasoning with the jury voice. "For awhile."

"I'll check his schedule and get back to you," Clayton said in his "oh the powa" voice. "You do know he's barely legal and in college?"

"I didn't check his ID, but I assumed so," Monrov said and stalked out on Clayton's smug chuckle.

"Hooked like a bass," Clayton thought coolly. If he hadn't been in the middle of the most expensive law firm in the tri-county area, he would have let loose a rebel yell to express his pleasure. Instead, he emailed Fran to call him at work and then very diligently went to work on the stack in his in-basket.

Clayton was not terribly surprised when Fran called to say he didn't exactly remember who Monrovia Dahlton-Rhys III was, he'd met so many new people at the barbeque, but he'd be delighted to go out with him and Clayton.

Some perverse instinct caused Clayton to change his mind about a nice dinner at Monrov's club and suggest they go to the Dipsy Doodle Inn that very night. Fran was on a break from school and Monrov's and

Clayton's case loads were manageable (as lawyers, they didn't sleep much anyway) so it could be a late night.

Monrov liked the idea and invited fellow lawyers Shilo St. Athenaeus and Tyndale Gottshock along as cover for his real plan: get Fran drunk and into his bed. The Dipsy Doodle Inn was perfect for that. He told Clayton he'd be delighted to meet them there.

The DDI, as it was more popularly known, only served beer and wine but the management, what there was of it, did not care what other illegal substances were brought in. The police rolled in now and then looking for outlaws, but never bothered to charge the owner of the DDI with anything. Once an overzealous prosecutor had closed the place for various offenses and the effect had been remarkable. All the lunatics who drank, danced and shot pool in relative peace at the DDI poured into other nearby bars, which were not equipped, physically or psychologically, to handle them. An unfortunate crime wave began because the police no longer had a central area to pick up banditos and also because the banditos had no acceptable place or way to let off steam. Not surprisingly, a mix of continuous bacchanal and riot ensued in the outlying areas of the highway, getting dangerously closer to the center of town as lesser establishments mysteriously burned down or were torn apart by the former DDI patrons, who were at least housebroken there. The Mayor and the Governor considered calling in the militia, but Wombat Morganthral, Esq., senior partner at Morganthral Morganthral Morganthral and Barstow LLC, the biggest law firm in the tri-county area and whose lawyers were some of the DDI's best customers (including Wombat in his wilder youth—and the Governor, too, although that's been thoroughly hushed up) suggested that if they just dropped the charges and let the DDI open again, things would calm down right away.

Wombat was right; Wombat was always right. The DDI reopened and all the nutcases went back to drinking, dancing and shooting pool in the rowdy chaos that was the bar and dance floor. The bikers were happy to have their juke joint back, the police were happy to have a one-stop place to pick up miscreants, the business community was happy the crime wave was over and they could drink in their little bars in peace again, and the staff and owner of the DDI were just happy to be back in business.

This was all ancient history, even before Clayton and Tyler blew into town. The Dipsy Doodle Inn was from sundown to two a.m. a whirling vortex of drugs, drink, loud music, loud sex, violence, dancing and billiards. And into this madhouse, Clayton, who'd lost his mind, decided to bring the adorable faun-like Fran.

They'd all lost their minds; in retrospect, the legal eagles realized they should have seen the hungry looks sooner. The bouncer at the door had spent a long time looking at Fran's ID and back at Fran and shaking his head before he let him in. During one of the runs for beer, the bartender leaned over and suggested that their young friend might like the ice cream store better than the DDI.

But it was all in vain. Clayton, Monrov, Shilo and Tyndale got drunk as skunks and never noticed the owner of the DDI, Hugo St. Victor, come out and give their party the once-over. He was a tall and rangy man, weathered and weary-looking after spending most of his life outdoors. His sad gray eyes had seen too much disappointment and looked out on the world expecting the worst. He still had his shaggy jet hair, going gray in an orderly fashion, and nights like this just made it more gray. At that particular gray-hair-making moment he was looking at Indamelo, one of his regular ex-con, violent-but-manageable nutcase customers, who was keeping an eye on the sweet young thing sitting with the preppie drunks. Actually, he'd come out to see what his bartenders and bouncers were freaking out about and, as it turned out, he agreed with them; that kid was way too pretty for the DDI. The biker, Bosco Calcutta, on one of his rare passes though that part of the country, was also watching discreetly from the pool table area.

Hugo considered tossing them out but he really didn't have any reason to. Besides, he knew the older guys worked for Wombat Morganthral, and Wombat Morganthral was the last person on earth he wanted to piss off. Nor did he want to see that kid hurt, and since he was feeling helpless at the moment, he decided to go into his office and think positive thoughts. He had to pass fairly close to Bosco, who waved him over.

"Nice night," Bosco growled under the band, blaring away behind their chicken wire screen.

"So far," Hugo said blandly.

"Since when do you let faggots in here?"

This seemed like a question, but Hugo knew it was some kind of weird accusation or demand or reality check or something. So he just said, "Always," which Bosco knew was true.

"Fucking excuse me if I was unclear," Bosco snarled. "How long have you let faggots in here that look like that one?" He waved in Fran's general direction.

"Think I should throw him out?" Hugo asked.

Bosco thought about it for a second and then nodded. "A kid like that is nothing but trouble," he said simply.

Hugo wondered if he had some personal experience with that kind of trouble but was distracted by a fight breaking out on the dance floor. One of his bouncers was dealing with it. As it turned out it was merely cover for Indamelo and his gang to grab the kid and head for the door. The back door, by the pool tables. "Aw shit," Hugo groaned, and headed for his office.

The kid was putting up a helluva fight, but Indamelo was simply much bigger and overpowered him. He was yelling for help, too, but the band, the fight and some women screaming about something drowned him out. What would happen when they got him outside was too horrible to contemplate. They might leave him torn up and bleeding in the alley, or they might drive him off to some deserted place and no one would ever see him again. This being the case, Bosco glanced at Hugo, who was no longer beside him, sighed and stepped into Indamelo's path.

"Outta mah way!" Indamelo yelled over the din.

"Put him down, muthafucka," Bosco said a little louder than usual. His gang knew his fighting stance and moved around behind him. The boss might let them have some of that kid when he was done if they could get him away from Indamelo in one piece.

"Like fucking who says?" Indamelo screamed, smacking Fran to keep him quiet.

"Me and fucking Mr. Pool Cue says so." Bosco squared off with Indamelo. He'd aim for the fucker's knees first. "Put him down."

The sound of a shotgun being pumped is unmistakable. Bosco didn't bother to look over his shoulder; he knew Hugo was there.

Clayton saw Fran slung over a very scary looking guy's back and was moving on adrenalin. Monrov, Shilo and Tyndale followed him, but they stopped at the sight of the stand off. They knew a shotgun did a lot of damage to a lot of people when it was fired.

"Put him down," Bosco said dangerously. "And git you and yer fag sociopaths outta here."

Indamelo figured the kid's ass might be worth fighting Bosco for, but it wasn't worth getting shot up over. He slung Fran in Bosco's general direction and stalked off.

White as a sheet and breathing hard, Fran scrambled under a pool table, behind his rescuers.

Hugo sighed, but didn't put the shotgun down; he simply looked over at Bosco. "Well?" he asked.

Bosco was not looking at him, but at Clayton and his pals. He reached under the table, hauled Fran up and threw him into Clayton's arms. "He yours?" he growled.

"Sort of," Clayton said, putting his body between Fran and the enraged, psychotic biker.

"Then take better care of him!" Bosco screamed. He walked away muttering something about assholes, faggots and idiots.

Hugo went into his office and put his shotgun away. When he came out again, the kid and his pals were gone. He sent a couple of beers over to Bosco on the house, but they never said anything else about it.

Clayton got Fran out of the bar and into his car in record time. On the way to his dorm, Fran started to shake. Clayton pulled over and put his arm around him. "I think you better stay at my place tonight," he said, when Fran had calmed down some. "You can sleep in Tyler's bed."

"Okay," Fran agreed shakily.

At home, Clayton poured Fran two fingers of brandy and made him drink it. "Are you going to be all right in there, Fran?" Clayton asked, standing at Tyler's bedroom door.

"I think so," Fran said. He leaned bravely into Clayton's one-armed hug and went into the empty bedroom.

About ten minutes later he tapped on Clayton's door and went in when he was invited. "I guess I'm not going to be all right," he said sadly.

Clayton patted the empty side of his bed and Fran burrowed under the covers.

"C'mere, Fran," Clayton said, stretching his arm out to him.

He curled into Clayton's arm and dozed while Clayton read some typewritten bound pages. "Were you scared?" he asked softly when the light was put out.

"A little," Clayton admitted. "It could have gotten very ugly."

"They were going to rape me, weren't they?" Fran asked, but it was really a statement.

Clayton considered lying to him, but what was the point in that? "Yes, I'm sorry I took you in there," he said. "I don't know what I was thinking."

"Clayton, don't feel bad," Fran said quickly. "It was fun for a while, you know."

"That's how most of life is, Fran," Clayton sighed. "Go to sleep."

Clayton woke up at first light with Fran cuddled up on his chest. He looked like a tousled angel who'd gotten some peaceful sleep. He had a bruise coming out on his cheek; Clayton wondered when in the scuffle he got it. Fran also had a hard-on pressing against his leg. There was no mystery in that; it was morning and Clayton had one, too. He got out of bed without waking Fran and took his into a freezing shower. And that was the end of that.

Fran was still sleeping, so Clayton made coffee and didn't read the paper because it got soaked in the unexpected rainstorm that morning. He read it off the website and noticed that the weather prediction was especially vague for that day: it might rain more, but then again, it might not. Fran was up by then and not especially hungry. Clayton drove him to his dorm because it might rain, but then again, it might not, and the kid had no rain gear. They did not mention the night before. Clayton assumed it was resolved for Fran. He'd been rescued and that was all there was to it.

But Fran was a cheerful brooder, so it was hard to tell what he was thinking. His school was on a break and he had nothing to do but think about the night before, what had happened, and what might have happened. The decision, once he made it, was fairly easy. He called the DDI to ask what time they opened. The answering machine said they started serving at four p.m. and closed at 2 a.m. Fran called up the bus route and schedule and found one that went fairly close and when he wanted to be there. Early, so he would miss all the crazies.

Because it was impossible to miss the crazies at the DDI, the bartender on duty, Bruno Segni, nearly had a heart attack when the soaking wet kid came in. "Jesus, you look even younger in the daylight," he said, handing him a bar towel.

"Sorry, it wasn't raining when I left," Fran mumbled, shaking with cold. "Were you here last night?"

"Yeah."

"Those guys...the one with the pool cue and the one with the gun...do you know them? Can I talk to them?" Fran asked between sneezes and sniffles.

"Well, one of them is here," Bruno said, and because the kid was getting too many hungry looks, he led him to Hugo's office. "Somebody to see you, boss," he said, ushering Fran in.

"Oh, fuck. What are you doing here?" Hugo got up from his desk in alarm. "Who's out there, Bruno?"

"Three guys too burned out to do much more than look. But still...I thought he'd be better off in here." Bruno said and left, closing the door behind him.

Hugo turned back to the beautiful child in front on him. "What in the flyin' hell are you doing here?" he asked, noticing the bruise on his cheek. "Courtesy of fucking Indamelo," he thought.

"I wanted to thank you," Fran said, sniffling.

"You're welcome."

"I wanted to thank the other guy, too."

"Bosco? He blew last night," Hugo said and then asked if Fran drove there. "No wonder you're soaked. That bus stop is about a mile from here."

Fran nodded, wishing he was home and dry.

"You'll catch cold if you stay in those wet clothes, kid." Hugo handed him a blanket. "We have a dryer in the kitchen," he said, keeping his gaze firmly on his desk while Fran undressed. "What's your name?" he asked, shaking a little water out of the jeans, t-shirt and briefs Fran handed him.

"Gilly La Farge," Fran—or rather, Gilly—said, wrapping the blanket around him.

"Well, have a seat, Gilly, and I'll be right back. I'm locking this door from the outside while I'm gone," Hugo said on his way out.

"My, my, that's fast work," Ladislaus Brindisi, washing up in the kitchen observed as Hugo tossed the wet togs in the dryer they used to dry bar towels and whatnot.

"Shut the fuck up, Lad," Hugo laughed and poured a mug of milk. He put it in the microwave and while it was nuking, he opened cupboards until he found some rum. Optimally he'd have liked some chocolate syrup for the drink, but the chances of that being within miles of the DDI were slim to none. He'd have settled for sugar, but, surprisingly, found some honey, which was better. "Where'd this come from?" he asked Lad.

"The guy lives next to Ignatius keeps bees," Lad said matter-of-factly.

"No shit? Has the fucking honeycomb still in it, yeah. Can I use some?" Hugo asked.

"Sure, that's what it's here for." Lad smirked. "Wanna see if we got a baby bottle, too?"

"Fuck off," Hugo laughed. He spooned a generous dollop of honey into the hot milk and brandy and walked back to his office stirring it.

Looking down at the shivering Gilly, he realized the kid would never get it down on his own. He sat down and put his arm around him. "Here," he said holding the cup to his lips.

"Thanks," Gilly said softly. "What's your name?" he asked between sips.

"Hugo St. Victor," Hugo said. "French, like yours."

About half way through the mug, Gilly got steady enough to handle it. He also got sleepy, so by the time he was finished, he was well on his way to dreamland.

"Was a time I didn't put 'em to sleep," Hugo thought, arranging the pillow and laying Gilly on it. "Back in the day..." Because he didn't have another blanket, he draped his coat over the sleeping beauty on his couch. "Yeah, back in the fucking day..." He turned the heat up a little and went back to his accounts while Gilly, pretty pretty Gilly, slept sweetly on his couch. Sigh...

Hugo had great hearing. He could hear the bar coming to life outside his office. Or rather, he could feel it coming to life. He could also hear

Gilly's peaceful breathing and felt very strongly that he had to get him out of there soon. He got up to open the door at Ignatius' soft knock; he knew all his crew's knocks, but this was a little softer than usual. "Thanks," he said, taking Gilly's dry and neatly folded clothes from Ignatius while not obscuring the other man's view.

Ignatius nodded, took one last look at Gilly and left.

Hugo put Gilly's clothes on the coffee table and looked at his watch. He'd let him sleep a little longer. The kid might be hungry when he woke up, so Hugo went out to the kitchen to see if they had any food. They never had food in that kitchen, but it was worth a try. On the way out he stopped to fiddle with the pile of stones they kept on the end of the bar. None of the patrons knew why there was a pile of stones at the far end of the bar, but they did add interesting specimens to it. Mainly smooth river rocks or sun-bleached desert stones; so beautiful in their simplicity even the hard-asses that frequented the DDI noticed.

Hugo's crew knew why the stones were there and they froze watching him contemplate and then move a few stones around with his long weathered fingers. He lowered his eyes, moved a few more stones and walked back to his office.

The minute his door closed, Bruno, Lad and Ig dropped what they were doing to study the new arrangement of stones. They murmured "yeah", "okay", and "yeah", until one of the patrons yelled for a fucking beer and right fucking now. "Yeah, okay, yeah," Ig yelled back and got the cretin a beer. It was a bar after all.

Back in his office, Hugo sat on the edge of the couch and gently shook Gilly awake. "It's time for you to go home, Gilly," he said softly.

"Wha' time is it?"

"Seven." Hugo got up and sat at his desk with his back to him.

Gilly briefly wondered if it that was a.m. or p.m., but decided it didn't matter. He put on his clothes and ran his fingers through his hair. "If it's raining, can someone give me a lift to the bus stop, please?"

"I thought I'd take you all the way home, if you don't mind," Hugo said, making sure he had his wallet and put on his coat. "If you're hungry, we can stop and have something on the way."

Gilly said that would be nice and Hugo led him out the back way, where fewer people would see him. Hugo stopped briefly at the bar to tell the bartender they were leaving. Gilly thought he recognized one of Clayton's friends at the bar, but Hugo was between him and the rest of the room, so it was only a fleeting glimpse and he wasn't sure.

One of the few pleasures Hugo still allowed himself was eating at Saint-Saveur-en-Puisaye, more commonly and barbarically known as St. Savor, now and then. He usually turned up in the quiet hours before the dinner rush, so the owner, Marc Chalon, was as surprised as delighted to see him at such a civilized hour. And with such a young and charming escort.

"Bonsoir, bonsoir, Hugo, ça va?" Chalon said graciously.

"Bien, merci, et toi?"

"Aussi. Ton table habituelle?"

"Merci." Hugo returned Wombat Morganthral's wave from one of the A tables and followed Gilly and Chalon to the little dinning room off the kitchen. Only staff and family ate there, and because long ago Hugo had arranged the garden outside the long windows so beautifully, the Chalon family and staff always seated him by a window that overlooked it.

Originally the restaurant had planned to put the A tables by those windows, but Chalon was protective of the peace and harmony of the view and didn't want to share it with just anyone. They could eat his food, but he would save the beauty of his garden for his loved ones. He counted Hugo St. Victor as a loved one (even if he did own the most awful bar in three counties) and someday Hugo would snap out of it and start living again. Although a discreet look at Gilly made him wonder if his old friend hadn't really gone over the edge; this child was young enough to be his son.

The food at Saint-Saveur-en-Puisaye was country French and very good. Chalon and his staff liked to experiment a little, and Chalon proceeded on a long, detailed description of a duck dish and side dishes and the wines that he thought went with it.

Hugo's French was adequate; he neatly processed what Chalon had said and was about to translate it to Gilly, when Gilly politely asked, "S'il vous plaît, je voudrais l'eau minérale au lieu du vin avec mon repas. Pardon, je n'aime pas le vin beaucoup."

"Bien sûr, monsieur..."

"Je m'appelle François Guillaume La Farge, mais tout le monde m'appelle Gilly," he said shyly.

"Enchanté, Gilly," Chalon said graciously. He shook hands with the younger man while making a hasty reevaluation of the situation. "Voudrais vous l'eau minérale avec gaz ou sans gaz?"

"Sans gaz, s'il vous plaît, et aussi s'il vous plait, pouvez me tutoyer, monsieur," Gilly said, blushing a little.

"Avec plaisir," Chalon said and meant it as he went off to get Hugo a dry vermouth and Gilly a mineral water.

When he was gone and Gilly turned his attention to him, Hugo raised his hand to forestall him. "Please, don't speak French to me," he said. "It wears me out."

"But you speak so well," Gilly said.

"Not really, just enough to get by." Hugo thought Gilly was a rotten, if charming, liar. "Where did you learn? You speak very well."

"At home, from my grandmother and aunts mainly," Gilly said. "We spoke English everywhere except at home. Where did you learn?"

"Mostly at school," Hugo said, nodding thanks at the drinks waiter and sipping his dry vermouth. He liked vermouth; he ought to drink it more. "My father was French, but we didn't have time to speak very much. He did read me French stories when I was little, and that helped when I learned it later."

"What did he read you?" Gilly asked, wondering if they'd heard the same stories.

"*Jungle Book* translated into French."

Their first course arrived and, realizing how hungry they were and how good the food was, they gave it their full attention. Almost their full attention: Hugo was glancing out the window occasionally and Gilly was taking those opportunities to examine his dinner partner.

The room was dim so the moonlight made the most of the garden, still glistening from the earlier rain. A waiter brought a few more candles and Hugo found Gilly especially charming by their light. "What are you thinking?" Hugo asked, finding Gilly studying him.

"What time is it?"

Surprised, Hugo looked at his watch. "Eight-thirty. Gotta date?"

"Just this one," Gilly said with a smile. "It's just seems like my life changed a lot in less than twenty-four hours."

"Last night? Yeah, you had a pretty bad shock," Hugo said, nodding. "Look, Gilly..."

"I thought I was in luck this evening!" Wombat boomed, looming over them.

"Wombat! You're gonna scare me straight one day," Hugo said, putting his tough guy bluster back on. "Have a seat, meet Gilly La Farge."

"A pleasure to meet you, young man," Wombat said suavely and hoped that Hugo checked his date's ID before they did anything illegal. Wombat was a genius lawyer, but it helped if his clients didn't break the law in the first place. "How are things at the DDI?" he asked, turning back to Hugo.

"Nonlethal lately," Hugo said coolly.

"Glad to hear it," Wombat said pleasantly. "Nice to see you here, Hugo, you don't get out much, do you?"

"I still like Marc's food," Hugo said, motioning the waiter forward with their next course.

"Who doesn't?" Wombat asked, rising. "Well, enjoy!" He sketched them a wave and strode back to his party.

"Who was that?" Gilly asked quietly when he was gone.

"My lawyer," Hugo said. "I never hired him and I've never paid him anything; he just decided to be my lawyer when there was a shooting at the DDI after I bought it. I don't know how he knows when I have to appear in court or give a police statement, but he always shows up. I never call him. He's a great lawyer."

Gilly nodded politely and went back to his excellent dinner. A wine glass filled half with wine and half with mineral water appeared at Gilly's elbow and he drank that with his meal. He still didn't like wine, but it did add more to the food than plain water.

Hugo just had a cognac for dessert and was very mellow. He was enjoying watching Gilly plow through Gaufres aux Pistaches. The bill came to less than the price of dessert, but arguing with Chalon was always a waste of time, so he just paid it and left a humongous tip as usual.

Seated in Hugo's battered pick-up truck, Gilly was quiet and trying to find a way to get Hugo to take him to his place and not to his dorm. He'd never seduced anyone in his life and he wasn't entirely sure he wanted to seduce Hugo; he just didn't want to leave him yet. He glanced over at the possible object of his possible desire and found he was being studied.

"Okay, Gilly," Hugo said softly, when he knew Gilly was with him again. "Where do you live?"

Because he couldn't think of a way around such a direct question, Gilly have him his dorm address.

"You're at the university?" Hugo asked, putting the truck in gear. "Studying what?"

"Finance, but I don't like it very much," Gilly said.

"Then why study it?"

"So I can get a job when I graduate," Gilly said, watching the city get thick around them.

"And spend your life in something you don't like?"

"Well, I don't hate it, but I can't think of anything else I want to study right now," Gilly admitted.

"Hm." Hugo really didn't understand this; he'd latched onto his focus in life so young, he'd nearly not recovered from the shock of losing it in mid-life. But then again, perhaps he did understand Gilly studying something he was only mildly interested in; Hugo was living an entire life he was only mildly interested in.

Hugo drove aimlessly around the dorm complex partly because Gilly was not navigating and also because he didn't want to not be with him.

He wasn't sure he wanted to take him home to bed, or read him *Jungle Book* in French, or shoot pool at the Reykjavík Bar; he just knew he didn't want the moment to end. The peace and quiet of the truck cab, the softness of Gilly's presence shyly reaching out to him was the most exquisite torture Hugo had had in a while. That made two pleasures in one evening: good food and sweetness and light. Okay, three, but he was way over his limit and knew it. Almost against his will, he found the address Gilly gave him and parked in front. "Well, here you are," he sighed, shutting the engine off.

Gilly cleared his throat. "Thank you for dinner," he said softly. "Um...can't I just go home with you?"

"Huh," Hugo said to cover his surprise. "Ah...well, that had crossed my mind..."

"Okay, let's go!"

"But we only just met," Hugo continued. "And I'm not sure either of us knows what we're doing here."

Gilly bit his lower lip, frantically forming a reply. "Hugo, I don't know what I'm doing, but I just know I don't want to not be with you now," he said in a rush, hoping it made sense.

"You don't know a thing about me, Gilly." Hugo laughed. "Is this how you always pick up strange guys?"

"I don't know. You're not strange and I've never picked up anyone before," Gilly said. "But I know I want to stay with you tonight and I don't care about anything else."

"How can you know that?" Hugo asked more gently. "We just met."

"Can't you know all at once sometimes about a person?" Gilly asked. "Can't I know I want to stay with you tonight? What's wrong with that?"

"Nothing, it's just reckless," Hugo said slowly, staring at Gilly's big dark eyes.

"Really?"

"Hell, yes," Hugo said. "Asking a man you've just met to take you home is incredibly reckless."

"Are you dangerous?" Gilly asked with a hint of playfulness.

"Sometimes," Hugo answered darkly.

"Like now?" Gilly asked seriously.

"Not really," Hugo admitted.

"Then it's not so reckless," Gilly said logically and finally. "It's kind of cold out here, don't you think?"

Hugo gazed at his logical, impulsive little French guy and sighed. "You're going to cause a lot of trouble someday," he said, reaching over to cup Gilly's cheek.

Dipsy Doodle Inn

Gilly nuzzled into Hugo's rough palm. "Really?" he asked, against the thumb caressing his mouth.

"Nah, it just sounded like a good thing to say right then." Hugo removed his hand and started the truck.

They drove to Hugo's apartment in silence. Neither noticed when they passed Tyler and Clayton on their way from the airport, making a detour to Gilly's dorm.

Tyler had a terrible reaction when Clayton told him about the near abduction and rape in the Dipsy Doodle Inn. "You did what?" he asked in a hollow but strangely furious voice.

"Tyler..."

"You took my innocent, virginal –"

"Tyler –"

"Little Gilly into to the DDI where every psychotic rapist, wannabe rapist, retired but–"

"Tyler–"

"...willing to unretire rapist, crazy motherfucking–"

"Tyler–"

"...father raping lunatic in the known world–"

"Tyler! Stop! You need to pray!" Clayton said, very near the end of his patience. "It was a mistake and he's okay. Fuck! This is the last time I take pity on one of your boytoys."

"Thank the Lord, and I hope you don't," Tyler snarled. "I mean, if you're going to toss them into the DDI like fresh meat–"

"Would you and your luggage like to walk home?" Clayton growled.

"My luggage and I would like to swing by Gilly's dorm and see if he's all right," Tyler shot back.

Clayton spun the car over three lanes and gunned it to Gilly's dorm.

There was no answer at Gilly's room and no one they talked to had seen him in two days.

"Well, I dropped him off this morning, Tyler, so it's only less than a day," Clayton said reasonably. "Maybe he went out. Did he know you'd be back today?"

"No," Tyler said, staring at Gilly's door. "Didn't you tell him I'd be back today?"

"In the rush of events, I forgot," Clayton admitted.

"Well, I can see how that could happen," Tyler said absently. Then he banged on doors until one of Gilly's neighbors gave him paper, pen and tape to leave a note on Gilly's door. "Guess that'll do until he calls me," Tyler sighed. "I am dying of jetlag, let's go home."

Clayton took the exhausted artist home and figured he'd gotten off easy for taking Gilly to the DDI. He would have been happier if he knew where Gilly was at that moment, but, like Tyler, he'd just have to wait for him to call, email or show up.

Hugo lived in a nondescript one-bedroom apartment in a huge complex on the outskirts of town, conveniently near the DDI. It was far enough from the highway that it was not noisy, except when a huge swarm of bikers were on their way to the DDI, which was Hugo's cue to go look after his establishment. It was too early in the year for huge swarms of bikers, so his place was quiet when he led Gilly into it.

It was tidy, too, as Hugo's methodical neatness had not deserted him. In many ways keeping his spaces clean and orderly were the best way to kill time and not think. Housekeeping was visible progress without much mental effort involved. Hugo was either busy at the bar or at home or sleeping in one place or the other. He ran on his narrow track and called it a quiet life: not a happy one, but one he could manage.

So bringing Gilly home really threw a monkey wrench into his works. Hugo brought people there to have sex with them (usually on the couch and then he threw them out), but Gilly wasn't in that category. Hugo wasn't sure what category Gilly was in. Anyway, because he never had people like Gilly in his place, he never saw how boring and threadbare his home was. "Like my soul," he thought, half hoping Gilly would ask to be taken home and never see him again.

But Gilly did nothing of the sort. He let Hugo hang up his coat and offer him a drink, which he refused. Wandering around the front room, he was waiting or hoping for Hugo to make the first move (whatever that was), Gilly gravitated very close to his host, who seemed to be waiting for him. "Um..."

"Um...what?" Hugo asked, cupping Gilly's pointed little face in his palms.

"What now?" Gilly asked, leaning into this minimal embrace.

"Whatever you want, Gilly," Hugo said softly, drawing him a little closer.

"I want to go to bed with you," Gilly sighed.

"Okay, but I get to take your clothes off slowly," Hugo whispered in his ear. "It's like Christmas and my birthday all in one." He laughed softly and led Gilly into his bedroom. If the kid was there, they might as well both enjoy it for as long as it lasted.

And it was exactly the long, slow tease they both needed. Gilly wasn't wearing all that much, just jeans and a t-shirt, but between kisses and tickling, it took quite awhile to remove them.

Because he was shy, Gilly had only managed to get Hugo out of his work shirt. Even in the dim light he could see the scars. "How did you get this?" He asked, tracking the trail from shoulder to bicep.

"Falling out of a tree in Japan," Hugo said, caressing Gilly's inner thigh. He knew better to proceed while the kid was distracted. This was one reason Hugo tried to stay dressed as long a possible, but Gilly was the exception to everything.

"And this one?" Gilly asked, tracking another scar across his ribcage.

"I didn't get out of the way of a boulder in Canada quick enough," Hugo said, letting his hand edge toward Gilly's erection.

"What were you doing?"

"Working," Hugo said and got his lips really close to Gilly's, in hopes that the kid would rather kiss him than interrogate him.

Fortunately, this was the case, and as Hugo skillfully pumped him to orgasm, Gilly forgot all about the beautiful map of Hugo's chest and arms. In fact, as he arched in his lover's strong arms and cried out his name, Gilly pretty much forgot everything he ever knew.

Hugo was pleased; only the young came that hard, but there was more poetry in Gilly than he'd realized. Or hoped for; Hugo never hoped for much anymore, but was always ready to be disappointed and glad when he wasn't. He laid the panting kid down and got a towel. Gilly was not a messy climaxer, but, hopefully, they'd need a towel later. He pulled off his jeans and crawled in beside him.

Gilly rolled into his arms to wrestle, something he liked a lot and Hugo seemed to enjoy, too. The light was out, so he couldn't see any more scars, but he could feel the hardness of Hugo's body and, soon, his cock. Hugo's skin over ropy muscles was not exactly soft, but it was softer than it looked and not at all unpleasant. He ran his hands over the broad powerful back as Hugo humped his erection against Gilly's answering rhythm. They made a lot of noise as they came, and not that Gilly in his inexperience would know, but Hugo took a long time to recover.

"What is it about this kid," he wondered, reaching for the towel and finding Gilly already using it on him. "Thanks," he panted. He lay contented on his back with Gilly in his arms, enjoying the warmth and silence and something he rarely got: afterglow.

And, God bless Gilly La Farge, he let him enjoy and drop off into peaceful sleep. Well, almost.

"Hugo?"

"Hugo is sleeping."

"I just wanted to know if you would have killed him," Gilly said softly.

"Who, baby?"

"That guy, last night," Gilly said softly. "You had a shotgun..."

"Honey, that gun is loaded with rock salt," Hugo said, three quarters asleep. "Slows 'em down enough to jump on 'em. It was Bosco I was worried about, he's no choir boy either."

"Who's Bosco?'

Hugo yawned. "The guy with the pool cue," he said. "Go to sleep."

The next morning, Clayton checked his email and his voicemail for a message from Gilly. There was none. He left Tyler sleeping off his jetlag and went to work, where there was also no word from Gilly. He asked Monrov if he'd heard from Gilly, or rather Fran as Monrov knew him and the other man was afraid he had not.

"Worried?" Monrov asked.

"Yeah, a little," Clayton admitted. "Tyler hit the ceiling when I told him about the DDI."

"Is Tyler after him?" Monrov asked, omitting the presumed "too."

"Yeah, but it might be more protective than sexual," Clayton said, omitting the "unlike you." "I'd like to round the kid up before Tyler comes to."

Monrov shrugged and said he'd let him know the second he heard from him.

Tyler woke up in his own bed for the first time in weeks and was glad to be home. Then he remembered Gilly and checked his email. Nothing. Voicemail. Nothing. He called Clayton and Clayton had nothing for him either. "Where the fuck is he?" Tyler asked, annoyed.

"Wish I knew, Ty," Clayton said, nodding to his secretary to bring in his next clients. "Maybe he's off having a good time."

"Like the one you showed him at the DDI?" Tyler snarled and got hung up on.

Ever intrepid (or at least he thought he was), Tyler pulled himself together and drove to Gilly's dorm. Maybe the kid was mad at him for going off without telling him. Well, he'd melt that iceberg in one second. He'd done some thinking in France and thought Gilly would make a wonderful lover to pass the time with. For awhile.

But his note was still neatly taped to Gilly's door and no one Tyler cornered had seen him in three days. "No, that's just one, Clayton saw him yesterday morning," he reminded himself. He cursed Clayton for not...not what? Locking Gilly in Tyler's bedroom until he got home from France? As interesting as that thought was, even he knew it was way over on the silly side.

The worst part, when Tyler looked critically at it, was that he didn't know Gilly well enough to know where he might be. He did know a few cafes and internet gamer places they'd been together but that was it. To feel less helpless, he drove to all of them. At each one, Tyler checked his email and had no message from Gilly. He asked around and no one there had seen Gilly in days, if not weeks, and a few didn't even know who he was.

This was becoming more and more upsetting to Tyler so he decided to go to Clayton's office and take it out on him. And Monrov. And anyone else handy.

Hugo woke up with gentle teeth on his nipple and a warm hand on his erection. He rolled on top of Gilly and kissed him until they both came, which was pretty damn quick. "Ummmm, shower, coffee," he groaned into Gilly's long white neck. "D'you drink coffee?" he asked.

"Sometimes."

"I have some really good coffee," Hugo said, dragging him into the shower.

Hugo had some really good soap and loofa sponges in his shower, too. There was some soapy wrestling and cuddling to go along with the exfoliation and steam. After the shower he smoothed some oil over Gilly's wet skin. "Not that you need this," he said, caressing his back and ass. "But it's fun for me." He reached around and brought Gilly off (again) in half a dozen strokes. When Gilly was able to stand on his own, Hugo turned to the task of oiling his own body.

Very considerately, Gilly offered to do his back. This was always welcome as Hugo lived alone and usually didn't get his back oiled well enough.

"This is why your skin is so nice," Gilly observed as he smoothed oil over muscle and scar tissue.

"My skin is so fucked up from weather and abuse, kid, if I don't do this is gets too dry and irritated," Hugo told him, moving his slim hand away from his cock. "Leave that alone or you'll never get any breakfast."

"Breakfast can wait," Gilly purred into his shoulder.

"Not as long as it would take me to come again," Hugo said, reaching for his robe and draping it around Gilly. "At my age these things take a while and I'm out of practice," he added, wrapping a towel around his hips.

Gilly followed him into the kitchen where he did indeed get very good coffee and some toast with jam because there was no butter.

They didn't talk much; there was no need in the comfortable silences they'd been enjoying since before dinner. Gilly finished his coffee and toast said he'd wait on more of both.

"Okay," Hugo said, putting the pot down. "Whaddya wanna do now?"

"Go back to bed with you."

Hugo thought about it for one nanosecond and said, "Okay."

Tyler's trip to Clayton's office yielded a clue to Gilly's whereabouts, and a disturbing one at that. One of the lawyers that worked with him told Monrov he thought he'd seen Fran leaving the DDI the day before with a tall, old guy.

"What tall, old guy?" Tyler asked, wondering who Fran was.

"I don't know him," the lawyer said. "And I'm not one-hundred-percent sure..."

"Well, you're not on the stand, pal, thanks," Monrov cut him off and turned to Clayton. "If Fran was at the DDI–"

"He wouldn't be stupid enough to go back there–"

"Who the fuck is Fran?" Tyler snarled.

"Fran is Gilly's real name," Clayton said, looking at his watch.

"Who's Gilly?" Monrov asked and exchanged looks with the lawyer, who shrugged and left them to it.

"Gilly is Fran, Fran is Gilly," Clayton snapped and picked up the phone. He dialed the DDI and got the run around. "Fuck! Tyler, let's just go out there and talk to them. Monrov, you're welcome to come along."

"Wish I could, but I've got a dinner meeting," he said, looking at his watch. "I'll leave my cell phone on in case you need me."

"Why, we always need you, Monrov, honey," Tyler drawled and followed Clayton to his car.

At the DDI, Lad recognized Clayton and Tyler from previous visits, but didn't tell either of them much of anything. "Guys, look around," he said, waving to the budding chaos that was "happy hour" at the DDI. "Ain't no way I can keep track of every kid that comes in here."

"But do you remember, the night before last..." Clayton began.

"I was off," Lad said firmly. He'd been off, but had heard all about it. "Look, I'll tell you what," he relented seeing their sad, worried faces. "If I see or hear of your friend I'll give you a shout. Where can I call you?"

The lawyer and the artist handed over business cards and wrote their cell phones, home phones, office and studio phones, friend's phones and emails on them, too. Lad was impressed and felt kind of bad that he couldn't just tell them where the kid was. He himself only had a very strong suspicion of where he was.

When they were gone he had a brief conference with Ig and Bruno and then called Hugo at home.

"Your friends are looking for you," Hugo said, coming back to bed. He was relieved that Lad was not calling to tell him the DDI had burned down or something equally annoying. But he was concerned that Gilly's friends were looking for him.

Gilly shrugged.

"You should call them," Hugo said, hugging him. "If they're looking for you, they're worried about you."

"Oh, all right," Gilly sighed and went to the phone. He called Clayton's home number because it was the first one he remembered and left a message on the machine, "Hi, Clayton, I'm okay and staying with a friend. See you later." He romped back into bed and rolled around with Hugo a little more.

"What do you want for dinner, darlin'?" Hugo asked, pinning him.

"More of you."

"I feel annoyed by this," Tyler said when Clayton refused to play Gilly's message again. "That message, I mean."

"I feel disturbed by it," Clayton said, relenting and replaying it one more time. "The timing sucks; like, the guy in the bar knew where Gilly was all the time and made him make that call."

"That's a little paranoid, isn't it, Clayton?" Tyler asked. He didn't like it either, now that it was pointed out to him.

"It's the DDI, Tyler."

"Oh, fuck! Let me make some dinner and then we'll go back." Tyler stomped into the kitchen and pulled together a nourishing meal. They'd need it if they were going to the DDI when it was in full swing.

"Thank you for swallowing. I wasn't expecting you to," Hugo said, trying to get his breath back. "What did you think?"

"Kind of salty," Gilly said, licking his lips. "But not bad at all." He drank some cold tea and ate a little more of the house chow mein they'd had delivered. "Want some of this?" he asked, waving the carton in Hugo's general direction.

"Maybe later," Hugo said, easing down Gilly's body to devour him.

"Well, that was humiliating," Tyler said in the car after they were thrown out of the DDI. "What now?"

"If we don't hear from him by tomorrow noon, I file a police report and let the cops talk to the DDI," Clayton said, wondering which one of the bartender/bouncer thugs was the owner.

"A lot can happen by then," Tyler said darkly.

"Then pray it don't, Tyler, because that's all we can do right now."

"Are you sure?" Hugo asked, removing his finger.

"Yes, that felt so great," Gilly said, laying on his chest, bathwater lapping around them.

"My dick is a lot bigger than my finger," Hugo said, sloshing water over Gilly's back.

"Don't you want to?" Gilly looked up at him with those irresistible dark eyes.

"Oh, very much. I just want you to know it might hurt," Hugo said, knowing he'd do anything the kid wanted. "But we'll stop if it hurts too much."

Gilly agreed and they rinsed off. Hugo skipped the oil since they'd be in the shower later anyway.

The bath had been Gilly's good idea. After Lad's second phone call that Gilly's friends had come back and hurt his feelings, Hugo had been annoyed enough to carry Gilly on his back to his friends, just to prove he was okay. But Gilly simply picked up the phone and left another reassuring message and then suggested they take a bath. Hugo loved baths and this one did wonders for his mood.

"Goddamnit! I'm going to the cops tonight!" Clayton yelled after he heard the second "I'm fine, just fine" message from Gilly.

"And tell them what? That our boyfriend never calls when we're at home?" Tyler asked, stomping into his bedroom.

Clayton called the police station, but no one he knew was there. He left a message for everyone he knew to call him as soon as they could and called it a night. "God damn Tyler's boyfriends," he thought and fumed for a while before he could sleep.

"Are you okay?" Hugo whispered when he was all the way in.

"Oh...yes!"

Hugo dropped a soft kiss on the back of Gilly's neck and began to move, slowly and gently. He could come this way and, reaching around to stroke his lover to climax, did come and hard from the ensuing clenching. When the shuddering subsided enough for him to pull out, he got up to dispose of the condom and came back to hold the still recovering Gilly.

It had been easy, easier than ever before with a virgin. And even though the kid was raring to go, it was obvious he was a virgin and Hugo took care not to hurt him. Or let him hurt himself; at one point it had been necessary to hold him firmly so his thrashing around didn't tear any delicate tissues. But once he accepted that Hugo was in charge, all had been well. There was a little tearing, that was to be expected, and Hugo refused to go again that night, no matter what Gilly wanted.

"It is time for all former virgins in this bed to sleep," he announced, turning the light off.

"Why?" Gilly asked, squirming around.

"Because they are very tired and very happy," Hugo said around a yawn. "And need sleep so they can make love like crazed weasels in the morning."

"Oh, well, in that case," Gilly said, cuddled up and went to sleep.

Hugo followed him in short order. Neither of them gave another thought to their bar, their school, their friends, their community, or anyone who might be looking for them. Like all new lovers deeply in love they were thinking only of each other. They were allowed to, at least for that night.

Hugo realized he was in love when he woke next to Gilly and saw landscapes in the shapes around him. It was an old familiar feeling, but that morning he welcomed it with joy instead of the usual ache and despair. "Well, enjoy it as long as you can, old man," he thought. "Take love and beauty where you find them, let the rest go by the wayside." And enjoy it he did, until the landscape faded back into shapes and the world was mundane again. But a mundane world was easier for Hugo to live in, at least that's what he told himself. However, just then Gilly woke up and wanted to play, so the world was not as mundane as it might otherwise have been.

Around midmorning, Hugo made a terrible announcement. "Gilly, you and I are going to have to get out of this bed eventually."

"Why?"

"Because you have school to attend and I have a bar to run," Hugo said, not actually moving from the bed.

Gilly snuggled a little closer. "I'm on break this week," he said.

"Really? And you couldn't think of anything better than to let those fools take you to the DDI?" Hugo asked, stroking his hair off his forehead. "I thought all you wild college boys did wild things on break."

"Only those who can afford it," Gilly said. "And I'm not really that wild."

"That's debatable."

"And I was using the time to get ahead on research for my final project," Gilly said. "I graduate next term or the one after, depending on how much I get done."

"So, I really should let you get back to it," Hugo said.

Gilly agreed but neither of them actually made a move to get up.

"Can I see you again?" Gilly asked shyly after a while.

"Hell, yes." Hugo held him closer. "I've been thinking about it. I keep crazy hours, Gilly. How about if I give you a key and we'll get together as often as we can?"

"Do you want me to move in?" Gilly asked, looking up at him.

"Not yet," Hugo said. "Let's see how it goes with us and you finish school, okay? I don't even know how you voted in the last election."

"I was too young, but I would have voted for Gore," Gilly said. "He won anyway, so it wouldn't have mattered if I could have voted for him, would it? Who'd you vote for."

"Gore," Hugo said. "Second guy to win the election and not be President. What a country, eh?" He hugged Gilly and then sat up. "These are very fucked-up times, are you sure you want to get involved with such an old guy like me?"

"Yes, as long as it is you, and not someone like you," Gilly said, getting up. "Okay, I can go now as long as I can come back. And we can take a nice, long shower and have coffee first."

"This might work out, darlin', that was my thinking exactly," Hugo said and chased his new lover into the shower.

About midmorning, Clayton was in his office and dialing the police department. He was going to make an appointment to report Gilly missing. He wanted to see one of the officers he'd defended for the firm, so it would get taken seriously; college boys disappear all the time, but this was different.

"Ah! Clayton! There you are!" Wombat descended on him. "I'm so glad I found you!"

Clayton put down the phone. One never asked a founding partner to wait. Especially when they were as nutty as Wombat. "How nice to see you, Mr. Morganthral," he said politely. "I do try to be in my office when you're looking for me."

"Yes, excellent for both of us!" Wombat flung himself into a chair. "Now, look here, I've heard rumors that you're looking for a young man who might have been in the DDI the other day. Based on Monrov's description of your young friend, I believe I saw him having a delicious meal at Saint-Saveur-en-Puisaye with Hugo St. Victor, the owner of the DDI and one of my most amazing clients."

"Really?"

"Absolutely! I've won every case for him and he's never paid me a cent," Wombat boomed on his way out. "That's an amazing client in my book or any other."

Clayton couldn't get into Wombat's client database, but he did find Hugo St. Victor in the phone book. He told his secretary he might be out for a longish lunch and called Tyler from the car. "I know where he is and I'm coming to get you to get him," he said.

Tyler was waiting outside when Clayton swung by. "Where?" he asked when they were on the highway.

"With Hugo St. Victor, know him?"

"No."

"He's the owner of the DDI," Clayton said.

"My, my, I never think of the DDI has having an owner, you know," Tyler mused. "It just seems to run on some kind of demonic energy, but I reckon someone has to order all that beer and mop up the blood."

"Yeah," Clayton growled, parking in front of Hugo's building.

"Okay, so who's your favorite poet?" Gilly asked when Hugo came back from answering the phone. They were dressed and having coffee, like civilized people.

"Dylan Thomas," Hugo said, sitting across from him. "And that was my lawyer, looking for you because your friends are looking for you. I believe next time you call your friends, you should actually speak to them so they know you're all right. Here." He handed over a key and a card with his address and home phone on it. "I never ever want to see you in the DDI again, understand me, Gilly?"

"Yes." He bent over the scrap of paper Hugo handed him. "Here's my phone, address and email," he said handing it over. "Can I come back tonight?"

"Sure, but I probably won't get here until two or three a.m.," Hugo said. "I've got to give the guys a night off since I've had two unplanned ones."

"That's okay, I'll bring some work and you can wake me up when you get home." Gilly smiled brightly.

"Ah, so there is something to look forward to," Hugo thought. "You expecting anyone?" he asked when the doorbell rang.

"No. You?" Gilly followed him to the door.

"Nope, unless...Who is it?" Hugo asked.

"Clayton Bob Marsh and Tyler Ray Cain," Clayton said because he had the louder voice. "We're looking for Gilly La Farge."

"Go away!" Gilly yelled.

"Now, honey, be nice." Hugo opened the door and Tyler rushed past him to grab Gilly in his arms.

"I have been so worried about you!" he said with more drama than necessary. "Oh, hello," he said to Hugo. Tyler could obviously be worried about one man and flirt with another while he was at it.

Hugo ignored him and addressed his remarks to Clayton, "I remember you from the other night," he said.

"I don't exactly recall..."

Gilly pulled free of Tyler and got between Hugo and his friends. "He was the one with the shotgun," he said defensively.

Comfortingly, Hugo put his arms around him, but didn't say anything.

Tyler strolled around the room and examined what he could see of the bedroom, especially the bed, from there. "What a charming place you have, Mr. St. Victor," he drawled, moving to where Hugo would have a good view of him.

"Why, thank you, Mr. Marsh, is it?" Hugo asked.

"No, Cain, Tyler Cain. This is Clayton Marsh. I guess we were too pressed by worry and events to properly introduce ourselves," Tyler put out his hand, but withdrew it when Gilly seemed coiled to strike. "Hm...well..."

"Tyler, I do believe we've misunderstood this situation from the gitgo," Clayton said reasonably.

"Might not have if we could have actually talked to someone about it," Tyler said, never taking his eyes off Hugo, who was suppressing a smile behind Gilly's head. "I don't suppose you'd like a ride home, would you, Gilly?"

Gilly turned to look at Hugo, who said, "It's okay, sugar; I brung you here, I'll take you home."

"Well, I suppose we'll see you later, Gilly," Tyler drawled. "If you have time, that is."

"I'm free for dinner," Gilly said, more pacifically.

"Then come over at seven," Tyler said, giving his arm a warm squeeze. "I'll make something you like."

"Sorry to have bothered you, Mr. St. Victor," Clayton said, extending his hand.

"Oh, well, nice to know Gilly has good friends," Hugo said, shaking hands with both of them.

"We try, but do fuck up occasionally," Tyler admitted charmingly.

"I do have one request," Hugo said. "Keep him the hell out of the DDI, okay?"

"Oh, my dear man, it goes without saying," Tyler drawled and herded Clayton to the car. "Well," he said when they were underway. "If Gilly has a daddy complex, I don't stand a chance in hell, do I?"

"If he's happy, I'd leave it alone, Tyler," Clayton said neutrally, but thought that Tyler didn't have a chance against anyone who faced down psychotic bikers on a daily basis either.

Hugo drove Gilly home. "People will talk," he said when Gilly asked him to walk him to his dorm room.

"They can all go to hell," Gilly said. "Or get used to the idea." He leaned up and kissed him.

"Do you like to camp, Gilly?" Hugo asked out the blue.

"Very much."

"Well, since you have time off, let's go to Goldsworthy Park day after tomorrow and come back the next day," Hugo suggested. "Do you have time?"

"Sure!"

"All right then, we'll do it," Hugo said, kissing him good-bye. "I'll see you later."

"You will, you will," Gilly said and went into his room.

Aside from the occasional dinner at Saint-Saveur-en-Puisaye and the even rarer camping trip, Hugo and Gilly settled into each other's lives without a hitch. The main reason for this was that wrangling the Dipsy Doodle Inn kept Hugo very busy, and Gilly was a full-time student. Gilly had a key to Hugo's place and spent most of his nights there, except when he had an early morning class. But Gilly was in love and knew he'd still be in love even if he didn't spend every waking second with his beloved.

This worked well for Hugo, who appreciated Gilly's logical approach to their love affair. Hugo just accepted the fact that he was in love, as unexpected and miraculous as it was, and enjoyed the time he spent with Gilly as if they were the last hours of his life.

Overall, they were like all new lovers: happy as if they had good sense.

Because all their friends, especially Clayton, Tyler and Wombat, approved, there was no opposition to their romance from any quarter. Tyler was still smarting from being outmaneuvered by "Dad", as he referred to Hugo, but contented himself with two new boyfriends and a series of gallery shows in the late spring. He was, as usual, too self-absorbed to notice what Gilly was up to and, for a change, too busy as well. He did send Gilly an invitation to his big solo show at the Wilfred Canterbury Gallery, the most prestigious gallery in the region. It would be the biggest show of his career thus far, everyone who was anyone in the arts would be there, and he intended to make it a huge success.

"Will you come to this with me?" Gilly had asked very charmingly, holding out the invitation.

"Ah, Wilfred Canterbury," Hugo mused. "It's the top of the gallery food chain."

"Is it?" Gilly asked. "Will you go with me?"

"I'm not a big fan of these things, Gilly," Hugo said, neutrally.

"I know, but Tyler is my friend and I'd like you to be with me." Gilly could be a firm little thing when he really wanted something.

So Hugo gave in. He let Ig, Lad and Bruno know he'd be in late that Friday night.

"You hate easel painting, Hugo," Lad reminded him when they'd finished laughing at him.

"Yes, I loathe easel painting," Hugo agreed. "But I love Gilly and–"

"And he has you so wrapped around his little finger–" Bruno said.

"Well, there are worse places to be, I assure you," Hugo said loftily and smiled when they laughed.

"Is this the show at Wilfred Canterbury?" Ig asked in his quiet way. "I saw it in the paper, Hugo, it will be a mad house. More riot then art opening. Not that you're not used to riots, but the art types will be out in full force."

"I know. We'll go early and leave early," Hugo said. "I doubt I'll run into anyone who knows me. It's been a long time and the art scene has a short memory."

"People who are serious about art have long memories, Hugo," Bruno said.

Hugo shrugged. "I can't do anything about the past, guys."

"Is it invitation only?" Lad asked.

"It was in the paper, so I guess not," Ig told him.

"I have the evening off, maybe I'll swing by and take a few pictures," Lad said ever so casually. "Never know, might be able to sell them to the Gallery or the paper." He smiled at Hugo. "You wouldn't mind, would you?"

"Nah, you're still the best photographer on earth. If you want to waste your time taking pictures of a bunch of effete faggots and poseurs, well, that's up to you," Hugo said. "At least you still do it," he added, and went into his office.

"Man, he must be in love to go to an art opening," Bruno said when the door was closed. "Get some pictures, Lad."

"I surely will," Lad said, nodding.

The day of the Wilfred Canterbury show, Tyler was nervous enough to spend the day at the spa, getting a salt scrub, a massage, a facial and his hair deep conditioned and trimmed. It was expensive, but one of his new boyfriends was rich enough not to feel it. He would be feeling Tyler blowing him later in the evening, so he could pay for some spa indulgence.

Tyler looked so great when he got home, even Clayton noticed. "Thanks," he said, smiling at the appreciative whistle. "You are still going with me tonight, aren't you?" he asked.

"Sure, Tyler, don't worry 'bout a thing," Clayton said reassuringly. He would go with Tyler and then hand him off to whichever lover got him that night. He knew Tyler only leaned on him when he was feeling very insecure, and he was not only used to it, he welcomed it. After all, what were friends for?

Tyler grimaced and took his fully-conditioned and very fine self off to change into his good suit.

Hugo and Gilly were unfortunately delayed by a shooting in the Dipsy Doodle Inn parking lot. Or rather, Hugo was, because no amount of arguing with the new Police Commissioner would convince him not to close the DDI until further notice. It was the first fatal shooting at the DDI in ages and the new Commissioner would not listen to reason. Hugo just figured Wombat or the Mayor would explain it to him. Hopefully, the bar would reopen before the militia had to be called in to restore order again, like the last time the DDI was closed.

So, that being the case, and being as late as he was, Hugo told his crew to take the night off. Without changing from jeans and a work shirt, he drove to Gilly's dorm to pick him up. "Honey, it's been a long long afternoon," Hugo said, when Gilly, in a suit, frowned at his attire. "And there are more important things in life than clothes." He proceeded to tell him about the shooting and the bar closing, in hopes that Gilly would let him off the hook. The best-case scenario would be if they could go back to Hugo's and go to bed early.

"Oh...I'm sorry," Gilly said, hugging him. "We won't stay long, okay?"

Hugo hugged him back and gave him a long, lingering kiss. Plan B was to get them into Gilly's bed. Actually, any bed would do at that point.

But Gilly was as single-minded in this as he often was in pursuit of pleasure and Hugo, who knew a fight he couldn't win when he saw one, gave in graciously and drove to the gallery.

It was so packed they had to park several blocks away. This gave Hugo hope that Gilly, who hated crowds, would want to turn back. When he didn't, Hugo decided to hope that there would be so many people there, they wouldn't stay long. Like only twenty minutes, tops.

Gilly did hate crowds and only planned to make sure he said hello to Tyler and leave. Hugo was in complete agreement with this plan. On their way to Tyler, Gilly waved to Clayton, Monrov, Ig, Bruno, and at Lad, who was engrossed in taking pictures and didn't see him.

Hugo figured he was a quarter of the way home, but then Arturo Gonzaga, director of the Local Art Institute, hailed him. "Hugo! How long has it been?" he boomed loud enough for Tyler to look over at them.

Unfortunately all the art mavens around Tyler looked over at the same time. "Dear God," Eustace Respigi squeaked. "Is that Hugo St. Victor? I thought he was dead!"

This was the general feeling and, unfortunately, there was a general move away from Tyler to Hugo. "Who the fuck is Hugo St. Victor?" Tyler snarled at his agent, Ermingilde Anderlecht.

"Well, darling, he once was the hugest genius in environmental art on the planet," she said coolly. "About fifteen years ago he came to teach at the Art Institute, did some incredible work around here and then burned out. I never knew what happened after that."

"What work?" Tyler asked.

"He usually did huge work in remote locations, but here in town, he did the Al-Alta Gardens and spaces between the Theon Polychronopolus buildings," Ermingilde said. "I'll think up some more after I introduce myself to him. This is the closest I've ever been to him."

Tyler thought back on the two places she'd named. He'd been in both and had been deeply moved by the simplicity and power of the environment. Not that he'd ever mentioned this to anyone, nor had it ever occurred to him that someone had actually arranged those spaces. They were just there in a way he could never really come to terms with. Those spaces attracted photographers, but seemed to defy painters. At least Tyler and the painters he knew well enough to admit that they felt overwhelmed by the harmony of art and nature in those environments. "Shit," he thought. "I'm supposed to be the only genius in the room tonight."

But Tyler was a realist, and knew he'd have to be charming to Hugo or look extra foolish. On his way over, he thought he recognized a bartender or two from the DDI and the guy snapping pictures like mad, but wasn't sure.

There was quite a crowd around Hugo, who had his arm clamped around Gilly, when Tyler got to him. "My, how nice of you to come to my little show," Tyler drawled at Gilly, who was looking very uncomfortable in all the fuss around Hugo.

"I...I think it's very nice, Tyler," Gilly said over the noise. "I think so, but it's hard to see with all these people."

Tyler smiled sympathetically and tuned in on Hugo, watching him while he listened to Oslo Praetextatus raving about some huge installation in the Canadian north woods. "Nice turn out for you, Tyler," Hugo said evenly.

"So far," Tyler drawled. "I don't imagine they'll have to call the riot squad."

"No, I'm sure they're more than occupied elsewhere tonight," Hugo said mysteriously. He turned his attention back to Oslo, who was hugely rich and making him want to work again, just to see if he still had it.

Tyler knew when he was dismissed, but retreated graciously as that photographer was still snapping away. In the course of the evening he would learn that the photographer was Ladislaus Brindisi, who was famous for photographing Hugo St. Victor's environmental art. The two bartenders from the DDI were Bruno Segni and Ignatius Fronto, sculptors who spent their careers working with Hugo on whatever there was to work on. Those three still made art and were selling here and there, but they stuck with Hugo in hopes that he'd start working again.

As the evening wore on and Tyler gradually pieced together these facts from various people, he also got the feeling that Hugo might be working again soon. The buzz in the room certainly sounded like deal-making in progress. And huge deal making; Tyler's paintings were expensive, but Hugo's alterations of nature sounded like they were hugely expensive in personnel, materials and earth moving equipment, not to mention land to move all that earth on.

Tyler slumped a little. If Hugo was sucking up all the available money in the room, no one was going to buy his work. But this was not at all the case, every painting Hugo praised suddenly had a bidding war and, because Hugo was making a point of praising the ones without red sold stickers next to them, Tyler's show sold out that night.

Taking a quick tour of the sold out room, Clayton winked at Tyler, who smiled back graciously. Clayton laughed to himself that even totally upstaged, Mr. Tyler Ray Cain was the finest Southern lady he knew.

Gilly was silent on the way back to Hugo's apartment and Hugo was too tired to drive and question him at the same time. Making art deals was exhausting, however elated Ig, Bruno and Lad were about it. Realizing that he'd made several potential environment and installation deals in three hours was shocking and left him drained. So he let Gilly brood on whatever it was he was brooding on.

"You're awfully quiet," Hugo said when they were in his place.

Gilly looked over at him. "I didn't know you were famous," he said, drifting around the room like he'd never seen it before.

"I'm not really," Hugo said, waiting for his lover to gravitate back to him. "I did some decent work that's famous. Not the same thing actually."

"Why did you stop?" Gilly asked.

"I stopped seeing what was possible...all my ideas seemed contrived," Hugo admitted. "It was less painful not to work than to think up bad work."

"But tonight you sounded like you wanted to work again," Gilly said, moving in front of him.

"I might. I haven't felt this way in a long time."

"About art?" Gilly asked.

Hugo cupped Gilly's face in his palms. "About anything."

"Why?" Gilly leaned into the minimal embrace.

"Because I love you," Hugo said, drawing him close. "And that makes all things possible."

Chase

Anastasia Witchhazel

The Game had been played for longer than anyone remembered—although there was a little less ceremony involved in times gone by. Once upon a time, if you were a Rahbet unlucky enough to be spotted aboveground by a member of the Hauk clan, that was it for you, end of story, no matter the time of day or the season of the year. The Hauks were the Chasers and you were the Chased, whether you wanted to play or not. These days, there was an appointed place and time, and specially-chosen players (although there was still a pretty good chance that the Rahbets involved didn't really want to play). The game was a reminder of their violent mutual history, and, more importantly, that history was in the past.

None of that mattered a whole hell of a lot to Bryer at that moment, though.

Once every turn of the seasons, a handful of his people were chosen to play The Game; this year, Bryer's lot had come up. The rules were simple: you ran, the Hauk pursued. If you made it back home, to the underground city of Ber'Roe, you'd get to live. If not...

It was a fair price to pay, the Council of Elders had long preached. For just one handful of lives a year—lives that might not even actually be lost, if the Rahbets in question were smart and fleet—the Hauks promised not to attack any other Rahbet that came above-ground for the rest of the season. It didn't even matter to the Hauks if any of the Rahbets were caught or not; they would honor that vow, so long as The Game was played. Theoretically, the fact that the rest of one's family and friends would live another year should have been a solace for a Chased. About ten minutes into The Game, though, Bryer realized that wasn't the case, at least not for him.

"Why do they insist on us playing this stupid game anyway?" he wondered, not for the first time. The Hauks had otherwise given up hunting other hominid beings for food centuries past. They even raised livestock. "Why this one hunt still, once a year, then?"

The leaves above him rustled, though there was no wind; a Chaser, skimming the trees. His heart racing faster than his feet ever could, Bryer backed against a massive tree trunk and froze, listening with his great, long ears for the sound to pass him by. He waited a few long minutes after that, just to be certain. Just as he'd decided it was safe to move again, he heard another rustling, coming from behind him this time: one of his own people this time, moving on the ground. Another few seconds, and the other Rahbet—Jehna, a girl he'd known since before he could walk—came into sight.

Bryer barely kept from jumping out of his skin as a great, gray form hurtled through the trees above, tackling Jehna. Her scream almost pulled an answering cry from his own throat; he felt like the Hauk had gutted him before taking off with his friend. But his survival instinct was strong, and kept him silent. Knees weak, he slid against the tree to the forest floor. Grief closed his throat, making it even harder to breathe than his fear did. "What kind of sadists call this a game?" he wondered silently.

He watched a small, lone feather, a remnant of Jehna's captor, slowly settle to the ground. "Plumed sadists, I guess." He closed his eyes and bit his trembling knuckles in an effort to calm himself—and stifle the hysterical laughter that threatened to betray his position.

He felt a hand close around his arm; by the time he opened his eyes, he was being vaulted skyward, slung over the shoulder of a Chaser in flight. He thought a last, desperate farewell towards the diminishing ground, before his own terror knocked him senseless.

The scents of crushed berries and mint, coupled with the sound of boiling water, slowly roused Bryer.

"Smells good, Mother," he sighed happily, not quite ready to open his eyes. He rolled onto his back, and was vaguely puzzled by the rustle of leaves beneath him. A memory flashed on the inside of his closed lids, of Jehna, her eyes wide in fear as she was carried off by a Hauk—just like he himself had been, a mere moment later.

His instincts screamed for him to remain still, an ancient imperative. He held his breath, thinking to himself, *"They only like living flesh; if it thinks you've died..."*

A nudge to his shoulder startled him into inhaling with a sharp gasp. He still refused to open his eyes, though. He refused to look Death in the eye; he'd never claimed to be brave.

Tiny bits of heat struck his face; he flinched, but otherwise remained as he was. The pinpricks came again; this time he felt something wet roll down his face after. Rain? On top of everything else? Maybe the god of the sky was weeping for him in advance. As if a sky god would care about someone who spent most of his time below ground; the thought made him laugh in spite of himself.

A chuckle in his ear snapped his eyes wide open, taking in the vast, darkening sky. Despite his best efforts to the contrary, he felt compelled to look to his left, where a smile with wings awaited him.

He'd never seen anything more beautiful in his life.

"Idiot!" he hissed at himself. "That smile is going to *eat* you! It's not beautiful, it's deadly!"

"Can't it be both?" another part of him wondered—doubtless the part of him that was attached to his now-stirring member.

"Kwyck always warned me not to think with *that* head," he reminded himself, "but I didn't think he meant it so literally..."

Another splash to the face, and his attention snapped back to his captor. The Hauk held out a mug to him, the contents steaming. Bryer could tell from the strong aroma that it was a tea of some kind. "Poisoned? Wouldn't that take the fun out of killing me? Or eating me, for that matter?" He met the Hauk's eyes, baffled. He grew even more confused with what he found there—or rather, with what he didn't find.

This Hauk didn't seem the slightest bit menacing.

No deadly glint in the amber orbs that watched him, no savagery in the man's now-closed mouth. The tilt of his head was undeniably questioning, in an open, earnest manner. The Hauk gestured again with the cup, clearly meaning for Bryer to take it: he did, gingerly, his nerves braced for the hands that offered it to strangle him next.

His eyes trailed up the Hauk's well-muscled arms—not too thick, but nicely-defined. The chest they were attached to was equally well-honed...as were the abs...

When Bryer caught himself wondering about what was beneath the Hauk's breeches, he shook his head violently, causing his very large ears to swing about comically. Or at least Bryer assumed it was comically, as the Hauk suddenly chuckled. "What a nice laugh he has," Bryer thought before mentally chastising himself again.

"Why am I even still alive? And why are you offering me tea? For flavoring, or what?" He glanced at the large sizable pot boiling over the fire. "Too small to cook me in—unless he chops me up first." Bryer shuddered, the fine brown fur of his head, back, arms, and legs standing on end, while the bare skin of his torso was covered in goose bumps. His nipples grew hard, but he had to admit that might be for an entirely different reason.

The Hauk rose to its feet. Bryer followed the winged man with his eyes as the Chaser went to the other side of the fire and messed with something on the ground. Bryer tensed, trying to work up the nerve to bolt, but in the next moment, the Hauk turned back to him, a blanket slung over his arm.

Still smiling, the Hauk knelt before Bryer again, and wrapped the blanket around the Rahbet's shoulders. His hands brushed against Bryer's skin, his fur, and the Rahbet felt warmth flood through him, warmth he couldn't blame on the blanket, or even from the still-warm mug of tea he had clasped in both his trembling hands. His member ached; he was thankful for the cup, which served to keep those shaking hands from wandering down his body and offering the Hauk, seated so close to him now, a little pre-dinner entertainment.

His people were a highly sexed race, so much so that they would take touch, caresses, anytime, anywhere and from just about anyone, regardless of gender—sometimes even regardless of race. (The Elders said the gods figured some actual reproduction would have to come out of all that at some point.) But never in a million years did Bryer think he would feel anything but fear or hate in the presence of a Hauk. Well, maybe the hate and fear were still there, but without an obvious, imminent threat, the instincts to run and hide that had hammered at him so hard just moments past had apparently softened enough to let other biological urges take center stage. "Too bad *you're* not ready to soften," his thought testily at his cock. "Maybe if I think scary thoughts..." He tried to imagine the Hauk tearing into his flesh.

He stared at the Hauk, almost daring his captor to attack. Kind, questioning gold eyes met his. The image in his head degenerated into the Hauk giving his neck playful little nips, followed by soft kisses.

He swore. The Hauk looked concerned now. Somehow, that just angered Bryer.

"What do you want already?" he snapped, his voice croaking from either disuse or a remnant of his fear—probably both. "If you're going to eat me, eat me, for Sol's sake!"

The Hauk did that maddening head tilt. The winged man pursed his lips in a slight frown, then seemed to brighten. He tapped his chest. "Cyril. Cyril." He tapped again.

"You're introducing yourself?" Bryer stared at the Hauk incredulously. "'Hello, I'm Cyril, I'll be your murderer today.' Nice to meet you, Cyril! I'm Bryer, and I'll be your main course..."

Cocking his head at Bryer's ramblings, Cyril repeated the gesture. Sighing heavily, Bryer tapped his own chest and said his name, then repeated it.

Cyril beamed. He picked up another cup and took a sip, then said an unfamiliar word, gesturing to Bryer's cup as he did. He repeated the motions, speaking the word again.

Chase

"You want me to drink?" Bryer asked his captor. He copied the Hauk's motions. "Drink?" he said again.

"Drink," the Hauk answered, then repeated his own people's word for the action.

Puzzled that the Hauk should see the need to teach his dinner his own language, Bryer took another sip of the tea. He stared at the contents of the cup in surprise; it was actually quite good. There didn't seem to be much in the way of a leafy taste, save for the mint, but plenty of fruit. To be honest, he found he didn't miss the bitterness of the leaves his people were so fond of. It struck him as rather odd that a predatory people would bother with plants in their diet.

He was even more surprised when Cyril handed him a warm bit of cake, which had been resting near the fire. It tasted of star-tree fruit, nuts and fire-spice; his own mother couldn't have made it better! He began to entertain the notion that Cyril was just fattening him up again, until he saw the Hauk take a hearty bite of his own bit of cake.

Cyril licked his lips. Bryer was struck by an urge to taste Cyril's lips himself, to have the Hauk's tongue play napkin to his own face. "Oh, to be a cake and have you taste me," he thought, inwardly reciting a popular bit of Rahbeteen poetry. He turned away and shook his ears again, trying desperately to clear his head of such thoughts. It was too bad he couldn't hear the rush of the Quicksilver River; a nice cold dunking would do wonders for his current condition—mental and physical. Well, it would, provided the Hauk would *allow* it. Then again, given Cyril's behavior thus far, he just might, at that! But it was a moot conjecture, given that they had to be a goodly distance away from the river; the Rahbet's sensitive ears would have picked up the sound of it if it were even a mile away.

Bryer was saved from his own inner ramblings when a soothing piping caught his attention. His oversize ears swiveled towards the sound a moment before the rest of his head did; when his eyes finally reached the source, they found a two-branched flute being expertly manipulated by Cyril's deft mouth and fingers. Beautiful as the music was, Bryer could think of better uses for the Hauk's apparently talented digits.

The melody and the warm crackling of the fire lulled Bryer's eyes closed. His last thoughts as he drifted off were of how funny it was that he had woken up fearing the Hauk's mouth, but now wanted nothing more than to feel it against his flesh.

The sounds that woke Bryer the next day were considerably less melodic.

He snapped to attention, swaying as he rushed to his feet. Holding a two-foot baton in one hand, Cyril was yelling something unintelligible; it took Bryer a moment to realize the words weren't aimed at him, and that he wasn't seeing double. Another Hauk, also armed with a baton, stood in the circle of their camp, his feathers just a tad darker than Cyril's, but his face, scarred over one eye and twisted in a sneer, was considerably less attractive.

Oh wait, Cyril's face was twisted in a sneer too. "Hmm. Not as pretty as last night but still better looking than this new one. I suppose if I had to choose which Hauk I wanted to be eaten by..."

Bryer's mind snapped free of the last tendrils of sleep. The Hauks were too busy threatening each other to pay him any notice! He turned and ran, not daring to look back. Despite his sizable ears, which were longer than his forearms, all he could hear as he ran was the thunder of his heart and, after a minute, his ragged breathing. He concentrated on the sounds, trying to keep an even rhythm.

He was so intent on the sound that he failed to notice the strange, red log on the ground until he tripped over it. Blood filled his mouth when his jaw struck the ground, causing his teeth to champ his tongue. The breath knocked from him, it took him a moment to gather his wits and scramble to his feet. When he finally looked up again, he was blasted in the face by foul, hot air that made his eyes water.

Stepping back instinctually, he lost his footing again, this time landing heavily on his back. Luckily the ground was soft; his head hurt when it connected with the dirt, but not enough to do any permanent damage.

"So where did that cracking sound come from, if not my skull?"

When the stars faded from his eyes, he could see nothing but red above him. He blinked his eyes, trying to clear his vision, until he realized it was already clear. The ceiling of red moved skyward, growing smaller; it was the underside of a scaly hiila's jaw! The sickening crack had been the sound of its massive teeth clapping together on empty air.

The creature was looking about, trying to figure out where he'd gone—it couldn't look down to see him. It moved forward, just barely missing stepping on him with a massive clawed foot. Hearing another crack, muffled this time, he quickly rolled out from under it before its hind legs could follow.

The muffled sound wasn't the hiila's teeth this time, but the smack of a wooden baton connecting with its snout. Cyril jumped back, the giant lizard's razor-filled maw missing him by only millimeters. Cyril cried out something as the lizard swooped in again. He held out his baton, shoving it in the beast's drooling mouth. The hiila bit down, applying pressure to the center of the wooden cylinder with its tongue; the wood snapped easily. Cyril tried to dodge while it was distracted, but he wasn't fast enough; the great lizard chomped down on his wing, and used one heavy foot to then pin him to the ground, its teeth slipping along his flesh and feathers.

Bryer didn't even think about what to do, his sense of self-preservation pre-empted by another: protect your comrades. Rahbets often stomped their large feet to make booming sounds, communicating over sizable distances with a staccato beat. He stomped one foot now, loud and repeatedly, drawing the attention of the lizard.

Cyril was hanging limp from the creature's jaw. Despite its immense size, the creature had a small brain; attracted to the sound, as predators tend to be, it forgot all about the motionless meat in its mouth in favor of chasing live prey. As it swiveled, with its claw still heavy on Cyril's back, its teeth slipped free of the wing.

Bryer had never been a very good runner—his lungs weren't sound enough—but he'd always been an excellent jumper. When the hiila made a lunge for him, he sprang skyward and landed astride the creature, just behind its head. As it swung its head around, trying to reach him (it wasn't bright enough to think of dislodging him), he wrapped his arms and legs tightly around its long neck.

The monster had been roaring the entire time of the attack, its harsh growls grating against Bryer's large and sensitive ears. Now a new screech joined in, one that instilled Bryer with a sort of blind terror. He was on his feet and running down the hiila's backside before he knew it. The hiila started moving too—in the opposite direction. Bryer stumbled, falling from the monster's back, landing heavily on his left shoulder. He rolled away and backed up against a tree stump. From there he watched, horrified, as the beast charged Cyril, who was also back against a tree—a very large, full-grown one that was easily twice as wide as the hiila!

Cyril ducked at the last possible moment. Bryer wasn't sure if the subsequent sound was that of the hiila's jaw breaking or the tree splintering. The beast fell where it stood—right on top of the Hauk. Without thinking, Bryer ran—straight for the beast's head!

All he could see was Cyril's hand, covered in blood. His own, or the monster's?

"Does it matter?" his sense of self-preservation asked. "*Run*, idiot! Before another Hauk finds you!"

There was a moan; Bryer's heart raced for a moment, until he realized it was coming from beneath the hiila, not the beast itself.

"I can't just leave him; he saved my life!"

Or he'd just saved his dinner...

"If that's true, then why didn't he sup on me last night?"

If Hauks didn't eat the Rahbets they catch, then what *did* they do with them? And wouldn't Kwyck have come back if he'd lived?

Thinking of his beloved elder brother, who'd been chosen for the Game one turn past and never made it back home, rekindled a familiar ache in his chest. Kwyck had been more than Bryer's brother; he'd been his best friend, had taught him everything he knew that had ever meant something to him and had never complained about Bryer's endless questions. When Kwyck hadn't come back, Bryer had felt as though the world had ended.

Kwyck had been their parents' first child (as it was rare for a Rahbet to have more than one in their first litter). And since all of Bryer's littermates had died during a particularly vicious outbreak of the Shudders, Bryer and Kwyck had developed a special bond that Bryer had never been able to duplicate with his younger sibs. He received little comfort from his parents, who had, by necessity, turned the bulk of their attentions to their numerous younger children. Sure, Bryer had other friends, like Jehna. (Jehna! He'd almost forgotten her—did she still live?) But friends didn't live in your house: they didn't hold your hand through the night when you were sick, or fix you cocoa when you'd come home after a bad day, or help you with your hangover, or cover for you when you were out past curfew. No, Kwyck would have come home if he were alive; he would never have abandoned Bryer, even if Bryer was old enough to take care of himself now.

He didn't know why this Hauk had been so kind, but Bryer would be a fool to believe Cyril wished him anything but ill.

A sweep of the hiila's long tail literally knocked the Hauk from his thoughts.

Scrambling backwards, Bryer's fingers closed on half of Cyril's baton, its broken side now wickedly sharp. He pushed himself to his feet, fist tight around the short, wooden shaft. He slowly edged back, eyes on the stirring monster, which rolled onto its side.

A cry of pain from Cyril stayed him; the Hauk was free but too injured to move, and the beast's thrashing forelegs were dangerously close to shredding him.

Not allowing himself to debate whether he was being a hero or an idiot this time, Bryer went around to the beast's backside, following its spine to its head. Once there, he found that its snout was horribly broken and bloodied, its eyes screwed shut in obvious pain. He felt a stab of pity, but kept to his plan; what he was about to do was a kindness, after a fashion. When it lifted its head in its thrashing, he scrambled under it. As it brought its own skull forcefully downward, in mindless agony, Bryer brought the pointed stick upwards and braced himself. The stick went through its eardrum, deep into its skull, the force driving him to his knees. It stiffened, then relaxed, finally dead. The sudden full weight of it pinned Bryer. He struggled, but he couldn't hold the head up and crawl out from under it at the same time.

And then suddenly the head was lifted off of him. He panicked a moment, thinking perhaps the thing wasn't dead after all. A sudden, strained, unintelligible word erased his fear; the Hauk was doing the lifting! He quickly rolled over and crawled free.

Cyril collapsed as soon as Bryer was free, crying out in agony as the motion jarred his injured wing.

The sound tore at Bryer's heart—but it didn't stop him from walking away. In fact, it encouraged him.

Their camp was a mess when Bryer returned to it, but the other Hauk, the one that had attacked Cyril, was—happily—absent. He prayed no one else would come while he gathered the spilled supplies and stuffed them into Cyril's pack. The fire had died; he found a spark box near it and shoved it in after the other supplies. The sand around the pit was well stirred from the Hauks' fight; as an afterthought, Bryer found a branch and smoothed it, then smoothed the trail behind him. His own people would never come looking for him; no point in inviting any other Hauks to follow them either.

Aching, he made his way back to the hiila kill as quick as he could—which wasn't very fast, now that the adrenaline had passed and his injuries began to truly pain him. It occurred to him once that he didn't have to go back to Cyril, that he could go home, but before the thought was even finished, he knew he wouldn't do it. He'd been certain yesterday that he wouldn't live to see today. All he really wanted out of his life *now* was *answers*, and he knew he would never find them back in Ber'Roe.

The Hauk lay on his stomach, one wing resting up against the hiila's back, while the other was stretched out along the ground. In the noonday sun, Bryer could see that the already dark gray skin (although it was a bit paler now than it had been before the battle) of Cyril's back was nearly black with bruises from the hiila's foot. The wing lying on the ground looked grotesquely mangled, with bared muscle and bone in the gashes where the hiila's teeth had ripped through the feathers and skin. At least the bones, by some miracle, didn't seem broken, but an awful lot of blood was pooling on the ground beneath the gray pinions.

Bryer dropped the pack unceremoniously on the ground, not caring if the small pot within squashed the cakes or broke anything else within it.

He hurried over to the fallen Hauk, then knelt carefully by the injured wing, so as not to bump it. Hand shaking, he brushed the long, dark, feathery hair from Cyril's brow. The Hauk's skin was cool to the touch; panicked, Bryer felt for his pulse. It was there, but faint. Bryer didn't let himself consider the fact that that was probably for the best. Quite the contrary: after laying both the blankets from the pack gently over the Hauk's backside, he scrambled about to gather wood and clear a spot near the hiila carcass for a fire.

The stench of the thing was horrid, but Bryer figured that worked to their advantage; what other predator would go anywhere near a hiila? Plus the massive beast's body would shield them somewhat from the cold night winds. And though the very notion made his stomach flop quite unpleasantly, if he had to, he could carve the beast up to feed to Cyril.

Once the fire was going, he found another problem, though: no water, save that which was in Cyril's canteen. The Hauk must have flown off to fill the pot and brought it back to the camp while Bryer was unconscious. And yet he didn't even tie Bryer up?...He'd puzzle over it later; at that moment, he was more concerned with deciding whether he should use some of the sparse water to clean Cyril's wounds. The river was at least a few hours away; he couldn't move Cyril that far, but was reluctant to leave the Hauk alone, defenseless, for so long.

He reached out absently with a hand and leaned against a sapling. He yelped when something cold and wet struck his ear. He reached up and touched his ear; nothing there but water. He looked up at the tree. It had cup-shaped leaves. A vague memory of a camping trip with Kwyck came back to him: "If you're far from the river and out of water, check the leaves." Bryer shook the tree again, lightly; more water sprinkled down on him. Grinning, he grabbed the pot and did his best to relieve the sapling and its nearby siblings of the water weighing down their leaves. It took a while, but he managed to fill the pot.

After setting it near the fire, he searched through Cyril's bag and, happily, found what he was looking for: a bar of soap and a small medical kit with bandages and sealant.

Grimly, he set to the task of cleaning Cyril's wing, then gluing the wounds closed with the sealant. Cyril stirred a little in the beginning, but that was all. Bryer was glad that Cyril was unconscious through the ordeal, but worried that it meant the Hauk might never wake up...

Knowing Cyril would need protein to replenish his blood (and, by now, being somewhat desensitized to the sight of blood and smell of the beast), Bryer set to the task of making a broth from a bit of the hiila's flesh. He hoped he was doing it all right; Rahbets were not meat-eaters, so he could only guess at best.

Leaving the broth to simmer, Bryer checked on his patient. Cyril's skin seemed less pallid, but still not as dark as it had seemed before—but did he really remember what the color was like before? Cyril seemed a *little* warmer; was he warm enough for a Hauk? Kwyck had told him that when anyone, a Rahbet or any other animal, was severely injured, you had to keep them warm. Surely that was true of Hauks too? But he already had a fire going and both blankets thrown over the man; how could he make the Hauk any warmer?

Kwyck's voice played in his mind, another scrap of memory from one of the many lessons in above-ground survival his brother had given him: "If you're out in the cold, the best way to warm up isn't with a fire, but your own body heat. Wrap yourself in a blanket, but don't keep it tight; make a pocket of air between you and the fabric. Getting naked first is the most effective method. In a little while, your body will heat the air trapped by the fabric."

Bryer looked at the Hauk, pursing his lips. The way Cyril was positioned, the blankets couldn't be cocooned around his spread wings, couldn't trap the air. He'd have to reposition him—and the Hauk was both taller and heavier than Bryer! But there was nothing for it, not unless he was willing to just let the Hauk die. Somehow that wasn't even an option to him anymore. He wasn't going to strip the man, though; that was just asking for trouble! Cyril's already-shirtless state would hopefully be enough...

Bryer laid out one of the blankets for Cyril to lie on, then knelt in front of the Hauk's head. Gingerly as he could, he slipped his hands under Cyril's chest and began to lift, then, when he'd gotten the Hauk off the ground enough, swiveled his hands so that he was pushing instead. He got the Hauk upright, so that Cyril was essentially kneeling—and then the man began to fall backward. Bryer fell painfully to his knees, making a mad grab for the Hauk, wrapping his arms around Cyril's chest and pressing it against his own.

A flash of heat coursed through Bryer as the Hauk's nipples rubbed against his. He let out a moan that was half desire, half dismay at that desire.

As if in answer, the Hauk let out a moan of his own.

Bryer's heart picked up its pace. On the one hand, the sound Cyril had made showed that there was still some life left in him. On the other, it might mean he was about to wake up, and without a common language, how was Bryer supposed to explain their current relative positions?

He carefully got to his feet, trying to keep the Hauk, who was still on his knees, at least upright, preferably leaning back. Unfortunately, at some point Cyril was once again leaning slightly *forward*, instead. His lolling head, of course, came forward as well, hitting Bryer squarely in the manhood. The Rahbet yelped and almost dropped Cyril; the act of catching the Hauk just pressed the man's skull into Bryer's groin even more.

Bryer quickly pushed him away, holding him by the shoulders. Cyril started to sag. Bryer quickly sank to his knees again, catching him. The motion jarred Cyril awake, his gold eyes snapping open as he cried out in pain.

"I'm sorry!" Bryer yelped, still holding tight.

For a long moment, they stayed like that, eyes locked, with Bryer's arms embracing the Hauk, and Cyril's hands reflexively gripping the Rahbet's shoulders. Their faces were barely more than an inch apart; Bryer could feel the Hauk's breath dance across his lips. Every cell in the Rahbet's body seemed to catch fire at once. His cock instantly strained against his breeches; he feared it would break right through the material!

The Hauk doubled over with a sudden spasm and cry of agony, effectively doused the Rahbet's raging libido. When Cyril was able to straighten up again, Bryer maneuvered himself under one of the man's arms and lifted him to his feet. Waiting a moment for the next wave of the Hauk's pain to pass, he slowly led him over to the waiting blanket. Cyril, either anticipating what the Rahbet wanted or simply wanting it himself, began to kneel, and, with Bryer's help, settled himself on his back, wings folded in as best as he could manage, so that Bryer could wrap the other blanket around him.

By then, Bryer had decided (or hoped, anyway) that the broth was ready, and poured some into a cup he'd found in Cyril's pack. The Hauk seemed almost eager; he surprised Bryer by requesting another cupful, then another, seeming to grow stronger with each one, eventually sitting fully upright and managing to feed himself. The pot empty and the Hauk's appetite finally sated, it wasn't long before Cyril was fast asleep.

His patient well on the mend, the stress of the day caught up with the Rahbet all at once, dropping him into an exhausted stupor on the bare forest floor.

Bryer woke shivering, the untended fire having gone out long before and the sun having set an hour past, taking its warmth with it. He got to his feet and restarted the fire, then, tucking his hands under his arms, walked over to check on Cyril.

The Hauk was awake, his gold eyes reflecting the friendly warmth of the fire. He lifted the blanket, gesturing, it seemed, for Bryer to join him under the covers.

The Rahbet's libido flared to life. Fists clenched tight, biting his tongue, Bryer struggled to keep it in check as he knelt near the blanket, but not on it. The hurt, confused look in Cyril's eyes made Bryer silently curse their language barrier.

"You're hurt! I don't want to cause you any pain!" he pleaded, gesturing to Cyril's wing.

Understanding lit Cyril's eyes. He shook his head, smiling, and sat up. He took hold of Bryer's hand. The Rahbet's breath caught in his throat, a wave of desire threatening to overwhelm him. Caught up in it, he didn't resist when the Hauk made him place his hand against the injured wing.

Cyril didn't cry out. Not only that, but Bryer couldn't feel the wounds under his hand. Granted, he had done a more than capable job of sealing the wounds, but the feathers were back and lay perfectly against the skin! He crawled closer—maybe it was just the lack of proper lighting, but the wing looked as though it had never been injured! As if to prove it, Cyril stretched the wing out with ease, not flinching in the slightest.

Cyril pointed to the hiila carcass, then to his wing.

Bryer glanced between the Hauk and the remains of the beast several times in disbelief. The broth had done *that*? He vaguely remembered Kwyck telling him once that lizards had amazing regenerative abilities, but this was ridiculous!

While he was staring at the hiila again, Cyril took advantage of the distraction and kissed him gently on the cheek, then brushed his other cheek lightly with the backs of his fingers. Bryer shivered, skin flushed, eyes drooping closed, lips parted in need. Cyril's fingers slipped behind his neck, thumb caressing his jaw. The Hauk's lips brushed against his own and paused, barely touching, but setting Bryer's nerve endings ablaze all the same. When Cyril drew away, the Rahbet whimpered, opening his eyes.

Cyril leaned back, his once-injured wing folded back behind him, out of the way. He held the cover blanket open in invitation once more, revealing that his breeches had at some point vacated the space.

Apparently the Hauk knew about that particular survival technique, too.

This time Bryer didn't hesitate, but hurriedly slipped in beside the Hauk, barely able to hold his hunger in check. Cyril leaned over him and pulled the blanket over them both, his wings holding the fabric up enough to create a pocket of air. He laid a hand on Bryer's stomach, the caress of his fingers causing the Rahbet's cock to beg for attentions that the Hauk wasn't willing to give—*yet*.

The Hauk was only slightly more forceful this time as he brushed his mouth against Bryer's again, capturing the Rahbet's lower lip between his own. He pulled away, and dove in again, going for the upper lip. He kissed the corner of Bryer's mouth, then moved to his jaw, then down his neck, each feather-light touch causing something to flare beneath Bryer's skin, like a spark box being ignited. The feeling intensified when Cyril began to draw his hand across Bryer's abdomen in little circles. The slender digits came tantalizingly close to the waistband of the Rahbet's breeches, then swept it up along Bryer's side. Bryer gasped and arched his back, baring his neck to the Hauk's slowly deepening kisses. He gasped again when Cyril brought his tongue into play, leaving a wet trail from his clavicle to his jaw, then blowing on it, a playful flash of cold in the midst of the heat they were creating. He moaned appreciatively as Cyril brought his hand up higher, brushing a nipple with his thumb. Cyril silenced him by capturing his mouth again. Bryer parted his lips in invitation, and Cyril gladly accepted, slipping his tongue between them, probing, tasting.

Bryer grew bolder, no longer willing to just lie there and be the Hauk's "victim." Reaching upward, his fingers stroked Cyril's chest, raising the nipples into hard peaks, then trailed around behind the Hauk, gently learning how the wings met the skin and muscles of the winged man's back. Bryer's hands trailed down, circling the Hauk's tight ass, then snuck to the front, circling around the Hauk's hardening member without ever actually touching it. His heart skipped erratically every time the Hauk moaned and sighed into his mouth, in a way it had never done with any other lover.

Cyril's own hand continued to caress and tease, slipping a little further below the waistline with each pass, until his hand suddenly swooped in, sliding down Bryer's rock-hard member, cupping it. The Rahbet arched his back again, thrusting hard into the Hauk's hand. When he relaxed, Cyril withdrew his hand, then undid the fastenings on the Rahbet's breeches. He slid his hand in sideways, caressing Bryer's hip, then pulling that side down a little. Bryer lifted his hips, giving Cyril room to slowly work the fabric down. Cyril moved in front of him, using both hands, caressing Bryer's buttocks in the process, fingers coming maddeningly close to the Rahbet's entrance. Once his breeches were past his ass, Bryer, getting impatient now, lifted his legs so Cyril could pull them free.

But Cyril, it seemed, wasn't ready to give him release yet. The Hauk lay half atop Bryer as before, pulling the blanket over them again. Cyril then resumed the fiery kisses, this time stroking Bryer's cock with feather-light, teasing caresses, his fingers trailing down the Rahbet's thighs. Bryer parted his legs expectantly and raised his hips for easy access. The Hauk positioned himself over the Bryer, his erection brushing gently against the Rahbet's own. Both males shuddered, pleasure shooting through Bryer. Cyril rocked his hips, causing their members to rub against each other again and again; Bryer enjoyed the electric jolt of each contact, and hoped Cyril did too. Slowly the Hauk lay himself against Bryer, until their groins were pressed hard together, and began to rock his hips once more.

While Bryer enjoyed what was being done to him, for a moment the Rahbet thought maybe the Hauk wasn't familiar with the way males made love among his kind. Was this all Cyril knew to do? Or was the Hauk afraid of hurting him?

"*Please!*" he begged, and by the warm look in the Hauk's eye, he could tell the man understood what he wanted. Bryer held himself open.

Cyril poised himself above his lover with both arms; it only took a moment for his swollen member to find the Rahbet's hole. Slowly, he lowered himself down, until the tip of his shaft pushed past the entrance; then he quickly hilted himself between Bryer's thighs, his need to be buried within the Rahbet as anxious now as Bryer's own need to be filled.

They lay like that for a long moment, then another, just enjoying the feel of each other. When they finally did move, the Hauk's movements were small and hesitant at first. Bryer, though, no stranger to this sort of lovemaking, began to thrust upwards insistently. Cyril took the hint, increasing his thrusts in kind.

The cover blanket fell off.

They didn't need it.

Bryer didn't ask where they were going. Not that Cyril could have answered, but point in fact, Bryer didn't much care. All he knew was he was happier than he ever remembered being. The Hauk could kill him tonight, tomorrow, in the next ten seconds, and it would be fine with him, because the Hauk wanted him. His parents had never really seemed to want him as their child. Kwyck had wanted him as a brother, but Kwyck was gone. Bryer'd had plenty of lovers, but they didn't want him, just his cock—and any cock would have done. He had friends, but he wondered now if they were his friends because they wanted to be, or simply because it was convenient? Did any of them mourn him now?

But when Cyril looked at him, he knew Cyril wanted him, had chosen him. He could have had any of the Rahbet players, but it was Bryer who he'd abducted. He'd defended his claim on Bryer against another Hauk and a hiila, had even nearly lost his life against the latter. And when they made love, Cyril was the only one who'd considered Bryer's own needs, the only one who wanted to be with him, beyond the satisfaction of lust, and hold him after. So long as Cyril had that warm look in his eye when he struck the killing blow, the look that made his heart melt, Bryer would die a happy Rahbet.

Truth be told, though, he rather doubted Cyril actually wanted him dead, so the question of where they were going was a good one. But Bryer hadn't cared enough to asked it—and Cyril wouldn't have been able to answer him anyway.

Four days later, Bryer was able to answer the question himself.

The trees had gradually been growing thicker, taller, and more spread apart the further they walked; the change was so subtle, Bryer hadn't really noticed the difference between the woods near Ber'Roe and where he was now until the last leg of their journey. In fact, he was literally standing right under the Hauk city of Kanno'Pii before he even noticed it. He would have gone on not noticing it, if not for Cyril stepping up to a tree, pressing a gold button embedded in the bark and looking skyward while he waited. Bryer followed his gaze and noticed that the light coming from very high overhead wasn't sunlight: it was too orderly to be natural. And the darkness between the circles of luminance was too thick to be made of branches.

An opening appeared in the tree; Bryer quickly realized it was an elevator. Intrigued, he stepped in, Cyril following after. Once upon a time, he would have been scared out of his wits; he supposed that Bryer, the one who'd expected to be eaten by a Hauk that first night out, had been "killed" by the hiila. Once upon a time, he would have been proud for conquering his fear; that Bryer had been killed, after a fashion, by Cyril. Now he just took things as they came, and accepted—even enjoyed—them for what they were.

They were met by a female Hauk in white robes. She seemed weak with relief to see them, hugging Cyril tight and then doing the same to Bryer. Cyril called her Ayleen.

Cyril seemed oddly expectant as Ayleen led them through the paths of the Hauk city, glancing almost nervously over his shoulder again and again. Bryer grinned, squeezing his hand reassuringly. It wasn't a false reassurance; he really did like Kanno'Pii, with its towering "buildings" (hollowed-out trees, mostly, but with additions added here and there) and delicate, leafy décor. The true sunlight, shining through the leaves overhead, gave everything a sort of gold-and-green glow. He gave a friendly smile to the Hauk citizens who rushed by, going about their daily routines.

He almost called out cheerfully, "Hello, I'm your dinner, nice to meet you!" but managed to stifle it.

Ayleen led them to a tree building that seemed much bigger than the others. Indeed, when they passed through its massive doors, they entered a great hall, one easily as big as any Ber'Roe had to offer. There were benches covering three-quarters of the hall. The floor slanted downwards, affording everyone a decent view of a dais at the far end. The seats were all empty, but the dais held several figures.

Bryer's eyes widened; he didn't know why it should shock him, considering his own circumstances, but at least two of the figures were undeniably Rahbeteen. His shock only grew as he got closer to them.

They were Jehna...and Kwyck!

His heart was a battleground, with relief and a sense of betrayal as the opponents. Speaking a mile a minute as she ran and threw her arms around him, Jehna seemed oblivious to his inner struggle—although she could have just been so happy to see him that she simply didn't care about anything else. It didn't really matter; she wasn't the one he felt betrayed by.

One of the other Hauks said things that seemed to be a welcome of some sort; he didn't care. He only had eyes, had thoughts, for two beings. One was Cyril, who kept casting alternating nervous and hopeful glances at his lover. For the first time since the battle with the hiila, Bryer began to question the Hauk's reason for capturing him. The other being had the bulk of his attention, though. Seeing that Bryer was making no move to come closer, the other Rahbet made the walk instead, the room silencing with his first step. It remained so, even after he halted, half a foot away. The silence was a living being, waiting expectantly for its dismissal. Bryer wasn't feeling terribly accommodating.

"Hello, brother," Kwyck said tentatively.

Bryer didn't bother stating the obvious, that his brother was alive. Instead, he grabbed his brother's hand, pulling him towards the door and proclaiming, "You're going to let everyone know the truth!" He might be small, but at that moment he felt as fierce as a hiila: just let some Hauk try to stop them!

Kwyck pulled his hand free. "No. They can never know, Bry. Do you really think I would have stayed away all this time, would have let you go on thinking I was dead, if it wasn't necessary?"

Bryer's eyes snapped to Cyril, all of his affection for the Hauk suddenly smothered by smoldering rage. "Why?" A year of grief and loneliness hadn't been banished by Cyril, only buried, as the Hauk had buried himself inside Bryer. Now the sadness burst forth like the climax Cyril had brought him to, again and again—only not in so satisfying a fashion. "Why are you keeping us prisoners here, if not to feed on us?"

The Hauk was obviously distraught, knowing his lover was angry but having neither the words to understand the Rahbet nor to explain himself.

"We're not prisoners," Jehna snapped. "We chose not to leave."

"But Kwyck just said—"

"You can return," Kwyck corrected, "if you do so within the next few days. So can Jehna—"

"Hell no!" Jehna said hotly.

"...but if you *do* leave, your memories of here and your time with Cyril would have to be erased, by order of the Elders. Our people cannot know the truth about The Game," he reiterated.

Bryer stared at Kwyck with a mix of utter confusion and disbelief. "And what *is* the truth? That the Elders know we're not eaten, but let us go on thinking we'll die if we're caught? That they let our families think we die—like I th-thought..." he began to choke on tears.

Kwyck's own eyes were less than dry as he took his brother in his arms. Bry tried to pull away at first, then wrapped his arms around his brother tightly.

"Do you remember those little pet myyse you used to have, Bry?" Kwyck asked.

Bryer pulled back but didn't let go, eyeing his brother oddly. "They were fodder for your miniature hiila first, if I remember."

Kwyck smiled. "Yes, and what happened when the hiila died?"

Bryer shrugged. "You gave the two that were left to me." He thought for a moment. "They bred like crazy—I had too many to feed after a while. They started attacking each other. Finally mom put her foot down and told me to just let them die."

"Lucky for us the Elders aren't like mom," Kwyck said dryly.

Bryer cocked his head in a questioning manner not unlike Cyril's.

"Bry, what do you think happened when the Hauks stopped hunting us, like when the hiila was no longer around to hunt those myyse?"

Bryer's eyes filled with horrified understanding.

"Our people refuse to leave Ber'Roe and come above ground, but they also refused to stop having sex, and refused to use any sort of birth control. Food grew scarce, fights broke out; the Elders had to do something. So what better way to convince people to leave than to tell them it's for a noble cause, that they're doing it to protect their loved ones? The Elders get to lay the blame for the losses at the Hauks' feet, and the people go on trusting them."

Bryer felt like he'd been sucker punched. All this time they'd been lied to, had lived in fear of the Hauks for no reason. "So...s-so we'll sneak back and just explain everything to everyone! If they know it's safe, maybe some of them will be willing to come here anyway!"

Kwyck raised a brow. "Would *you* have come willingly? Even if you knew for certain that I was alive?"

"Yes!"

The elder Rahbet ruffled his brother's hair affectionately. "Well, maybe you would—you're braver than most. But I think the Elders are right—most people would prefer to let 'someone else' leave, and then no one would go. Maybe someday that will change, but for now... Listen, little brother, if you try to go back without a memory wipe, the Elders will have you killed. They can't afford to have the people lose faith in them."

Bryer shuddered. What *else* were his people capable that he never would have imagined of them? Then again, in the past few days he'd done things *he* never would have dreamt of. He glanced at his Hauk lover, feeling desire stir again. It really wasn't so surprising that the Elders had needed to take such drastic measures; when the urge for sexual pleasure came on, it was very hard to stop for niceties like contraceptives, much less curb the desire altogether! He did his best to cast his lust aside now, though, focusing on what his brother was—and wasn't—telling him.

"So you...you liked it so well here that you didn't want to come back to Ber'Roe, huh? To me..."

Kwyck cursed. "If I had, we'd both be stuck there! You can't tell me you were all that happy there, Bry! So I arranged for *you* to be in the lottery for choosing the Chased this year."

"*You* arranged...?!" Bryer felt the floor shift under him; it took him a moment to realize it was him, and not the tree, that was moving. Cyril grabbed his shoulders from behind to steady him. Bryer was torn between a fierce need to have the Hauk do more and the anger that made him want to pull away. He turned his accusing eyes on his brother. "You could have gotten me killed!"

Kwyck scowled. "Hauks don't eat us anymore!"

"No, but hiilas sure as hell do!" Bryer said through clenched teeth.

Kwyck, Jehna, and even Ayleen paled.

"So that's why you were so late," Kwyck whispered, settling heavily on one of the benches.

"And the other Hauk that attacked Cyril probably slowed us up," Bryer added, muttering.

Kwyck nodded, sighing. "It doesn't happen often, since there are usually more Chased than Chasers, but every now and then a Chaser who fails to catch one of us will try to take a Rahbet from its original captor."

Bryer had a new thought, one that made his insides twist unpleasantly. "Did you also 'arrange' for Cyril here to be my Chaser?"

Cyril jumped at the sound of his name, but didn't let go.

Kwyck smiled wanly. "No, I didn't—that was either Fate's Design or pure dumb luck!"

Bryer's eyes narrowed. "Why should it be anything, if you didn't arrange it?"

Jehna laughed. "Oh gods, it's so obvious, Bry, that you two got cozy while you were out there!"

Bryer nose twitched. "Why's it obvious?"

She giggled. "Because most of us had to be tied and carried by our Chasers, and were about ready to crawl out of our skins for want of a good tumble by the time we got here! But you, you just strolled on in here on your own two feet, not bound, with that big ol' satisfied grin on your face!"

Bryer blushed. "So what's that have to do with anything?" he asked defensively. "You still got here, right? Bound or not! Aren't the chances that I still have gotten here with another Chaser about the same as my chances were with Cyril?"

"Probably," Kwyck conceded. "The dumb luck comes in because the Chaser who did choose—and catch you—just happened to a)," he ticked off a finger, "be attracted to males, b) be attracted to Rahbets, c) be attracted to you in particular, and, most importantly, d) be someone you could be attracted to in turn, enough so that you could get past the fear he might eat you."

"Is there a point to all this?"

"He's just saying that it's something of a miracle that you could be captured by the one Chaser you could—and did—end up mated to!" Jehna snapped, exasperated.

Bryer goggled at her. "What do you mean, mated to?"

Kwyck eyed him warily. "I don't know how to break this to you, Bry, but...well, most Hauks don't have casual sex—they mate for life."

Bryer quickly turned to Cyril, eyes wide. The Hauk's eyes were both frightened and hopeful, and held the same warmth they'd always carried.

"He *did* choose me," Bryer breathed in wonder, mostly to himself. "He chose *me*!"

But there was still one niggling doubt.

"That other Hauk...why would he want to capture me if the Hauks don't eat us? Why do they even play The Game at all?"

"Ah. That other Hauk would have been Manius, I'd wager, seeing as he came back empty-handed and in a seriously bad mood," Kwyck said, nodding thoughtfully. "You see, the Hauks have developed a use of their own for The Game: it's a sort of a..." he waved a hand, looking for a good description,"...proving ground for their youths. Those who catch a

Rahbet and bring it home—on foot, once they reach the half-way point—earn a cash prize and a coveted position in Kanno'Pii's Guard."

Bryer's heart sank; maybe Cyril did eventually fall in love with him, but likely he was seeking fame and glory first and foremost, and that love was just a bonus. Maybe the odds weren't so unlikely as Kwyck thought; maybe Cyril would have fallen for any Rahbet he might have captured.

"Cyril surprised everyone by being rather insistent on coming along for The Game this year—I guess now we know why, 'ey?" Kwyck grinned. "Anyway, can't say as I blame Manius for his attack, seeing as, to his mind, Cyril would have had no use for you."

"How do you mean?" Bryer asked, tilting his head in that Hauk way again, making Jehna smile knowingly.

"Well, Cyril here is actually of noble blood and one of the richest men in the city," Kwyck informed Bryer. "So it's not like he needs the money, much less the position. He also hasn't studied the Rahbet tongue, like most Chasers do before playing. They say he's never even shown an interest in The Game before, not even to wager on a Chaser! But Ayleen here," he pointed to the robed Hauk who'd brought them to the hall, "is a Seer, and his elder sister. She told him that if he didn't go out this time, love would be forever lost to him. She also told me, when I arrived, that I should arrange to get my brother here. I wasn't sure that I should listen, until she pointed out that, if you really didn't like it here, we could always send you home. But I don't think we'll need to do that," he added with a smile.

"No, I don't think you will," Bryer replied, smiling back.

"So let me give you a little wedding present." Kwyck got to his feet and embraced his brother, whispering in Bryer's ear as he did so.

Bryer blushed, and faced Cyril. The only doubt he had now was whether he'd ever be worthy of the adoration he felt when standing in the Hauk's line of sight.

"*I love you,*" Bryer said, clumsily repeating the Hauk words Kwyck had just told him.

Eyes shining, Cyril smiled, and to Bryer, it lit the whole hall. The Hauk moved to embrace his love, but Ayleen stayed him, standing on tiptoe to whisper in her brother's ear. When she was through, he nodded thanks and went to Bryer, taking him in his arms and kissing him in that sensual, maddening way. When they broke, Cyril fondly brushed a lock of hair from his mate's brow and declared in hushed Rahbet words,

"I am yours to devour."

Permissions

Steve, © Molly Kiely, 2007
The Lawn Fags, © Turk Albany, 2007
Humu Humu, © Lene Taylor, 2007
Nul Gravity, © Valessa Smith, 2007
The Accompanist, © Amy Throck*-Smythe, 2007
Jewel of My House, © Colleen Wylie, 2007
Mage Vows, © Kathryn L. Ramage, 2007
Chiaroscuro, © Ginger Mayerson, 2007
The Fall, © Laura Dearlove, 2007
The Omega Men, © Kitty Johnson, 2007
The Dipsy Doodle Inn, © Karmen Ghia, 2007
Chase, © Anastasia Witchhazel, 2007

Many thanks to Molly Kiely for the proofread and her patience.
Many thanks to Robin Austin for the fabulous cover design.
Please visit our website for more information on this title.

The Wapshott Press
www.WapshottPress.com

www.ingramcontent.com/pod-product-compliance
Lightning Source LLC
Chambersburg PA
CBHW022358040426
42450CB00005B/233